KOREAN SECURITY
DYNAMICS IN TRANSITION

EDITED BY
KYUNG-AE PARK
AND DALCHOONG KIM

palgrave

KOREAN SECURITY DYNAMICS IN TRANSITION
© Kyung-Ae Park and Dalchoong Kim, 2001

First published 2001 by
PALGRAVE
175 Fifth Avenue, New York, N.Y. 10010 and
Houndmills, Basingstoke, Hampshire RG21 6XS.
Companies and representatives throughout the world

PALGRAVE™ is the new global publishing imprint of St. Martin's
Press LLC Scholarly and Reference Division and Palgrave Publishers Ltd
(formerly Macmillan Press Ltd).

ISBN 0–312–23874–6 hardback

Library of Congress Cataloging-in-Publication Data available from the
Library of Congress.
A catalogue record for this book is available from the British Library.

Design by Letra Libre, Inc.

First edition: June 2001
10 9 8 7 6 5 4 3 2 1

Printed in the United States of America.

Transferred to digital printing 2005

CONTENTS

PART THREE
THE DYNAMICS AMONG MAJOR POWERS
AND KOREAN SECURITY

Notes on the Contributors

BRUCE CUMINGS is the Norman and Edna Freehling Professor of International History and East Asian Political Economy, University of Chicago. He received a BA from Denison University and a Ph.D. from Columbia University. He previously taught at Swarthmore College, University of Washington, and Northwestern University. Cumings is author or co-author of eight books, including a two volume study, *The Origins of the Korean War* (Princeton University Press, 1981, 1990), *War and Television* (Visal Routledge, 1992), *Korea's Place in the Sun: A Modern History* (Norton, 1997), and *Parallax Visions: Making Sense of American-East Asian Relations at Century's End* (Duke University Press, 1999). He also has contributed more than 70 articles to various journals. He is the recipient of fellowships from the Ford, National Endowment for the Humanities, and MacArthur Foundations, and the Center for Advanced Study in the Behavioral Sciences. He is a winner or finalist for four book awards and was elected as a Fellow of the American Academy of Arts and Sciences in 1999. Cumings is a frequent contributor to *The Nation, Current History,* and the *Bulletin of Atomic Scientists.*

L. GORDON FLAKE is Executive Director of the Mansfield Center for Pacific Affairs. Prior to joining the Mansfield Center, he was a Senior Fellow and Associate Director of the Program on Conflict Resolution at the Atlantic Council of the United States. Before moving to the Atlantic Council, he served as Director for Research and Academic Affairs at the Korea Economic Institute of America. As a conference participant and lecturer, Flake travels frequently to Japan, Korea, China, and other countries in Asia. He has traveled to North Korea on four occasions. He is a regular contributor on Korean and Asian policy issues in the American and Asian press. Flake received his M.A from Brigham Young University. He lived in Korea for a number of years and speaks both fluent Korean and Laotian.

SUNG-JOO HAN currently serves both as a professor of political science and the director of the Ilmin International Relations Institute at Korea

University. Before returning to Korea University in 1995, he was the Republic of Korea's Minister of Foreign Affairs. He also served as the United Nations Secretary-General's Special Representative for Cyprus (1996–97) and a member of the United Nations Inquiry Commission on Rwanda Genocide (1999). He is a graduate of Seoul National University (1962) and a recipient of a Ph.D. degree in Political Science from the University of California at Berkeley (1970). Previously, Han taught at the City University of New York (1970–78), Columbia University (1986–87), and Stanford University (1992) among others, and was a distinguished fellow at the Rockefeller Brothers Fund (1986–87). Han is a frequent contributor to professional and news journals both in Korea and abroad and was an international columnist for *Newsweek* (1984–93). He has authored many publications on Korean and international politics.

SELIG S. HARRISON is a Senior Scholar of the Woodrow Wilson International Center for Scholars, a Senior Fellow of the Century Foundation, and Director of the Foundation's Project on the United States and the Future of Korea. He has visited North Korea six times and met the late Kim Il Sung twice. In June 1994, on his fourth visit, he met Kim for three hours and won a public pledge of agreement to the concept of a freeze of the North Korean nuclear program in exchange for U.S. political and economic concessions. President Carter, meeting Kim Il Sung a week later, persuaded him to initiate the freeze immediately, opening the way for negotiations with the United States that resulted in the U.S.-North Korean nuclear agreement of October 21, 1994. Harrison is the author of five books on Asia and is currently an Adjunct Professor of Asian Studies at George Washington University.

DALCHOONG KIM is Professor of International Relations in the Department of Political Science at Yonsei University, in Seoul. He has served as President of the Sejong Institute and also as Dean of the Graduate School of Public Administration, Dean of the Graduate School of International Studies, and Director of the Institute of East and West Studies at Yonsei University. He graduated from Yonsei University with a BA, from National Chengchi University in Taiwan with a ML, and from the Fletcher School of Law and Diplomacy, Tufts University, with a Ph.D. He is currently President of the International Political Science Association. He also served as President of the Korean Association of International Studies. Kim has been serving as Program Chair of the Seoul Forum for International Affairs since 1986 and as Chairman of the National Committee of the Council of Security Cooperation in the Asia-Pacific (CSCAP) since 1996. He is author, co-author, editor, or co-editor of 13 books.

B. C. KOH is Professor of Political Science at the University of Illinois at Chicago. A native of Seoul, he was educated at Seoul National University (LL.B.) and Cornell University (M.P.A. and Ph.D.). Koh has taught at Louisiana State University in Baton Rouge, Louisiana, Temple University Japan in Tokyo (as a visiting professor in the summers of 1989 and 1990), Seoul National University (as a Fulbright lecturer in 1991), and Yonsei University (as a visiting professor in 1999). In the summer of 1993, he was a visiting researcher at the University of Tsukuba in Japan. He is the author of four books, including *The Foreign Policy Systems of North and South Korea* and *Japan's Administrative Elite*, both published by the University of California Press. He has contributed articles to journals such as *Asian Survey, Comparative Political Studies, Comparative Politics,* and the *Journal of Politics,* and chapters to numerous anthologies.

STEPHEN E. NOERPER is an international affairs specialist, focusing on Korean security and external relations development. He served as Associate Professor of International Relations at the Asia-Pacific Center from 1996–2000. Previously, Noerper was a Visiting Fellow at the East-West Center and Director of Washington Programs for the Nautilus Institute for Security and Sustainable Development. Noerper also served with the Institute for Foreign Policy Analysis, Edward R. Murrow Center, and Stone Foundation. He was a Visiting Scholar at the Institute for Foreign Affairs and National Security in Seoul, Korea. He holds a MA and Ph.D. from the Fletcher School of Law and Diplomacy, as well as a MS in Economics from the London School of Economics. His recent publications include "China-South Korea Relations: Quietly Building Trust" in *Comparative Connections,* "Regime Security and Military Tension in North Korea" in *Understanding Regime Dynamics in North Korea,* and *The Tiger's Leap: The South Korean Drive for National Prestige and Emergence in the International Arena.*

HAN S. PARK is Professor of Political Science and Director of the Center for the Study of Global Issues at the University of Georgia. Included in his extensive list of publications are *Human Needs and Political Development, China and North Korea* (co-author), *North Korea: Ideology, Politics, Economy* (editor), and *North Korea: The Politics of Unconventional Wisdom* (in press). He received his education in China, Korea, and the United States, with advanced degrees from Seoul National University, American University, and the University of Minnesota. Park has visited North Korea regularly since 1981, more frequently in the 1990s. He has initiated and participated in Track II negotiations designed to alleviate tension on the Korean peninsula. He has organized seminars and workshops involving social scientists, policy advisors, and agricultural experts from North Korea. As an expert analyst, he has appeared regularly on CNN International and PBS. He also serves as a consultant/analyst for ABC News. His remarks have been regularly cited in major newspapers such as *The New York Times* and *Asahi Shimbun.*

KYUNG-AE PARK teaches in the Department of Political Science and holds the Korea Foundation Chair of the Institute of Asian Research at the University of British Columbia, Canada. Park received a BA from Yonsei University, Korea, and her MA and Ph.D. from the University of Georgia. She previously taught at Mercer University and Franklin and Marshall College in the United States. She is currently President of the Association of Korean Political Studies in North America. Park is co-author of the book, *China and North Korea: Politics of Integration and Modernization,* and has contributed many book chapters and articles to various journals, including *Comparative Politics, Journal of Asian Studies, Asian Survey,* and *Pacific Affairs.* She also has presented numerous papers at academic conferences and has given many talks at the invitation of various universities, research institutes, academic associations, and government agencies in the United States, Canada, China, and South Korea. She recently has made three trips to North Korea.

C. KENNETH QUINONES, after retirement from the Foreign Service in 1997, worked with non-governmental organizations to promote better understanding between the United States and the two Koreas. Currently, he is affiliated with Mercy Corps International as the director of the Northeast Asia Project. During the past two years, he has published a dozen articles about U.S.-DPRK relations in academic journals and news magazines in the United States, Korea, and Japan. His recollection of the U.S.-DPRK nuclear talks, *The Korean Nuclear Crisis—Off the Record Memories—1992–95,* was published in Seoul and Tokyo in 2000. As a Foreign Service Officer, Quinones concentrated on Northeast Asia, particularly the Korean Peninsula. He was the first U.S. diplomat to visit Pyongyang (December 1992), the first to cross the DMZ from North to South (1993), and the first to visit the Youngbyon Nuclear Research Center (1994). Between 1994 and 1997 he was the State Department's representative on numerous delegations to the DPRK, including the U.S. Spent Nuclear Fuel Team and the U.S. Joint Recovery Team for U.S. Servicemen Missing in Action.

ROBERT A. SCALAPINO is Robson Research Professor Government Emeritus, former chair of the Political Science Department, director of the Institute of East Asian Studies, and editor of *Asian Survey,* published by the University of California, Berkeley. He is a member of the American Academy of Arts and Sciences, Trustee of the Asia Foundation, Pacific Forum, the Atlantic Council, and the Japan Society of Northern California, and director emeritus of the Council on Foreign Relations and the Asia Society. He has received the Order of the Sacred Treasure from the Government of Japan, the Order of Diplomatic Service Merit, Heung-In Medal from the Government of Korea, the Friendship Medal from the Government of Mongolia, the Berkeley Medal, the University's highest honor, and numerous other awards. Scalapino has written some 38 books and monographs and more than 500 articles. His books include *Communism in Korea* with Chong Sik Lee, *Modern China and Its Revolutionary Process* with George T. Yu, *Asia and the Road Ahead, The Foreign Policy of Modern Japan,* and *The Last Leninists: The Uncertain Future of Asia's Communist States.*

SCOTT SNYDER is the Asia Foundation's Representative in Seoul, Korea. Previously, he was Program Officer in the Research and Studies Department of the U.S. Institute of Peace, where he conducted research on Asian security issues and wrote a book entitled *Negotiating on the Edge: North Korean Negotiating Behavior.* In 1998–99, Snyder conducted independent research in Tokyo and Seoul as an Abe Fellow of the Social Sciences Research Council. In addition to numerous articles on Northeast Asian security affairs with a focus on Korea, Snyder has written on the political/security implications of the Asian financial crisis and on regional island disputes in Asia, including the conflicting maritime claims in the South China Sea. Prior to joining the U.S. Institute of Peace, Snyder served as Acting Director of the New York-based Asia Society's Contemporary Affairs program. Snyder received his BA from Rice University and an MA from the Regional Studies East Asia Program at Harvard University. He was the recipient of a Thomas G. Watson Fellowship in 1987–88 and attended Yonsei University in South Korea.

LIST OF ACRONYMS

ADB	Asian Development Bank
APEC	Asia Pacific Economic Cooperation
ARF	ASEAN Regional Forum
ASEAN	Association for South East Asian Nations
CBM	Confidence Building Measure
CFC	Combined Forces Command
CIA	Central Intelligence Agency
CPPCC	Chinese People's Political Consultative Conference
CSBM	Confidence and Security Building Measure
CSCAP	Council for Security Cooperation in the Asia Pacific
CSIS	Centre for Strategic and International Studies
DMZ	Demilitarized Zone
DPRK	Democratic People's Republic of Korea (North Korea)
GDP	Gross Domestic Product
EU	European Union
HC	House of Councilors
HR	House of Representatives
IAEA	International Atomic Energy Agency
ICBM	Inter-Continental Ballistic Missile
IMF	International Monetary Fund
JDA	Japan Defense Agency
JSA	Joint Security Area
KADO	Korean Peninsula Agricultural Development Organization
KAIDZ	Korea Air Identification Zone
KCIA	Korean Central Intelligence Agency
KEDO	Korean Peninsula Energy Development Organization
KPA	Korean People's Army
LWR	Light-Water Reactor
MAC	Military Armistice Commission
MCM	Military Committee Meeting
MFN	Most Favored Nation
NAPSNET	Northeast Asia Peace and Security Network
NATO	North Atlantic Treaty Organization

NEACD	Northeast Asia Cooperation Dialogue
NEADB	Northeast Asian Development Bank
NGO	Nongovernmental Organization
NMD	National Missile Defense
NNSC	Neutral Nations Supervisory Council
NPT	Nuclear Nonproliferation Treaty
OPEC	Organization of Petroleum Exporting Countries
PBEC	Pacific Basin Economic Council
PNTR	Permanent Normal Trading Relations
PRC	People's Republic of China
ROK	Republic of Korea (South Korea)
SCM	Security Consultative Meeting
SCC	Security Consultative Committee
SOFA	Status of Forces Agreement
TCOG	Trilateral Coordination and Oversight Group
TMD	Theater Missile Defense
UN	United Nations
UNC	United Nations Command
UNESCO	United Nations Educational, Scientific and Cultural Organization
USFK	U.S. Forces Korea
WTO	World Trade Organization

PREFACE

The Korean peninsula has long been a source of conflict and alarm to the international community. The world has watched North Korea with suspicious eyes, labeling it as a rogue state that is mysterious and unpredictable. Controversies surrounding North Korea's nuclear facilities and missile technology throughout the 1990s increased fears of another conflict on the Korean peninsula, and North Korea's economic disarray, reflected in its shortages of food, energy, and hard currency, accentuated the instability of the Korean peninsula.

However, the Korean security system is undergoing a swift change at the beginning of the twenty-first century. South Korea's policy toward the North has fundamentally changed under the Sunshine Policy of the Kim Dae Jung government, and the North, which has long been isolated, is aggressively reaching out to the international community. North Korea normalized relations with Italy, Australia, and the Philippines in early 2000 and joined the Association for South East Asian Nations Regional Forum in July 2000. Its diplomacy in 2000 was nothing short of unprecedented. North Korean leader Kim Jong Il made a rare foreign visit to China in May. He surprised the world by holding the landmark inter-Korean summit meeting in June. Kim also hosted a summit meeting with Russian President Putin in July, whose visit marked the first trip ever to North Korea by a Russian head of state. He held another meeting with the former U.S. Secretary of State Madeleine Albright, in October, making her the first American cabinet official to visit Pyongyang. Kim Jong Il's diplomatic offensives have continued into 2001 as reflected in his visits and planned visits to China, Russia, and South Korea in the first few months of the year.

In response to the rapprochement on the Korean peninsula, the Cold War atmosphere surrounding the two Koreas began to thaw. The stalemated relations of North Korea with the United States and Japan gained momentum following the Korean summit. The visit of Kim Jong Il's special envoy, General Jo Myong Rok, to Washington in October 2000 and Albright's return visit marked a breakthrough in North Korea-U.S. relations. North Korea and Japan resumed normalization talks, which had been frozen since 1992. All these groundbreaking developments will restructure the security dynamics on the Korean peninsula in the coming years.

This book provides an assessment of the new security structure of the Korean peninsula. The book critically analyzes the key factors and issues that are shaping a newly emerging security regime on and around the Korean peninsula at the beginning of the new millennium. The authors examine emerging inter-Korean security relations by analyzing the nature and structure of the legitimacy competition between the North and the South and new security strategies of the two Koreas. They also offer insight on the future of the American military presence in the peninsula, North Korea's ability to influence the United States, and security ramifications for South Korea of the changing U.S.-North Korea relations. One of the book's important contributions is its focus on the contentious relations among the major powers of the region and the implications of these relations for the Korean peninsula.

This book brings together the work of eleven distinguished scholars and leading experts on Korean politics. It is a joint effort by scholars who are longtime observers of the Korean peninsula and leading policy-makers who have helped form U.S. policy toward North and South Korea. Most of the contributors rely on first-hand knowledge obtained from their visits to both Koreas. Given the fact that few Western scholars have had the opportunity to visit North Korea, this book benefits from the authors' first-hand analysis.

We express our deep appreciation for the financial support by the Sejong Institute and for the assistance of Annwen Rowe-Evans and Hakhyun Nam. Thanks are also due to the staff at Palgrave, including Anthony Wahl.

Kyung-Ae Park
Dalchoong Kim

PART ONE

INTER-KOREAN
SECURITY RELATIONS

CHAPTER ONE

THE NATURE AND EVOLUTION OF THE INTER-KOREAN LEGITIMACY WAR

HAN S. PARK

Without understanding the nature and structure of inter-Korea competition, the relationship between the divided halves on the Korean peninsula, including the prospect of unification, cannot be properly comprehended. This relationship is predicated upon the premise that both systems cannot be simultaneously legitimate (one of the systems must be illegitimate and, therefore, disintegrated). The historical climate peculiar to the evolution of inter-Korea relations is unique. Each system has developed a political culture that contrasts with and often contradicts that of the other. As political institutions, domestic policy behavior, and foreign policy postures are all founded on the norms and values that constitute the foundation of regime legitimacy. The understanding of the political culture involving system legitimacy is particularly crucial in explaining and forecasting system characteristics and behaviors of the two Korean systems. By limiting analysis to the study of leadership characters or international contextual factors, even the most informed observers have consistently been puzzled by the unconventional nature of inter-Korea dynamics.

The purpose of this chapter is to discern the nature of the legitimacy competition and its ramifications for inter-Korea relations. Although the "legitimacy war" itself has never ceased, the pattern has shown appreciable transformation due to contextual changes in domestic policy priorities and the international political climate. This evolution will also be examined.

CONTRASTING BASES OF REGIME LEGITIMACY

Analytical and empirical distinction may be made between two bases of legitimacy. One is regime *performance* in meeting basic needs and promoting prosperity of the people. In this case, people as the governed will authorize and support the regime in exchange for its performance in delivering what the people need and want. This basis of legitimacy is consistent with classical democracy's theory of a social contract as advanced by John Locke and adopted extensively by both participatory democracy and socialism. This basis of legitimacy simply suggests that the ruling elite can find the justification to possess and exercise power by helping people satisfy their needs and attain prosperity in material and physical life. The second basis on which a regime pursues legitimacy is *ideology*. The ideological basis is more of a question of psychology and mass belief systems. In any political culture, there are a certain set of accepted norms and principles that cannot be easily compromised. In a liberal democracy, for instance, basic political rights such as speech, assembly, and due process are assumed to be so fundamental that they cannot be undermined if the polity is to be sustained as a legitimate system. Communist systems, on the other hand, uphold principles of distributive justice and centrist allocation of values. In reality, all systems are mixed systems in the sense that both performance and ideology are utilized in varying degrees of relative importance to maximize regime legitimacy.[1] However, some systems tend to weigh ideology more heavily than the utilitarian performance of the system. Both regimes in the Korean peninsula have not undermined the centrality of their relative ideologies. Indeed, the two systems have employed ideologies that are mutually incompatible to the extent that one system's ideology is predicated upon the rejection of the other's ideological system. Yet, the two systems have encountered contextual changes in both domestic policy priorities and the international environment, forcing them to alter their basis of legitimacy to some extent. While North Korea has almost always emphasized ideology, South Korea has shown flexibility to pursue pragmatic economic interest.

THE ASCENSION OF THE COMPETING SYSTEMS

In the formative stage of both regimes of Korea, two factors decisively contributed to the shaping of their political systems. First, the fact that the nation's partition was engineered by the external forces of the emerging superpowers affected the nature of the Korean regimes. Following the Japanese surrender in 1945, the occupied forces of the United States and the

Soviet Union imposed on Korea a period of trusteeship until an independent Korean government could be established. The external forces were there for the caretaking job of accepting the Japanese surrender and facilitating the establishment of a Korean government. However, the post–World War II period was quickly filled with the hegemonic conflict between the two victors of the War, paving the way for the prolonged occupation of Korea. The United States was determined to curtail the Communist forces that were riding the tide of global expansion. Thus, the country was divided along the 38th parallel with the United States occupying the south and the Soviets occupying the north. The line gained permanence due to the perpetuation of the conflict between the ideologically opposed hegemonic powers in the peninsula. At the formal conclusion of the trusteeship governance in 1948, the occupying powers helped establish two separate governments with handpicked leaders.

Within two years of the establishment of governments in both halves of Korea, a civil war ensued.[2] The civil war (1950–1953) on the peninsula became an international conflict between the hegemonic adversaries, placing the two Koreas on the front line of the Cold War. During the war, the Korean people were devastated not only by the loss of many lives but also by the separation of millions of people from their families. In the process of the bloody conflict and the ensuing decades of system developments sponsored and master-minded by the super powers in the Cold War era, the two regimes have established not only mutually incompatible, but fully hostile system characteristics.

Since the Korean War, the peninsula has been in a virtual state of war. Even the end of the Cold War world order could not help terminate the division. No longer do the international forces commission the division. In this sense alone, the Korean partition is fundamentally different from the case of German division. Intense mutual distrust and latent hostility grew on the peninsula with the support system for the external context of the Cold War world politics. Each system defines its jurisdiction and territorial boundary inclusive of the entire peninsula. The conciliatory gestures displayed by both governments following the historic summit meeting in June 2000 should not be construed as altering their fundamental stance that there can be only one legitimate state.

LEGACIES OF THE KOREA WAR

What sets the Korean experience apart from the German experience is the fact that the divided Koreas engaged in brutal intra-ethnic conflict for three years. The conflict itself and the ensuing politics in both systems helped them further solidify their power bases and legitimacy.

The Korean War was alleged as a "moral war" for South Korea in that it fought for the values and accompanying institutions of democracy. Needless to say, it was the United States as the "master" superpower that guided the politics of the surrogate power. Massive economic and military aid from the United States helped the Rhee regime (1948–1960) establish a "democratic" system that upheld, at least in the constitution, the ideals and institutions of participatory democracy in a country that had just been liberated from four decades of oppressive Japanese rule (1910–1945), a period of trusteeship by the United States (1945–1948), and three years of a bloody conflict (1950–1953). Prior to the Japanese occupation, Korea had been under centuries of dynastic rule. Thus, it is an understatement to say that South Korea was not prepared for the alien ideology and institution of democracy. Nonetheless, the American tutelage and the Communist threat left the Rhee and ensuing regimes with no alternative but to adhere to the norms and institutions of western democracy. This course has been bumpy with a series of Constitutional revisions, military juntas, and trial and error. The consistent presence of security interest on the part of the United States and its allies and persistent threat from the North allowed the South Korean governments little room to maneuver away from the transplanted democratic ideology. American influence through educational and socialization processes has been so pervasive that democracy has found a relatively stable footing in the elite culture and mass belief systems.[3]

North Korea, on the other hand, has been induced to follow a completely different course. The Korean War was regarded as a continuation of nationalist struggle against foreign domination, this time against the United States and its "surrogate" powers. North Korea found a great sense of pride and fulfillment by representing itself in the signing of the armistice agreement, as its counterpart was not South Korea but the more formidable body of the United Nations. Since then, Pyongyang has shown reluctance to treat South Korea as a sovereign system. At the same time, North Korea has campaigned almost single-mindedly for national sovereignty under the banner of *juche* ideology. Although there have been various phases in the evolution of that ideology, no one can dispute the fact that it is a form of ultra-nationalism.[4]

DIVERGING IDEOLOGIES:
DEMOCRACY VERSUS NATIONALISM

From the inception of their respective systems, the two regimes evolved politically along separate paths. In the South, the American-educated Syngman Rhee assumed power with the blessing of the United States, setting the stage for democratic institutionalization. Power consolidation under Rhee was harshly anti-Communist. The Constitution was little more than a carbon copy of the U.S. Constitution with some elements of the British Constitution. There was nothing indigenous about the institutional development in South Korea. What may be "indigenous" is the uneasy footing of democracy showing mal-symptoms ranging from violence to corruption. In the end, state-engineered capitalism faced profitable, yet, precarious, encounters with the international market paving the way to "dependent" development.[5]

Conversely, North Korea was consolidated under the leadership of a young Soviet military officer, Kim Il Sung, who had education and political experience in the underground nationalist movement.[6] He was able to consolidate his power base by eliminating factions sympathetic to the Soviets and to the South Korean leftist movement. In the meantime, the Chinese Communist Revolution was in full swing, most vigorously in Northeast Asia where some 1.8 million ethnic Koreans had immigrated and established their residence. Mao's revolution has been largely attributed to the initial success in the Northeast region to which the Korean residents made significant contribution. China literally rescued North Korea from certain defeat in the war by intervening with massive numbers of ground troops. It is estimated that a majority of the Chinese soldiers were "volunteers" from the Korean community in the region. One notable event was that Mao lost his own son in a battle on Korean soil. These series of events helped the two Communist countries develop a fraternal relationship for the ensuing decades.[7] The fact that Maoist ideological orientation was more in line with nationalism than Soviet style Communism made Mao's China exceptionally appealing to Kim Il Sung's North Korea. In fact, North Korean communism has always been predicated upon the premises and ideals of nationalism.

"State Capitalism" Versus Juche

Since the 1960s, the process of diverging development between the two systems progressed at an accelerated pace, resulting in even more intense legitimacy competition. While South Korea found the basis of legitimacy in capitalist development, the North established a firm grounding in nationalist consolidation.

The trial course of South Korean democracy has been nothing but bumpy. The Syngman Rhee regime was toppled by a military takeover in 1961. An interim government took control and wrote a new constitution that replaced the presidential system with a parliamentary system. Yet another constitutional overhaul occurred when Park's Third Republic was established in 1963. Park's regime lasted until 1979 when the president was assassinated in a bizarre incident in which his own director of the Korean Central Intelligence Agency assassinated him. After another interim government with Choi Kyu Ha as the president, General Chun Doo Whan forced his way into power through another military insurrection. As expected, a new Constitution was installed, this time, limiting the term of presidency to five years and a single term. The Chun regime was succeeded by another military-turned politician, Rho Tae Woo. When a "civilian" government was installed in 1993 under the leadership of Kim Young Sam, with the help and blessing of the Rho government, the two generals (Chun and Rho) were subjected to a public trial on charges of corruption and both were eventually imprisoned. The Kim Yong Sam government quickly became a public nuisance for gross corruption, especially fiscal irregularities involving Kim's son and hand-picked conglomerates *(chaebols).*[8]

Finally, this quasi-civilian regime was replaced by a genuine civilian government when the long-time internationally renowned human rights activist and opposition leader Kim Dae Jung won a highly contested election in 1998. But the civilian government inherited a massive economic problem.[9] Kim Dae Jung's government was immediately forced to manage the enormous amount of foreign debt, more than $150 billion, with a virtually depleted foreign currency reserve, due to inefficient management on the part of conglomerates. Furthermore, they were faced with the imperative of restructuring the financial and economic system, making new loans, and accommodating intervention by international lenders such as the International Monetary Fund (IMF). While the initial phase of the Kim Dae Jung government was plagued by enormous economic difficulties and labor disputes, the regime has shown its commitment to the principles of democracy. How successful has the current Kim Dae Jung regime been as a system of democracy? Only history can make a complete evaluation.

The above brief account of regime changes in South Korea and cursory observation of the political dynamics help us understand a few characteristics of the polity. First, democracy has never been firmly established in South Korea, but the system could never abandon the ideology of democracy. Despite irregularities and turmoil with the institution of democracy, no one advocated for socialism or communism at any time in the country's history other than the most radical student and worker protesters. On the contrary, political integration and power consolidation have been promoted through the ideal of anti-Communism. This phenomenon may be accounted for by the presence of North Korea as an *antithesis* system based on a form of legitimacy that is diametrically opposed to that of South Korea. Secondly, the South Korean polity has always been centrist in that the center of power exercises almost unlimited influence. When this is coupled by "political monism" whereby politics overwhelms all other sectors, the central power becomes almost omnipotent. The role of government has always been vital to the success of economic growth, yielding a pattern of development referred to as "state capitalism."[10]

Nowhere was this phenomenon more evident than Park Chung Hee's Third Republic. Park, as the *junta* leader who assumed power through military coup, lacked legitimacy as a democratic leader. His regime was in need of supplementing his shaky basis of legitimacy by advancing system performance as the prime raison d'être of leadership. It was Park Chung Hee who installed multi-year economic plans with strong government intervention in all sectors of national economic construction. This practice meant a drastic deviation from the laissez faire principle of capitalism. Nevertheless, the South Korean ideology of democracy could have never distanced itself from claiming capitalism no matter how unconventional the practice might have been. This again is due to the imperative of self-identity that must be opposed to the North Korean system. And even though Park was anything but democratic, he still claimed democratic credentials.

In short, South Korea's practice of strong government over civil society is in part due to the imperative of maintaining legitimacy against the presence of perceived and real threat from the North. To cope with this threat, the military institution has exploded to the extent that the entire society has embraced the norms and values consistent with militarism. The military culture has deterred the maturation of democracy, as militarism and democracy are often mutually incongruent in their value systems and operational dynamics. Militarism upholds such values as uniformity, hierarchical authority structure, centralism, and enemy-driven belief systems. But democracy promotes diversity, articulation and aggregation of opinions from the bottom, pluralist civil society, and bargaining and negotiation as consensus building mechanism.

North Korea, on the other hand, developed a unique breed of nationalism under the banner of *juche*. This ideology has systematically adhered to the premise that whatever South Korea stands for is wrong and illegitimate. This ideology defies any form of reliance or dependence upon external powers. The self-reliance doctrine has led the system to alienate all foreign sources and, in doing so, the people are blocked off from the outside. The evolution of *juche* has shown a variety of phases and philosophical refinements but one salient feature has always been nationalism.[11]

The extreme nature of North Korean nationalism continues to tax foreign relations, economic development, technological advancement, and functional literacy on the part of the people into a new millennium. Yet, Pyongyang is not in a position to embrace reforms and openness that would induce economic growth. It fears that such a drastic move might endanger system stability and even cause system collapse as evidenced by European socialist systems. More importantly, the North Korean leadership cannot risk regime legitimacy by adopting open and reform policy measures that in effect negate its ideological legitimacy vis-à-vis South Korea.

With the demonstrated military capability that might include weapons of mass destruction, the Pyongyang regime is not expected to give in to foreign pressures and be swayed to embrace reforms. In fact, the Pyongyang system has sufficiently demonstrated that it can endure economic hardships and diplomatic isolation. Furthermore, North Korea has a formidable enough military force to maintain a significant bargaining leverage in the international community. However, the greatest strength of the North Korean system lies in its ideological solidarity; the ideology of *juche* has evolved in the legitimatization process as the *antithesis* to the South Korean system. The norms, values, and beliefs of a significant proportion of the people will not be altered overnight.

RAMIFICATIONS FOR UNIFICATION: THE SUMMIT AND BEYOND

Any meaningful analysis of the prospect of reunification must focus on the motivational factors surrounding the dynamics of the legitimacy competition. As long as each side maintains its insistence on system legitimacy, a path of compromise for negotiated settlement toward reunification is not likely. All politically engineered gestures by either party are simply designed to demonstrate its relative superiority as a legitimate system.

Undoubtedly, the summit meeting between South Korean president Kim Dae Jung and North Korean leader Kim Jong Il that took place in Pyongyang on June 13–15, 2000 was an historic event. What is troubling is that most observers did not give enough attention to the psychological motivations on the part of the two leaderships, especially that of the North. For that reason, there have been several erroneous accounts of the event. First, a major mistake was to see the summit meeting as the ultimate success of South Korea's Sunshine Policy.[12] If the Sunshine Policy was designed to open up North Korea and eventually foster the system's move toward accommodating economic, social, and political reform, the summit meeting itself may have had nothing to do with that objective.

Related to this mistaken account is the widespread expectation that North Korea is surrendering its reclusive system to the world capital market in order to alleviate economic difficulties. Nothing is more remote from reality than this ideologically charged assessment. North Koreans have never shown the intention to change by altering policy orientations. Then, what was the motivation behind Kim Dae Jung's resolve to aggressively seek a summit meeting with Kim Jong Il and the latter's acceptance of the proposal? The answer is simple. They both calculated that the meeting would strengthen their respective systems' claims for legitimacy.

For South Korea's Kim Dae Jung, the meeting would indicate a resounding success of his Sunshine Policy, thereby legitimizing the ideology of capitalist democracy. He would have expected that North Korea would be forced to open its door to South Korea's investment and human entries that would inevitably lead to system reform and social change. In this eventuation, Kim Dae Jung's policy would have given the Seoul regime a victory in the legitimacy competition. Furthermore, President Kim as the first South Korean head of state who brought out his reclusive North Korean counterpart to the summit meeting could demonstrate his political capability in handling the North, thereby strengthening his political base. It was in this calculation that the announcement of the agreement to convene a summit itself was made on the eve of a general election in South Korea. Kim Dae Jung's personal desire to contend for the Nobel Peace Prize might too have had some influence on his decision making process. Certainly the summit meeting would gain him support for that effort. All these were the outcome of a rational calculation. The only risk at the outset was the possibility of North Korea's non-compliance. In fact, Kim Dae Jung made the same overture to the North through such channels as Mr. Chung Joo Young of Hyundai Corporation and Mr. Park Po Hee of the Unification Church. President Kim conveyed his desire to convene a summit meeting with Chairman Kim Jong Il, but the latter did not responded with any positive reply until April 2000.[13]

Observers were stunned when Pyongyang announced its willingness to accept President Kim's proposal. There were numerous speculations about Pyongyang's motivation and intention behind such an unexpected response. But most of them suggest that North Korea is finally coming out of the closet, and it is a matter of time for Pyongyang to reform and change in order to habilitate the failing economy through participation in the world market. Following the summit, a ranking official from Seoul made a pointed remark to an American audience in Washington that was widely shared by experts on North Korea: Kim Jong Il's coming out of the traditional enclave and embracing the South Korean leader at the airport is a direct evidence that North Korea has surrendered to the South because of its failure as a socialist system. Nothing can be more wrong than this. Pyongyang never gave in to anyone, let alone conceded defeat in the competition with the South for system legitimacy.

There are a few tangible events justifying the above observation. First, recently, the Pyongyang authorities reiterated the significance of an historical event that took place in May 1948 when Kim Il Sung assembled a group of nationalist leaders from throughout the peninsula, including a delegation from the South. On a little island on Daedong River a commemorative tower was erected on which the names of the participants were engraved. Mr. Kim Ku, a prominent nationalist leader and a political figure, headed the Southern delegation to the meeting. The North was not led by Kim Il Sung, but by Kim Chaek who was a close comrade of his. Kim Il Sung was elevated to the position of the over-arching leader who actually presided over the meeting, thus, demonstrating that he was the leader of all nationalist leaders. The meeting took place in no other place than Pyongyang, suggesting that the city is the legitimate locus of unifying forces.

It must have been on the minds of North Koreans that a summit meeting that replicates the historical event could be a symbolic victory in the legitimacy competition. If this scenario were to prevail, the summit meeting is expected to boost North Korea's stance as a more legitimate government vis-à-vis the South. This calculation may have indeed been a decisive element in making the decision to host the summit meeting. Similarly, Pyongyang probably thought it could gain material and economic advantages from the South, while gaining ground in the ongoing legitimacy competition.

There is strong evidence to support this possibility. First, at the time of initial contact in Beijing to prepare the procedure of the summit meeting, the North Korean delegation headed by Mr. Song Ho Kyong, vice chairman of the Korean Asia Pacific Peace Committee, insisted that the meeting must convene in Pyongyang and that it should take the format of North Korean leader Kim Jong Il responding to the South Korean president's *request*. Second, the North Koreans insisted that the meeting in Pyongyang be the only meeting, without obligating the North to a reciprocal visit in Seoul by Kim Jong Il. This reinforced the symbolic implication that Pyongyang is the only locus of a unified Korea. Third, the North Koreans initially refused to name Kim Jong Il as Kim Dae Jung's counterpart with the intention of naming Kim Young Nam as the nominal head of state. In this case, Kim Young Nam would be equivalent to Kim Chaek in the aforementioned meeting of 1948. The North Koreans appear to have played out this scenario. They secured the concession from the South that the summit meeting be convened at the request of the South Korean president at least in their version of the Agreement. It should also be noted that Pyongyang was never ambiguous to report that the summit-meeting took place between Kim Dae Jung, President of South Korea, and Kim Young Nam, President of the Presidium of the Supreme People's Assembly of the Democratic People's Republic of Korea.[14] Even though it is obvious that Kim Jong Il is the actual leader and the summit meeting was between him and South Korea's Kim Dae Jung, the North Korean people have been led to believe that their beloved leader received the visitor and the practical business meeting involved Kim Young Nam. In fact, Kim Jong Il himself conducted his hosting chores with the clear intention of showing his warm hospitality and demonstrating his leadership attributes as the reigning leader for the entire Korean people. The typical recount of the meeting is as follows:

> The historic Pyongyang meeting of the leaders of the North and South in June was a product of the respected Kim Jong Il's firm will for reunification, tireless efforts and patriotic determination. . . . Kim Jong Il warmly greeted President Kim Dae Jung and his party who visited Pyongyang and throughout their stay in Pyongyang had informal conversations with them with his clairvoyant wisdom, broad-minded magnanimity, noble morality and profound knowledge.[15]

North Korea was led to believe that the terms of the Agreement signed by the two leaders in Pyongyang on June 15, 2000 were basically consistent with what the Pyongyang has advocated for decades. Article 1 on the agreed agenda was that "the North and the South agreed to solve the questions of the country's reunification independently by the concerted efforts of the Korean nation responsible for it."[16] This is seen as affirmation of self-reliance. This also suggests that the stationing of U.S. troops in Korea cannot be justified. Article 2 of the Agreement accepts the notion of Confederacy as an initial approach toward unification; the "low level" of North Korea's Koryo Confederacy is similar to the initial stage of South Korea's (Kim Dae Jung's) Three Stage Approach.[17] For the first time in inter-Korea relations, the concept of North Korea's Confederacy was accepted as a legitimate approach by the South Korean government. The North deemed this a significant victory in the longstanding struggle with the South for regime legitimacy. Article 3 involves two humanitarian concerns. First, South Korea secured Pyongyang's concession to help arrange the reunion of separated family members, the number of which was believed to be in the millions. Second, the South side agreed to return

North Korean war prisoners who were detained in the South. There may be over 100 such prisoners, each of whom is documented by North Korea. Pyongyang has been demanding their return for decades. There was a precedent in 1994, under the Kim Young Sam government, of South Korea's returning one of the prisoners of war, Mr. Lee Yin Mo. Upon his return home, Mr. Lee was given a hero's welcome and inducted to a selected group about whom the film series Nation and Destiny was made. The return of additional prisoners will help North Korea's cause of stimulating patriotism and enhancing relative legitimacy. Article 4 of the Agreement spells out the principles of facilitating the entire peninsula's economy by developing economic integration. This article is interpreted as South Korea's resolution and willingness to divert considerable economic and technological resources into the North, without necessarily obligating Pyongyang to open the system or to reform economic and political measures. This means an enormous economic gain on the part of the North, at least in the short run. Finally, Kim Dae Jung's invitation for Kim Jong Il to visit Seoul was dealt with as a peripheral issue. The Agreement simply states that Kim Jong Il will visit South Korea at an appropriate time. When that "appropriate time" will be or what conditions might create the appropriate time were not clarified.

In the final analysis, it is erroneous to assume that Pyongyang's acceptance of the summit meeting is a prelude to a fundamental change in North Korea's system characteristics. On the contrary, Pyongyang's rational calculation prevailed: the summit meeting will enhance North Korea's position in the legitimacy competition with the South and, at the same time, will promote much needed economic assistance. Furthermore, the conciliatory gestures surrounding the summit meeting will also help Pyongyang in securing cooperation from the United States and other Western countries. One should notice that Washington did not waste time in easing trade sanctions against North Korea. The lifting of U.S. sanctions became effective almost immediately following the inter-Korea summit. Other countries including Japan and Canada have shown their desire to improve relations with Pyongyang. The South Korean side, on the other hand, has its own scenario that favors the capitalist democracy as the dominant force that will stimulate the North to compromise its longstanding ideology of *juche*. In short, the two leaders had "different dreams in the same bed."

SUMMARY AND CONCLUSION

We have witnessed the passing of the Cold War, the endemic fall of socialist systems in Europe following the demise of the Soviet Union, and the drastic economic and legal reforms in China. All of these, however, were unable to change the Korean peninsula from its Cold War status quo. The thesis of this chapter has been that the stagnation of inter-Korea relations is due largely to the emergence of a new kind of war, namely the legitimacy war.

This chapter maintained that in order to properly understand the history and dynamics of inter-Korea relations, one must focus on the root of the legitimacy competition between the two systems. The competition has never slowed down, let alone settled in favor of the market economy oriented South Korea. Since the inception of the two separate regimes, following Japanese surrender, the difference between the competing systems grew to the point where they became mutually incompatible. The process of this diversion was fueled by Cold War politics in which the two Korean governments confronted each other as enemies. More significantly, they have advanced and refined ideologies and system characteristics that are mutually exclusive. Each has sought regime legitimacy on the grounds of rejecting what the other stands for. The politics and policies in both Korean systems, as well as inter-Korea relations, suggest clearly that it is the legitimacy competition that explains the underlying motivations and ensuing policy behaviors for both regimes.

The recent inter-Korea summit meeting was an historic event, and the world was stunned by the unexpectedly conciliatory gestures extended especially by North Korea's Kim Jong Il. The media hype surrounding the meeting has led not only Koreans but foreign observers as well to raise their hopes high for a speedy improvement of inter-Korea relations and for rapid structural and political reforms in North Korea. Yet, all indications in this young post-summit era suggest that these hopes are raised too high and prematurely. One certain thing is that North Korea has not given in to external pressures to compromise its reclusive policy. The legitimacy competition continues.

In this sense, the Korean conundrum is uniquely complex. One must dig into political culture and system characteristics to shed light on the seemingly endless string of mysteries posed by the behavior of the Korean systems toward each other.

NOTES

1. On the basis of legitimacy along this line, John Schaar makes an analytical discussion in his book, *Legitimacy in the Modern States* (New Brunswick, NJ: Transaction Books, 1981). For more extensive references on this topic, see Han Shik Park and Kyung Ae Park, *China and North Korea: Politics and Integration and Modernization* (Hong Kong: Asia Research Service, 1990), chapter 2.

2. On the origins and detailed account of the Korean War, see Bruce Cumings, *The Origins of the Korean War*, volumes 1 and 2 (Princeton, NJ: Princeton University Press, 1981 and 1990) and William Stueck, *The Korean War* (Princeton, NJ: Princeton University Press, 1995). The two authors offer conflicting interpretations about the origins of the war.

3. The evolution of democracy in South Korea is carefully examined by John Ki-chiang Oh. See his *Korea: Democracy on Trial* (Ithaca, NY: Cornell University Press, 1968) and *Korean Politics* (Ithaca, NY: Cornell University Press, 1999).

4. The ideology of *juche* was conceived as a simple form of anti-foreignism, but because it was used as an instrument for regime legitimacy, its content has evolved to counter the South Korean ideology of capitalist democracy.

5. The concept of "dependent development" is used as the antithesis to the *dependencia* school of thought that decries the intervention of external powers, as they will exploit and impoverish indigenous economies.

6. For an extensive discussion on this process, see Dae-Sook Suh, *The Korean Communist Movement, 1918–1948* (Princeton, NJ: Princeton University Press, 1967); also see, Chong-sik Lee and Robert Scalapino, *Communism in Korea*, 2 volumes (Los Angeles: University of California Press, 1972).

7. On September 5, 1952, during the Korean War, the Chinese government granted the Northeast region, heavily populated by ethnic Koreans, the status of "autonomous region." This policy action was generally regarded as a reward for the contribution that the Koreans in China made to the Chinese involvement in the Korean conflict. See Ma Nin, ed., *Jungkuk sosuminjok sangsik* (*The Chinese Minority Nationalities*) (Beijing: Nationalities Publication House, 1983).

8. For a concise and credible discussion on the leadership crisis and economic difficulties in this period, see John Kie-chiang Oh, *Korean Politics* (Ithaca, NY: Cornell University Press, 1999), chapter 9.

9. The outstanding external liabilities at the end of 1997 was 154 billion U.S. dollars, of which 68 billion was short-term debt.

10. The initiative role of government in the economic sector is observed in other East Asian countries including Japan, Singapore, and Taiwan, which are celebrated as representing the "miracle" of economic development.

11. On the evolution of *Juche*, see Han S. Park, "The Nature and Evolution of *Juche*" in Han S. Park, ed., *North Korea: Ideology, Politics, Economy* (Englewood Cliffs, NJ: Prentice Hall Publishers, 1996).

12. The Sunshine Policy of South Korea was designed to help North Korea reach out to the international community and to promote inter-Korea interactions in politically insensitive areas. In so doing, South Korea expects the Pyongyang government to become more conciliatory toward the outside. This policy is in line with the Engagement Policy of the Clinton administration, allowing Seoul to co-ordinate its policies with Washington.

13. This factual information is based on the author's conversation in Pyongyang with top officials on March 10, 2000.
14. Article 11 of the Constitution adopted in 1998 designates the president of the Presidium of the Supreme People's Assembly as the head of state. All official reports from North Korea since the summit meeting have been consistent in stating that the summit meeting was held between Kim Yong Nam, not Kim Jong Il, of North Korea and Kim Dae Jung of South Korea.
15. Press Release, DPRK Permanent Mission to the United Nations, no. 20, August 16, 2000.
16. For a complete text of the agreements, see *Pyongyang Times,* June 17, 2000.
17. For a detailed introduction to Kim Dae Jung's "three stage" concept, see *Kim Dae Jung's Three Stage Approach to Korean Reunification* (University Park, CA: Center for Multiethnic and Transnational Studies, University of Southern California, 1996).

CHAPTER TWO

South Korea's Approaches to North Korea: A Glacial Process

C. Kenneth Quinones

An old Korean adage proclaims, "The beginning is half the journey." The epic meeting of Korea's two leaders, South Korea's President Kim Dae Jung and North Korea's Supreme Commander Kim Jong Il on June 15, 2000 in Pyongyang took fifty years to accomplish. If the Korean adage is accurate, reconciliation between the two Koreas could require another half century. We would do well to look back now and recall the long, arduous journey to the Pyongyang summit. Such awareness should enable us to accept the reality that we have just reached the mid-point in the journey to reconciliation. Without this awareness, tempering impatience will be impossible. The price of impatience could be frustration that might convince either or both Korean governments to revert to their earlier practices. The result could be renewed confrontation and heightened tension that once again might lead to war on the Korean peninsula.

We should further broaden our perspective with an awareness of the potential geo-political consequences if the Koreans' efforts at reconciliation fail. The Korean peninsula's role as a flash point in the intense superpower rivalry of the Cold War has undergone profound alteration since the Soviet Union's demise in 1990. The once highly unstable intersection of superpower interests at the Korean peninsula between the United States and Japan, on the one hand, and the Soviet Union and China, on the other, is gradually giving way to an increasingly sturdy *détente*. The diminished tension has benefited the process of Korean reconciliation.

Looking back, it is indeed obvious that the pace of reconciliation has quickened since 1990. The two Koreas amazed the world in December 1991 by committing themselves to making the Korean peninsula free of nuclear weapons and by signing the Agreement on Reconciliation, Non-aggression, Exchanges, and Cooperation. Only a year later in September 1992, mounting distrust fostered by evidence that North Korea was attempting to conceal the extent of its previous production of nuclear weapon grade plutonium undercut the process of reconciliation. By June 1994, the crisis had escalated to one of virtual war that would certainly have involved the United States and possibly even China. Peace was preserved, but not by the conventional means long utilized on the Korean peninsula.

Making an accurate assessment of inter-Korean relations also necessitates discarding many assumptions we normally apply to relations between other nations. For example, we assume diplomacy between nations is essential for the resolution of disputes. Not so in the case of the Korean peninsula. The institutions of diplomatic communication between Seoul and Pyongyang were not formally instituted until 1991. They still are not in place for Seoul's primary supporters, the United States and Japan. In Korea's case, the only institutionalized, politically accepted and functioning channel of communication for many years between the two Koreas was the Military Armistice Commission (MAC). The purpose of the dialogue between representatives of hostile armies still technically at war was to perpetuate the military stalemate, not to resolve the conflict's underlying causes, nor to promote reconciliation or to pursue a durable peace. To describe the dialogue at Panmunjom as negotiation would be a gross inaccuracy. The MAC became the stage upon which two armies berated and belittled one another. In short, Seoul and Pyongyang equally disdained diplomatic contact and dialogue between their citizens and foreign supporters. Washington, Moscow, Tokyo, and Beijing readily aligned themselves with this perspective to demonstrate their unwavering support for the Korea of their choice.

Within this ideologically rigid and politically stark reality, the pursuit of reconciliation was foremost a futile exercise in rhetoric, at least until after 1990. Before then, the language of reconciliation was distorted and tainted with negative connotations. Reconciliation was affiliated with wavering disloyalty, even treason. Compromise, the essence of diplomacy and democracy, was associated with appeasement. Inducements and concessions, the key elements of international accords, were berated as signs of weakness.

Only since several long-term obstacles have been dismantled and replaced with new practices and perceptions has it been possible for the process of reconciliation to commence in earnest. This change dates from August 1971 with the first tentative official contacts and exchanges of official visits between Seoul and Pyongyang. The period of mutual exploration waxed and waned for two decades, restrained by the dynamics of continuing superpower rivalry and domestic political instability in South Korea. The Cold War released the two Koreas from their ideological strait jackets. The series of North-South High Level Talks that commenced in September 1990 institutionalized and expanded the channels of communication between Seoul and Pyongyang. Compromise and cooperation for the first time in North-South dialogue acquired positive connotations. The United States-Democratic People's Republic of Korea (U.S.-DPRK) nuclear negotiations from June 1993 to October 1994 preempted the war of words long waged in Panmunjom, shifted the resolution of bilateral issues to diplomatic channels, and restored compromise as a legitimate approach to resolving differences with North Korea.

CONTAINMENT—A QUESTION OF LEGITIMACY

A cornerstone of South Korean policy toward North Korea since 1948 has been its claim that as the Republic of Korea (ROK) it is the sole legitimate government on the Korean peninsula, and that the regime in Pyongyang (the Democratic People's Republic of Korea) is illegitimate and unworthy of diplomatic recognition and communication. This policy was forged in the heated rivalry between the former Soviet Union, which championed Kim Il Sung as the leader of all of Korea, and the United States, which preferred a long time resident of Hawaii, Dr. Syng Mann Rhee.

In May 1947, when North Korea refused to permit the United Nations to conduct a plebiscite in the northern half of the Korean peninsula, the United States declared, on August 12, 1948, that the government in Seoul was "the Korean Government" and established formal diplomatic relations with it.[1]

Long ignored has been the United Nations Resolution on Korea, adopted by the General Assembly on December 12, 1948, regarding the situation on the Korean peninsula. The pertinent section referring to the May 1948 plebiscite conducted in South Korea reads:

> Declares that there has been established a lawful government (the Government of the Republic of Korea), having effective control and jurisdiction over that part of Korea where the (UN) Temporary Commission was able to observe and consult and in which the great majority of the people of all Korea reside; that this Government is based on elections which were

a valid expression of the free will of the electorate of that part of Korea and which were observed by the Temporary Commission and that is the only such Government in Korea . . . [2]

The resolution's wording does not specifically address, thus leaving ambiguous, the issue of whether the ROK is the sole legitimate government on the entire Korean peninsula. Rather, the statement clearly indicates that the United Nations (UN) General Assembly recognized the government in Seoul as being "lawful" and having jurisdiction over the southern half of the peninsula.

Subsequent action by the United States and its allies in the UN firmly defined the basic parameters of ROK-U.S. policy toward North Korea in the half century after the Korean War. The ROK came to be viewed by most of the nations allied with the United States as the sole legitimate government on the Korean peninsula. Prompted by the United States, the UN Security Council, on June 25, 1950, condemned North Korea for its invasion of South Korea. Pyongyang's grievous misconduct earned it the label of international outlaw and, for many nations, confirmed its illegitimacy. The U.S. Congress imposed on North Korea strident economic sanctions as provided for in the Trading with the Enemy Act of 1918. The Korean War Armistice halted hostilities on July 27, 1953, but the war's legacy of distrust and hostility continued unabated. The ROK-U.S. alliance was affirmed by the signing of a mutual defense treaty on October 1, 1953. The essence of the treaty, as approved by the U.S. Senate, obligates the United States to the ROK'S defense only in the event of external armed attack. The treaty has remained unaltered since the date it entered into force, November 17, 1954.[3]

Until the early 1990s, Seoul and Washington worked in tandem to apply a policy of containment to North Korea while working simultaneously to make South Korea a showcase for democracy and capitalism. The two allies' intertwined policy provided that the United States would follow the ROK's lead regarding the formulation and implementation of policy involving Pyongyang. Seoul established and Washington accepted a list of "sticks and carrots" to be applied to or withheld from the North depending on whether its conduct was deemed good or bad.

Any official, diplomatic contact between Washington and its allies with Pyongyang was absolutely taboo. Nor was there to be any commercial intercourse. The aim was to diplomatically and commercially isolate Pyongyang from the mainstream of international society. For some people in both South Korea and the United States, the policy of containing and isolating Pyongyang nurtured the expectation that Korea's unification would someday bring about the northern regime's collapse. Such an expectation ignored the fact that Pyongyang found ample military and economic benefit in its alliance with the so-called Communist bloc nations. At the same time, Seoul linked its economy to that of the United States. From 1954 to 1976, the Seoul government absorbed large amounts of foreign aid from the United States. Eventually the endeavor reaped spectacular results as South Korea's economic dynamism finally burst forth in the later 1970s. The establishment of democracy took longer.

The ROK-U.S. policies of containing and isolating the DPRK during the three decades following the Korean War fell short of their intended goal. Pyongyang grew stronger from its association with the Communist bloc. The estrangement between the two Koreas, on the other hand, rigidified and their rivalry intensified. Tension on the Korean peninsula was heightened and sustained. Their contest projected itself far beyond the Korean peninsula, and often turned violent. They competed militarily not just along the DMZ in Korea, but also in Vietnam. South Korea, with U.S. help, prevented North Korea from gaining diplomatic respectability and entrance into markets outside the Communist bloc. None of this was conducive to reconciliation. Gradually but steadily, South Korea achieved diplomatic ascendancy over the North on the international stage. North Korea, on the other hand, made impressive strides in building economic and military prowess, both largely dependent however on the Soviet Union's continued viability.

North-South rivalry infected all aspects of communication between the two societies. Under South Korea's now notorious National Security Law, citizens of South Korea were not permitted to have contact of any kind with North Koreans, including kinsmen, without explicit written permission. Possession of any materials, especially printed literature from or even about North Korea and communism was similarly outlawed. Early on, even the exchange of mail with relatives in North Korea was considered a subversive act. North Korean television and radio broadcasts were jammed. Disobeying the law was punishable by execution. Conditions in the North were even harsher.

To demonstrate its loyalty to the ROK, the U.S. government took great pains to prevent any conduct by its officials that might make the South Korean government uncomfortable or which might imply a softening attitude toward the North Korean regime. U.S. diplomats were forbidden to speak to North Koreans and even to attend social and diplomatic functions where North Koreans were expected to be present unless prior, explicit written permission was obtained from the State Department in Washington, D.C.

Not until 1984 were these rules relaxed slightly when Washington instituted so-called "Smile Diplomacy." Thereafter, U.S. diplomats could attend diplomatic functions where North Koreans were present. If approached by a North Korean, an American diplomat could respond politely about the weather or some similarly innocuous topic. Any discussion of substantive issues was strictly banned. Only after 1988 were American diplomats able to engage North Korean diplomats on substantive issues, but all such encounters were limited to specific, brief engagements at a social club in Beijing. Each meeting was carefully scripted and the American diplomat was limited to exchanging letters and talking points. No American diplomat was allowed to visit North Korea until December 18, 1992 when then Department of State North Korea Affairs Officer Kenneth Quinones accompanied Senator Bob Smith (R. New Hampshire) to discuss future cooperation regarding the recovery of the remains of U.S. military personnel who died and were left behind during the Korean War.

DETERRENCE

Another cornerstone of ROK-U.S. policy until 1991 was deterrence. The goal of this policy was to perpetuate the status quo, that is, a military stalemate. The pursuit of a durable peace and reconciliation was not part of the equation. Effective deterrence relies on a balance of terror manifested through the amassing of armies and weapons. In the case of Korea, both sides amassed huge armies backed by modern air forces and navies. Neither side possessed nor had any need for its own nuclear arsenal, at least not until the fall of the Soviet Union. Instead, both Koreas relied on their respective superpower allies' "nuclear umbrellas" to reinforce their deterrence capability. Such an arrangement, however, created the possibility that the failure of deterrence could escalate rapidly into a nuclear holocaust both on and far beyond the Korean peninsula.

Deterrence was actually designed to ensure that at least one of the superpowers, specifically the United States, would be drawn into any resumption of hostilities. A division of U.S. infantry has straddled the main avenue of attack from north to south since 1953. Supporting the division are elements of the U.S. Air Force and a carrier battle group stationed near Tokyo, Japan. Additional land, sea, and air reinforcements are posted on Japan's southern island of Okinawa. Neither Russian nor Chinese combat units are present on the peninsula, but both nations' proximity to Korea make quick deployment from either possible.

Deterrence is a double-edged sword. It has restrained each side's impulses to resume hostilities, while at the same time it made the peninsula one of the world's most volatile places. Upwards of one million heavily armed men backed by large numbers of tanks, artillery, combat aircraft, ballistic missiles, and war ships stare at each other day after day anticipating a resumption of combat. Tens of thousands of soldiers, sailors, and airmen stand ready elsewhere throughout Northeast Asia to rush to the Korean peninsula to wage war. The Soviet Union's collapse in 1991 reduced Moscow's ability to project its military might toward the Korean peninsula, diminishing its ability to rush to North Korea's defense as provided for in their mutual defense treaty. This significantly altered the balance of terror on the peninsula. No longer could then North Korean leader Kim Il Sung rely on Soviet military might to deter U.S. military might. To restore the balance while also keeping his options open, Kim appears to have pursued a duel track policy. On the one hand, he engaged Seoul in dialogue while at the same time he hastened the development of an indigenous nuclear capability. The policy of deterrence, in short, did nothing to deter such a pursuit. On the contrary, Kim Il Sung's determination to perpetuate the balance of terror, as required by deterrence, appears to have contributed to his decision to build a nuclear arsenal.

Deterrence is a highly risky arrangement, one that obstructs rather than promotes reconciliation and durable peace. Nevertheless it remains a fundamental element of ROK-U.S. policy toward North Korea. If anything, Seoul has taken steps over the past decade to reinforce deterrence by engaging in increasing levels of military cooperation with Japan.

BEFORE DIALOGUE—
THE MILITARY ARMISTICE COMMISSION (MAC)

The ban on diplomatic contact with Pyongyang required reliance on some other mutually agreed upon channel of communication. Given the narrow range of options, responsibility for preventing war on the peninsula was placed in the hands of military men who represented two intensely hostile armies. The Military Armistice Commission, or MAC, assumed this role immediately after the Armistice had been signed. Initially, the MAC was established primarily to implement the Armistice, and to resolve disputes arising from clashes along the 151-mile DMZ that bisects the Korean peninsula from east to west. It conducted its business in the neutral Joint Security Area (JSA) located mid-point within the DMZ, due north of Seoul and south of Kaesong in North Korea.

Membership in the MAC consisted of officers of the North Korean People's Army (KPA), the Chinese People's Volunteers (as the People's Republic of China [PRC] referred to its army in North Korea), and the United Nations Command (UNC). The UNC was established at the beginning of the Korean War to oversee the armies allied against North Korea and its supporters. Eventually it engaged the Korean People's

Army (KPA) in the negotiations that led to the signing of the Korean War Armistice. The UNC maintains its headquarters in Seoul in the same compound across the street from the headquarters of U.S. Forces Korea (USFK). The same U.S. army general serves concurrently as the Command in Chief of UN Forces (CINCUNC) and commander of U.S. Forces Korea. Until 1993, the UNC staff, except for a ceremonial honor guard, consisted primarily of members of the U.S. armed forces.

The MAC shared responsibility for the Armistice's implementation with its "neutral" counterpart the Neutral Nations Supervisory Council (NNSC)—Sweden, Switzerland, Czechoslovakia, and Poland, also established by the Armistice. The NNSC's theoretical role was to serve as a board of arbitration between the two intensely antagonistic armies. Early on it became apparent to the NNSC's representatives that it would be best for them not to project themselves and their views into the almost perpetual verbal crossfire between the KPA and the UNC. The NNSC, its assigned role effectively blocked, early became a ceremonial adjunct to the MAC.[4]

The Armistice, like deterrence, has outlived the Cold War, but not without changes. The MAC's role as the sole channel of communication between North and South Korea has lessened significantly. Since 1972, the Korean governments have gradually expanded the number of officially sanctioned channels of communication. In 1993, one of the NNSC's original members, Czechoslovakia, split into two nations. When neither sought to fill the vacant NSSC seat, no other nation sought to occupy it. Then the Korean People's Army (KPA) pressured the recently democratized Poland to vacate its seat on the NNSC, effectively disbanding the commission.

Membership on the MAC has also changed significantly. The Chinese People's Volunteers, as the People's Republic of China preferred to call its military forces assigned to the Korean peninsula, pulled out of the MAC in 1994. Meanwhile, South Korea succeeded in claiming a position on the MAC although not a party to the Armistice. ROK President Syng Man Rhee (Yi Sung-man), South Korea's ruler during the Korean War, adamantly refused to sign the Armistice in 1953. The KPA declared the ROK's eventual acquisition of a position within the MAC to be illegal under the terms of the Armistice and unilaterally proclaimed the MAC dysfunctional. Pyongyang announced its withdrawal from the MAC and began urging the adoption of a new "peace mechanism." To draw attention to its claim, the KPA in April 1996 alarmed the world by dispatching a heavily armed infantry platoon into the Joint Security Area (JSA). The situation has since stabilized and KPA personnel do occasionally meet their U.S. counterparts when the situation requires.

The UNC continues to profess its conventional role, but in reality it functions less and less as a crucial entity for preventing hostility on the Korean peninsula and increasingly as an oddity of Cold War politics. Direct dialogue between Seoul and Pyongyang via their respective liaison offices at Panmunjom and increasingly frequent contacts in Beijing and elsewhere have diminished greatly the MAC's former role as the conduit of North-South communication. Although the United States and North Korea have yet to establish formal diplomatic relations, they maintain several channels of communication outside the MAC, including regular communication between the DPRK Mission to the United Nations and the Department of Defense's Office of Missing In Action Affairs. As for the process of reconciliation, the UNC has not and does not play a constructive role.

DIALOGUE'S FALTERING START: 1970–1979

In spite of the impressive obstacles described above, South and North Korea have been able to gradually build a dialogue that has become increasingly substantive and productive. They have focused on reconciliation rather than reunification. Their dialogue has alternated between protracted stalemate and spurts of progress. But the general trend is one of shortened hiatus between periods of dialogue and longer periods of increasingly intense engagement. Each new start has built upon the accomplishments of the previous phase, gradually broadening the common ground between the two Koreas. The range of issues has gained in substance, moving from procedural concerns toward the politically neutral areas of separated families and cultural and athletic exchanges. Economic cooperation, particularly in the areas of trade, tourism, and investment by the South in the North, continues to expand and gain momentum. The level of the dialogue has also climbed, beginning with intelligence officials conducting secret meetings, and moving through the exchange of prime ministerial visits to the June 2000 summit meeting.

Seoul's softening of its stance toward Pyongyang dates from 1971. The U.S. disengagement from Vietnam and the pursuit of *détente* with Beijing appear to have influenced the ROK's third president, former general Park Chung Hee, to initiate secret contact with his northern counterpart soon after President Nixon visited Beijing in February 1971. The swiftness and secrecy of the two superpowers' rapprochement surprised North Korea's Kim Il Sung and South Korea's Park Chung Hee. When the first round of North-South dialogue occurred at Panmunjom in August 1971, *détente* between "Red" China and a still staunchly anti-Communist America was well underway.

Precisely why the two Korean leaders decided to commence direct dialogue remains unclear. One possible explanation is their shared distrust of the superpowers. After all, both Koreas held the common conviction that their respective champions, the United States and the Soviet Union had agreed at the end of World War II to divide the Korean peninsula without regard for the wishes of the Korean people. Possibly to check against another secret accord that might adversely affect Korea's interests, the two Korean leaders opted to communicate with one another. This is also to suggest that the avowed purpose of the initiative, the pursuit of reunification, was more rhetorical than actual.

Progress in the Korean dialogue initially appeared promising. On July 4, 1972, the two sides issued the first North-South Joint Communiqué. Item one of the agreement has since become a pillar of North-South dialogue: "First unification shall be achieved through independent efforts without being subject to external imposition or interference." These were oblique references to foreign, particularly superpower intervention in the dialogue between the two Koreas.[5]

The first round of dialogue quickly sputtered into an impasse. Neither side, after all, had taken any steps to defuse their mutual hostility and to foster an attitude of reconciliation. Both Koreas persisted in insulting the other, belittling each other's legitimacy, and alleging barbaric conduct. At no time did inter-Korean rivalry—military and diplomatic—abate. Still the commencement of inter-Korean *détente* after a brutal war and two decades of total estrangement excited the Korean people, at least south of the DMZ. They were consumed in an emotional tidal wave of hope. Their yearning for national reconciliation and unification blinded them to the harsh political realities of the time. But there was no common meeting ground. Each ruler firmly stood his ground, confident in themselves and their allies. Each had successfully reconstructed their war-torn economies, built a huge armed forces, and established firm alliances with their respective superpower champions. Neither Korean leader had anything to gain by striving to cooperate and compromise with one another.

Yet the rigid mold set in place by the Korean War had at last been cracked. The legitimacy of dialogue between the two Korean governments had been established; so too had the principle that the two sides should pursue reconciliation without regard for foreign concerns. During the brief period of dialogue, the two sides also cautiously sought to broaden their channels of communication beyond the formal, rather rigid dialogue conducted at Panmunjom. On August 15, 1972, President Park, in a speech commemorating Korea's 1945 liberation from Japan urged, "the north Korean Communists" to " . . . exhibit their fraternal love by beginning the humanitarian task of reducing the pains of the separated families." Almost one year later, on June 23, 1973, Park in a special announcement stated, "We shall not object to our admittance into the United Nations together with north Korea, if the majority of the member states of the United Nations so wish, provided that it does not cause hindrance to our national unification." Within hours of the announcement, Kim Il Sung summarily rejected Park's proposal regarding the UN.[6]

More than a decade would pass before Korea's separated families could begin meeting one another. Two decades passed before both Koreas simultaneously entered the United Nations in 1991. Given the still intense estrangement between the two Koreas in the early 1970s, not to mention the Cold War rivalry between their respective superpower champions, such proposals were indeed bold. Though they achieved nothing at the time, both identified common ground for future dialogue and cooperation.

In the subsequent decade, 1973–1982, the two Koreas resumed their mutual hostility. By 1974, President Park was convinced of the futility of pursuing engagement with North Korea. A year earlier, in 1973, North Korean agents planted a bomb at the entrance to South Korea's national cemetery, apparently in an attempt to assassinate Park who was scheduled to visit the site the next day. The bomb's premature explosion during its installation killed the North Korean agents, but fortunately spared Park's life. A year later on August 15, 1974, a Korean resident of Japan, sympathetic to North Korea, attempted to shoot Park during a ceremony at the national theater in Seoul. Tragically, Park's highly respected wife was killed instead. Thereafter, Park demonstrated increasing signs of paranoia, not only toward his foes in the North but critics in the South. For Park, any criticism of his rule was equated with pro-Communist subversive activities. He made extensive, ruthless use of the anti-Communist National Security Law to torture and imprison any and all critics. Even contact between kinsmen in the two halves of Korea was suspect and forbidden. President Park rationalized his oppressive authoritarian rule by repeatedly pointing to the threat of North Korea and its Communist ideology. Given this stance, any effort at national reconciliation, much less reunification, was futile.

After 1975, South Korea was preoccupied with its own internal political problems. President Park's intensified oppression of dissent created a police state. He claimed criticism of his administration weakened the nation and invited invasion from North Korea. Park's paranoia and ruthless mistreatment of his critics tarnished his substantial accomplishments regarding South Korea's post war reconstruction and pioneering efforts regarding dialogue with Pyongyang. As the Western adage proclaims, "He who lives by the sword also dies by the sword." Park was assassinated by the man he had appointed director of the Korean Central Intelligence Agency (KCIA).[7]

DECADE OF DIALOGUE AND TERRORISM: 1980–1989

Before inter-Korean dialogue could resume, Seoul had to put its house in order. Chun Doo Whan, South Korea's new ruler emerged from the same mold as his predecessor Park Chung Hee. Chun was an ambitious army general who forcefully seized power on December 12, 1979, three months after Park's assassination. Over the next six months, Chun carefully consolidated his power base within the military and Korea's intelligence bureaucracy. In May 1980, he struck decisively and ruthlessly against his primary opponent—Kim Dae Jung, another man destined to become president of the ROK. Chun imprisoned Kim on charges of inciting pro-Communist riots in his home province and then ordered the brutal suppression of the demonstrators who were also described as pro-Pyongyang Communist sympathizers.

For the next seven years, Chun ruled South Korea with an iron hand. Anyone who criticized him or his policies exposed themselves to the possibility of imprisonment under the National Security Law for undermining national "harmony" and making the nation vulnerable to invasion from the north. Thousands of professors, students, journalists, politicians and other professionals were imprisoned, black listed, denied employment, or forced to flee the country. A small number like Kim Dae Jung were labeled pro-Communists and sentenced to death for having challenged Chun's rise to political power.

The new U.S. Administration headed by President Reagan struck a "gentleman's agreement" with the Chun administration. Washington promised to ensure South Korea's safety from invasion by North Korea if Kim Dae Jung's life was spared. Also, Washington promised not to intervene in South Korea's internal political affairs if Chun would actively pursue dialogue with Pyongyang. Kim Dae Jung's life was eventually spared and he was allowed to travel to the United States.

In retrospect, Chun's confidence in U.S. support for his administration and iron fisted rule at home enabled him to achieve remarkable progress when recasting Seoul's approach to the Communist bloc and its Communist neighbors, North Korea and China. He was able to launch a comprehensive policy of engagement with Communist nations despite still vivid memories of the Korean War, three decades of intense anti-Communist sentiment and education in South Korea, plus two horrendous acts of violence against South Koreans by Moscow and Pyongyang in the fall of 1983. In the first incident on September 1, 1983, a Soviet combat fighter blew Korean Airlines Flight 007 out of the air. This was a civilian passenger Boeing 747 that had mistakenly flown into Soviet air space. All aboard were killed, including a U.S. Congressman. The second incident occurred in October 1983 when North Korean commandos exploded a bomb in Rangoon, Burma where Chun's government ministers had gathered for a ceremony. Half of the South Korean cabinet was killed. Korean television crews filmed the explosion and its aftermath, but the government banned the film from being shown on Korean television for fear of the South Korean people's reaction.

South Koreans were understandably outraged, even without having viewed the film. They were willing to risk war to get revenge. Chun shared similar sentiments. After both incidents, he sought to launch retaliatory raids against North Korea. The United States quietly and firmly restrained Chun by reminding him that the United States controlled all the military assets—ammunition, bombs, and fuel—needed for such raids. After the Rangoon bombing, the United States bluntly told Chun that if he launched a retaliatory raid against North Korea, which he intensely wished to do, the U.S.-ROK defense treaty would not apply. The United States, candidly stated, could not act to defend South Korea since the ROK would have initiated the attack on the North.

Washington's restraint of Chun's basic impulses enabled the ROK to perpetuate its engagement policy toward the Communist bloc. The United States attempted to keep Chun's attention focused on the bigger picture, that is, Seoul's hosting of the entire world at the 1988 Olympiad. Washington applied a "carrot and stick" policy to the situation. Repeatedly Chun was reminded of the "carrots" for pursuing engagement and reconciliation with Communist nations—the possibility of a bountiful harvest of international respect, diplomatic recognition, and economic gain. The "sticks" on the other hand were painted in bleak terms—a failed Olympiad and embarrassment before the entire world.

By 1984, the Chun Administration had developed a comprehensive new foreign policy designed to engage all the Communist nations of the world, including Pyongyang. The outward aim was to ensure full and safe international participation in the Seoul Olympiad. The underlying objective was less apparent but equally important—to reinforce the Seoul government's stature as the sole, internationally recognized, legitimate government on the Korean peninsula, while at the same time further isolating North Korea from the international community and expanding the market for South Korean goods into the Communist bloc. Simultaneously, the Chun Administration would engage and pursue reconciliation with Pyongyang to defuse its hostility toward South Korea and hopefully deter it from committing terrorist acts that could greatly reduce participation in the Seoul Olympiad.

The effort was successful beyond everyone's expectations. Within three years of its initiation, Chun's policy of *Nordpolitik* enabled South Korea to establish athletic and cultural ties with almost every nation in the Communist bloc. Commercial ties also were established with several former enemy nations, including China and the former Soviet Union. South Korea's stature in the eyes of the international community soared to new heights, along with its foreign trade because of rapidly broadening access to new markets.

The inter-Korean dialogue seemed to make parallel progress. In September 1984, North Korea stunned the South and many of its allies by offering humanitarian assistance to the victims of devastating floods in South Korea. With some nudging from the United States, South Korea accepted the goods—mostly rice and cloth. The frequency of contacts at Panmunjom increased. Communication via both sides' liaison offices at Panmunjom became routine, eliminating any need to communicate via the Military Armistice Commission. A special channel was established for the exchange of mail and arrangement of meetings between family members long separated since the nation's division in 1945 and the Korean War of 1950–53. Discussions about economic cooperation commenced in the fall of 1984, but ultimately faltered. Nevertheless, the frequency of contacts increased in 1984 and 1985, and the range of issues discussed broadened.

Progress toward reconciliation, however, was blunted on November 29, 1987. Two North Korean espionage agents planted a bomb on Korean Air Flight 878, a South Korean civilian airliner, when it stopped in the Middle East while en route to Seoul via Bangkok. The agents, an elderly man and a young woman, deplaned at the next stop but left the bomb behind in a radio. Over the Gulf of Thailand, the bomb destroyed the aircraft and killed everyone on board. Tracing the terrorist act back to Pyongyang would have been impossible except that the two agents were captured while attempting to return to Pyongyang. The elderly man succeeded in killing himself, but the woman was captured alive and subsequently revealed that Pyongyang had masterminded the entire misdeed.

The international community justifiably responded with outrage. North Korea's terrorist act cost it condemnation around the world at a time when South Korea was winning accolades for its efforts to host the Seoul Olympiad, while also making impressive economic progress and persistent efforts to democratize its political process.[8]

TOWARD RECONCILIATION: 1988–1992

The balance of power on the Korean peninsula underwent a reversal during the decade of the 1980s. Pyongyang in 1980 seemed destined to achieve superiority over Seoul. North Korea's economy was a showcase of socialist accomplishment. Modern mining and manufacturing facilities enabled it to export impressive quantities of gold, zinc, and coal to Communist bloc nations. Its grain production soared to all time highs, yielding a surplus of rice for export. North Korea initiated an extensive modernization of its armed forces. It equipped its army with Soviet designed armored vehicles, and initiated research and development programs in the areas of ballistic missiles and nuclear weapons. Pyongyang's two superpower champions, China and the Soviet Union, competed with each other for North Korea's loyalty. Politically, North Korea's ruthless authoritarian ruler Kim Il Sung, backed by the unwavering loyalty of a million man army, dominated all aspects of government and politics.

Meanwhile, South Korea's generals pursued political power and lined their pockets with gifts from prosperous businessmen. Pyongyang was a picture perfect city of two million well-fed and well-clothed people. In the South, the government sought food aid from the United States in 1980 and 1981. Seoul's streets were narrow and chaotic. The poor and unemployed rioted in government built slums. Tear gas filled college campuses and nearby neighborhoods where students spent much of their time demonstrating against the Chun Administration. Frequent labor disputes were suppressed harshly, journalists jailed, and politicians corrupted. South Korea's export and light industry oriented economy was depressed by mounting competition from Taiwan, Hong Kong, and other newly awakening economies in East Asia. While Kim Il Sung proudly proclaimed his society "a workers' paradise," Chun was criticized severely at home and abroad for his heavy-handed rule.

Beginning in 1987, however, South Korea began to recover its political and economic poise. Politically, President Chun's harsh rule discredited military dominated authoritarianism, and set the stage for democratization. That spring, a violent, nation wide outpouring of popular indignation compelled President Chun to keep his earlier promise not to seek re-election. He stepped aside to allow a fellow retired general, Roh Tae Woo, to seek election to the presidency. Roh's late 1987 victory over a divided opposition in a relatively corruption free election calmed a decade of often violent domestic political turbulence.

Unprecedented economic prosperity accompanied South Korea's successful hosting of the 1988 Olympiad. For this, Chun deserves some credit. His tight controls on wage increases and heavy handed halting of labor disruptions attracted foreign investment, especially from Japan and the United States. At the same time, South Korea's workers deserve considerable credit. After all, it was their self sacrifice, technical competence, and hard work that transformed South Korea from an aid dependent and small agrarian nation into one of the four economic dragons of East Asia, the others being Hong Kong, Singapore, and Taiwan. By 1986, South Korea was on the verge of emerging as a major international exporter of light industrial goods. Simultaneously, Chun's efforts to entice the entire Communist bloc to attend the 1988 Seoul Olympiad proved a double edged sword. By establishing commercial ties with the Soviet Union and its allies in Eastern and Central Europe, South Korea was able to undercut North Korea's export market by offering superior quality goods at reasonable prices. Seoul's commercial gains were also converted into expanding political ties with socialist nations that had long aligned themselves solely with North Korea.

Within the single decade of the 1980s, South and North Korea traded places. Seoul's intense preparation to host the 1988 Olympiad had transformed the nation. Democratization and the production of high quality goods at reasonable prices won it international accolades. It had become a power in the world market, a producer of goods for export that ranged from the world's most advanced computer chips to seaweed. Prosperity transformed the nation into an urban industrial society with a well-educated and culturally cosmopolitan middle class. Seoul had become a city of parks, colorful nightlife, cultural diversity, and respected academic institutions. Problems persisted, but increasingly South Koreans were acquiring the material means and political practices to deal with their society's shortcomings. As for the once politically potent South Korean army, it quickly assumed an apolitical attitude and concentrated on using the nation's new found wealth to modernize its arsenal and to upgrade the combat readiness and technical expertise of the nation's 600,000 military personnel.

By 1990, North Korea on the other hand was perched on the verge of international condemnation and economic bankruptcy. Excessive use of chemical fertilizers had depleted the soil's fertility, undermining grain production. Aid from Moscow and Beijing dwindled in the late 1980s as the Soviet Union moved toward bankruptcy and China focused on its own economic development. Pyongyang, having invested too heavily for too long in building a highly modern and mobile war machine, had allowed its civilian transportation and industrial infrastructures to fall into disrepair. Pyongyang by 1990 had lost its markets in Eastern Europe and Central Asia. Food, like foreign currency, was increasingly in short supply. Then disaster struck—the Soviet Union collapsed. North Korea in

1990 began descending into an economic abyss just as South Korea was soaring to unprecedented economic and political accomplishments.

FROM CONTAINMENT TO ENGAGEMENT

Roh Tae Woo, South Korea's second democratically elected president, aspired in 1988 to exceed his predecessors' accomplishments by initiating an enduring process of engagement and reconciliation with North Korea. One of his first steps was to expand his predecessor Chun Doo Whan's *Nordpolitik* policy of engaging Communist nations to include North Korea. North Korea initially seemed determined to frustrate Roh's overtures with its destruction of Korean Airlines Flight 878 on November 29, 1987. Once the understandable public outrage had subsided, Roh extended an olive branch to North Korea in July 1988. He coordinated his effort with the United States in what has come to be called the "modest initiative." Roh bracketed his approach to Pyongyang with major policy statements aimed at restarting North-South dialogue. He urged Pyongyang to set aside its animosity and to embrace a new era of reconciliation. The United States confirmed Roh's earnestness by offering to begin bilateral U.S.-DPRK trade in "basic human needs" and to open the so-called "Beijing channel" to facilitate the first formal diplomatic contacts between Washington, D.C. and Pyongyang. This so-called "modest initiative" achieved its short-term goal of a safe, peaceful Seoul Olympiad.[9]

President Roh, much more so than his predecessor, had a vision of a peaceful, prosperous, and unified Korea. His overtures of reconciliation with North Korea continued after the Seoul Olympiad. Roh's proposals became increasingly moderate in tone and specific in formulation. Gone was the harsh Cold War rhetoric of President Park's pronouncements from his several public statements in 1989 about reconciliation and reunification. In his August 15, 1989 commemorative address, Roh urged, "It is . . . imperative that we establish an interim stage toward unification in which the South and North should, first of all, seek coexistence and co-prosperity on the basis of mutual recognition."[10]

As always, Pyongyang's initial responses to Seoul's overtures were cautious. Before engaging in dialogue, Pyongyang always seems intent on first assessing its potential dialogue partner in terms of his political prowess and the earnestness of his public rhetoric. North Korea additionally seeks to determine whether the United States supports the initiative of its ally South Korea and, naturally, the extent to which a positive response might benefit the Democratic People's Republic of Korea. Early on the United States had confirmed its support for Roh's overtures to

Pyongyang with the "modest initiative." The consistency in Roh's public statements suggested earnestness in trying to restart dialogue. Pyongyang's hesitancy may have been because of uncertainty over Roh's political prowess.

Only a politically strong leader with the support of his political party and the general public can follow through on any agreements that might be reached during inter-Korean dialogue. Both Presidents Park and Chun were politically strong because they headed authoritarian regimes only moderately sensitive to the ebbs and flows of opposition politicians' criticism and public opinion. But Roh was a new species of politician— the product of a democratic election, which made him highly sensitive to public opinion and to the concerns of the National Assembly.

Pyongyang's growing uncertainty about its future—the Communist bloc's collapse, the Soviet Union's bankruptcy, the Chinese flirtation with capitalism accompanied by South Korea's impressive diplomatic and commercial gains around the globe—may have proved decisive in convincing Kim Il Sung to engage in dialogue with Roh Tae Woo. Whatever the case may have been, once Kim decided in 1990 to deal with Roh, North-South dialogue lunged forward.

Seoul and Washington's teaming up in a coordinated program of economic and diplomatic inducements for Pyongyang pushed North-South dialogue to previously undreamed of heights in 1991 and the first months of 1992. All the while, the two allies maintained a highly visible and audible policy of deterrence. Seoul excelled in holding forth economic inducements—inter-Korean trade and investment and technology transfer. Washington loosened its grip on its long time diplomatic embargo on Pyongyang. The conventional rhetoric condemning North Korea as an international outlaw and illegitimate state was shelved, at least temporarily. Beyond opening the "Beijing channel," Washington sanctioned Japan's diplomatic approach to the DPRK. France made its own unilateral overtures to Pyongyang. The major diplomatic breakthrough in the ROK-U.S. campaign was the simultaneous admission of both Koreas into the United Nations in October 1991.

North-South dialogue by the fall of 1991 had broadened to include security issues, an area previously unexplored by the two sides. Here too, Seoul and Washington pursued a carefully crafted and jointly implemented program of inducements and disincentives. With deterrence firmly in place, President Bush announced in September the withdrawal of U.S. tactical nuclear weapons from around the world. President Roh followed with a call to turn the Korean peninsula into a nuclear free zone. Kim Il Sung's response was prompt and positive. The North-South Declaration on the De-nuclearization of the Korean peninsula and the

Agreement on Reconciliation, Non-Aggression, Exchanges, and Cooperation followed in December 1991. By the spring of 1992, North Korea had allowed the International Atomic Energy Agency to begin inspections at the DPRK's once top secret Nyongbyon Nuclear Research Facility, the U.S.-ROK annual joint military exercise Team Spirit had been discontinued, and Seoul and Pyongyang had established several joint commissions to formulate implementation accords for their earlier, basic agreements. Reconciliation and reunification suddenly seemed realistic possibilities in our time.

What made the dialogue so successful in 1991? Pending study by future historians, we can only conjecture now about what was responsible for the North-South *détente*. North Korea's sense of insecurity after the demise of the USSR must have been a major factor. No longer could Pyongyang secure its survival, economically and militarily, with a balancing act between Beijing and Moscow. Kim Il Sung's diplomatic dancing with these two partners had gained him the essentials for building a prosperous economy and a mighty army. Without the Soviet Union to rely on, and a China more interested in pursuing capitalism than preserving communism, Kim Il Sung had little choice but to turn outward and away from the collapsing Communist bloc and—as Seoul had begun doing a decade earlier—embracing the enemy.

Equally important must have been South Korea's tremendous gains—economically, diplomatically, and politically—between 1980 and 1990. South Korea had, within a decade, become attractive to Kim Il Sung. It had everything he needed—capital, technology, access to the world market, and at long last political stability. Additionally, South Korea's political leadership had moderated its stance and rhetoric toward Kim Il Sung and his domain. Roh Tae Woo was publicly and convincingly urging dialogue and coexistence. Kim was prepared to engage in dialogue if he gained diplomatic parity and coexistence with the South.

If these considerations got the dialogue restarted, what kept it going and propelled it to new heights? The impressive array of inducements tabled by Seoul, Tokyo, and Washington certainly contributed. Prior to each substantial agreement, Seoul and Washington held up the possibility of significant inducements. Both Koreas shared some of these. Their dialogue and cooperation won them accolades around the world. Both were admitted to the United Nations. Increased stability and improved peace prospects on the Korean peninsula attracted impressive amounts of investment from abroad. For North Korea, this translated into Japanese investment in its newly establish free trade zone, Najin-Sonbong. Meanwhile, South Korea's trade with the world continued to boom. Both halves of the Korean peninsula benefited from improved security arrangements. For the first time, North Korea began the process of making its nuclear program more transparent in exchange for an end to the annual U.S.-ROK joint military exercise Team Spirit. Pyongyang also received assurances that there were no nuclear weapons in South Korea, a major concern for the North.

DIALOGUE DISSOLVES INTO CRISIS: 1992–1994

Within a year of both Koreas' admission to the United Nations, the process of dialogue and reconciliation had halted, and the process swiftly slid backward toward the Cold War patterns of confrontation and hostility. The immediate causes have been amply scrutinized. International Atomic Energy Agency (IAEA) inspections suggested the possibility that North Korea had not reported fully its inventory of fissile nuclear material. Then U.S. intelligence revealed that North Korea had concealed beneath camouflage a nuclear waste site. When North Korea repeatedly denied the IAEA access to the site, the nuclear crisis of 1993–1994 was born.

History allows us the luxury of looking back and placing developments into a broader perspective. Several additional explanations for the rupture of dialogue late in 1992 become apparent. Underlying the progress of 1991–1992 was the legacy of intense mistrust that has pervaded both Koreas' perceptions of one another since 1950. This distorted and emotionally charged misunderstanding was intensified and perpetuated during the Cold War as both Koreas strove to please their dueling superpower champions with exaggerated effort to project absolute loyalty either to Moscow or Washington.

In short, the process of dialogue exceeded the capacity of either society to sustain the implementation of agreements reached by small teams of negotiators. The staff of each side's bureaucracy shared similar misgivings about the other side, particularly those in the military responsible for national defense. Possibly, this was less a problem in Pyongyang because of its authoritarian government. There the leader could direct his subjects to follow his lead. Nevertheless, there were indications that this may not have been entirely the case. Kim Il Sung was aging. His son and successor had long been groomed to succeed his father, but the transition could not begin until after the father's death. It is possible that the more assertive and conservative elements of North Korea's government sought to slow, even halt, the pace of opening the nation to the outside world and of pursuing reconciliation with South Korea. These elements could have been responsible for the faltering implementation of North Korea's agreements, particularly with the IAEA. A more certain explanation, however, must await future study by historians.

One thing is certain, the process was much more complicated in increasingly democratic South Korea. President Roh constantly had to nurture a political coalition that would support his dialogue and methods with North Korea. As his presidential term drew to an end in September 1992, criticism of his approach to Pyongyang intensified. Elements of South Korea's bureaucracy, particularly the conservative Agency for National Security Planning, moved to halt the dialogue with Pyongyang until a new president could be elected.

Actions by the United States in September and October 1992, likewise disrupted the dialogue. Washington appears to have expected too much, too soon. Washington's natural preoccupation with domestic U.S. politics tends to diminish the impact of foreign reality on the formulation of foreign policy. In the fall of 1992, American policy makers responsible for North Korea policy were concerned increasingly with the U.S. presidential election. Domestic political priorities surmounted those of foreign policy. It was more important to the incumbent Republican Administration headed by President Bush that he appear tough on rogue nations like Iraq, Iran, and North Korea. Perpetuating North-South dialogue was subordinated to projecting a hard line. This manifested itself at the October 1992 annual U.S.-ROK Security Consultative Meeting at which the United States agreed with South Korea to resume their annual joint military drill Team Spirit unless North Korea cooperated with the IAEA.

Given the choice between asserting its sovereignty and sense of independence versus submitting to pressure from the U.S.-ROK alliance, Pyongyang naturally opted to demonstrate its sense of national self-esteem and self-determination by rejecting the U.S. pressure. On March 12, 1993, Pyongyang announced it would withdraw from the Nonproliferation Treaty of Nuclear Weapons (NPT). Once again, dialogue had dissolved into crisis.[11]

THE ROUGH ROAD BACK TO DIALOGUE

North-South Korea dialogue has become a persistent progression of disrupted encounters. Each encounter gradually has broadened the common ground between the two governments and societies, better defined and prioritized the issues of mutual concern, and confirmed each side's willingness to coexist with the other. Despite the process' relatively significant gains in this regard, the still common, intense mistrust between the people of North and South Korea persists virtually unabated. In other words, the dialogue's mounting accomplishments continue to be built upon an unsteady platform of mistrust. For two years, between the fall of 1992 and of 1994, mistrust not only disrupted North-South dialogue, it almost led to war on the Korean peninsula.

Fortunately for all concerned, the United States intervened diplomatically for the first time. Washington's assumption of dialogue with Pyongyang was unsettling to the South Koreans, but it accomplished what their political leadership was hesitant to pursue—a negotiated resolution of the nuclear crisis. The U.S.-DPRK Agreed Framework of October 21, 1994 set the stage for the pursuit of a durable peace on the Korean peninsula. The risk of superpower rivalry over the peninsula had already diminished. Now the risk of a nuclear war was also reduced significantly.

The process of reconciliation between Washington and Pyongyang, like that between Seoul and Pyongyang in 1991, also proved short-lived. Just two months after its commencement, the United States and North Korea were once again on the verge of war. The apparent cause was the North Korean People's Army downing of a U.S. Army helicopter that had flown mistakenly across the DMZ into North Korea. A less obvious but more fundamental cause of the renewed tension was the profound mistrust the Korean War still aroused between Americans and the people of North Korea. The North Korean soldiers made no effort to communicate with either the helicopter or the U.S. Army. They assumed it was on a spy mission and fired a shoulder-mounted missile at it, killing the pilot and destroying the helicopter. Fortunately, however, diplomacy was put into practice and peace was perpetuated. Nevertheless, the incident's resolution did nothing to assuage the two sides' mutual mistrust. Ever since, official U.S.-DPRK relations have languished in a diplomatic limbo characterized more by pervasive mistrust and less by growing cooperation.

Looking beyond the Agreed Framework's apparent shortcomings, the accord nevertheless helped set the stage for the Korean summit of June 2000. The collapse of North-South dialogue and reconciliation in the fall of 1992 had excited serious doubts about their effectiveness. Had efforts to forge a diplomatic solution to the 1992–1994 nuclear crisis failed, the policy of diplomatic engagement and economic inducement, first initiated by South Korean President Roh Tae Woo in 1991, would have been discredited totally. A return solely to deterrence would have once again escalated tensions, just as it had in May and June 1994. Another possible consequence could have been North Korea's decision to respond in kind by attempting to preserve the balance of terror, which deterrence requires, by quickening the development of nuclear warheads for its arsenal of ballistic missiles. Had that occurred, the dynamics of deterrence without diplomatic engagement surely could have brought the

Korean peninsula to the brink of war. Fortunately for all the concerned parties, the Agreed Framework confirmed diplomatic engagement and economic inducement as effective methods for dealing with the peninsula's crises as well as with North Korea.

At the time, however, an intense debate ensued from 1995 to 1997, regarding the utility of pursuing a policy of balancing deterrence with diplomatic engagement accompanied by economic inducements. The champions of deterrence found vocal advocates both in Seoul and Washington. In Seoul, they tended to cluster around then ROK President Kim Young-sam. They argued that the Clinton Administration's extension of economic inducements such as heavy fuel oil, construction of nuclear reactors, and food aid verged on appeasement. Pyongyang, in their view, was on the verge of collapse. Korea's reunification could be hastened, the champions of deterrence contended, if only Washington would restore Seoul's leadership in the formulation of policy toward Pyongyang and end its alleged appeasement. In Washington, Republican Congressmen and their supporters in some of the think tanks along Massachusetts Avenue voiced similar criticism. They too argued that the Clinton Administration had usurped Seoul's traditional leadership in the forging of policy toward North Korea, undermining President Kim's ability to deal decisively with Pyongyang. Japan was drawn belatedly into the debate when North Korea, on September 1, 1998, launched a multi-stage ballistic missile across northern Japan. The enraged Japanese public intensely challenged the wisdom of diplomacy and economic inducements as tools for dealing with North Korea.

Paradoxically, as the debate raged in Seoul, Washington, and Tokyo, war was twice averted, and the freeze on North Korea's nuclear program was preserved by diplomatic engagement and economic inducements. Because of the Agreed Framework, the International Atomic Energy Agency was able to maintain a comprehensive regime of monitoring North Korea's nuclear facilities. When an intelligence leak in Washington aroused suspicions about the possibility that North Korea was building a secret underground nuclear facility at Kumsongni, diplomacy and economic inducements gained access to the site. The suspicions were soon confirmed as being groundless. Tensions on the peninsula also peaked when twice North Korean submarines intruded into the territorial waters of the ROK, apparently to off load heavily armed espionage agents. Deterrence prevented war, but it took diplomatic engagement with Pyongyang to defuse the crises.

Seoul and Washington, in April 1996, teamed up to propose "Four Party Talks" with Pyongyang. China, the fourth party, withheld its response to the proposal pending Pyongyang's reaction. Only after considerable diplomatic dueling, and the offering of sizable amounts of food aid, did North Korea finally agree to join the talks. The process yielded little progress toward restarting substantive North-South dialogue. Implementation of the Agreed Framework floundered in Washington and Seoul as efforts in both capitals focused on promoting the Four Party Talks. All the while, the critics of engagement and economic inducements pointed to the lack of results as proof these techniques were ineffective when dealing with North Korea.[12]

By the spring of 1997, the policy of engagement was under severe, sustained assault in Seoul and Washington. There was ample reason to question its effectiveness as a policy to win concessions from North Korea. Pyongyang's participation in the Four Party Talks seemed designed to obtain maximum economic benefit in the form of food aid in exchange for minimal concessions on substantive issues. At the same time, it gained the regime time to head off collapse as it quietly courted China and exported ballistic missiles to acquire oil and other essential commodities. Beijing responded positively to Pyongyang's overtures and quietly moved, in the spring and summer of 1997, to shore up the Kim Jong Il regime with large amounts of food aid, plus some credit and investment.

The chorus of protest against engagement intensified. For a time, the distinction between the policy and its faltering implementation were blurred. In Seoul, domestic scandals early in 1997 discredited Kim Young-sam's presidency. His perpetual vacillation between "soft" and "hard" lines toward North Korea disrupted policy coordination with Washington and Tokyo. In Washington, Republican control of Congress gave opponents of engagement a highly visible forum from which to proclaim the policy ineffective.

Belatedly, the Clinton Administration reacted by naming former Secretary of Defense William Perry coordinator of U.S. policy toward North Korea. Candidly speaking, the move appears to have been primarily a political device aimed at stilling Republican criticism of the Clinton Administration, less as an effort to enhance the effectiveness of the engagement policy. Perry more or less confirmed this in a private conversation in Seoul in March 1998. The White House had just delayed release of his report critiquing engagement and its implementation regarding North Korea. His visit to Pyongyang in June 1998 produced nothing substantive. The so-called Perry Process ultimately proved ineffective in terms of improving implementation of engagement. President Clinton's domestic political problems and eventual impeachment, far more than the Perry Report, deflected the focus of criticism away from engagement and toward the personal character of the president.

Meanwhile, the Asian Financial Crisis that enveloped South Korea in December 1997 shifted the focus of concern among Koreans away from Pyongyang and back to their own domestic situation. The debate over engagement verse deterrence was stilled, at least for the duration of the period of "conditionality" imposed on the Korean government's management of the economy by the International Monetary Fund (IMF). For South Korea's new President Kim Dae Jung, South Koreans' preoccupation at the start of his presidency with their domestic economic woes afforded him the time he needed early in his new administration to rally international support for his policy of engagement with North Korea. Foreign support, especially that rendered by the United States, Japan, Russia and China, lent prestige to his engagement policy toward North Korea and quieted, at least initially, the ardent domestic foes of engagement.

In December 1997, South Korean voters elected Kim Dae Jung, the aging champion of Korea's democratization and favorite son of prominent politicians and human rights advocacy groups around the world. He was very likely elected more because of the electorate's disgust with his predecessor than because of a conviction that he would make an excellent president. Certainly public opinion regarding his formula for dealing with North Korea was ambivalent at best. In any event, he assumed the presidency in the midst of economic turmoil and intense uncertainty about South Korea's future. Lurking in the background was a fear that North Korea might exploit South Korea's vulnerability in some unsavory fashion.[13]

ENCOUNTER IN PYONGYANG

Change on the Korean peninsula persists at a glacial pace, despite the recent appearances projected by images of the two Korean leaders embracing one another at Pyongyang International Airport. The June 2000 North-South summit between Kim Dae Jung and Kim Jong Il was indeed of epic proportions, but nothing accomplished at the meeting or since was unprecedented other than the meetings between the two men. As we have seen, all the accords leading to the summit, as well as those since, continue a process that commenced in 1972 and that reiterate previous agreements. For example, the North-South Joint Declaration of June 15, 2000, Article 1, reiterates the July 4, 1972 accord. Articles 2, 3, and 4 refer to items agreed upon in the December 1991 Basic Agreement on Reconciliation, Non-Aggression, Exchanges, and Cooperation. The June 2000 accord's final item holds out the pledge of an exchange of visits between the two leaders to each other's capital. Such a promise was originally agreed upon in principle in June 1994 between the now deceased Kim Il Sung and retired former ROK President Kim Yong Sam.[14]

Possibly the summit's most important aspect is that the two key participants represent a new generation of leadership in both halves of the Korean peninsula. Unlike his predecessors, Kim Dae Jung is less burdened by the concerns of generals and businessmen; Chun Doo Whan discredited military interference in politics and Roh Tae Woo's garnering of an enormous fortunate in bribes discredited the *chaebol*. Nor does Kim owe his political legitimacy to the U.S.-ROK security alliance. The source of his political success is the electorate of South Korea. Political reconciliation and coexistence are Kim Dae Jung's priorities, not preserving deterrence's balance of terror or the legitimacy of the UN Command. His plan of economic cooperation is motivated more by a desire to defuse North Korea's insecurity and hostility rather than to promote profitable trade and investment. Kim Dae Jung, nevertheless, does not necessarily have a wider range of flexibility than his predecessors. Bracketing Kim's flexibility are political realities in South Korea and Pyongyang.

Political reality in South Korea encompasses an enormous reservoir of mistrust for the North Korean regime. Already this mistrust is being manifested in an increasingly audible debate over how much and how soon South Korea should accommodate North Korea's economic needs. This economic argument is certain to spill over into the area of security. The debate is beginning to address the issue of whether engaging Kim Jong Il will enhance South Korea's security or strengthen North Korea's ability to assault the South. As the debate intensifies, the pace of progress toward reconciliation is certain to slow. How Kim Dae Jung intends to deal with these dynamics, and the extent to which he is successful, remains to be seen.

In Pyongyang, Kim Jong Il's current dealings with South Korea are a continuation of his father's legacy, not a pioneering venture. Kim Jong Il has made this amply clear in his publications on unification. As the Kim Dae Jung Administration was organizing itself in Seoul, Kim Jong Il published a major essay on reconciliation and unification, *Let Us Reunify the Country Independently and Peacefully Through the Great Unity of the Entire Nation*.[15] In establishing his position on these issues, Kim Jong Il carefully linked his views to those of his father, "The *Juche*-oriented idea of great national unity elucidated by the respected Comrade Kim Il Sung. . . ." The younger Kim proclaims his father formulated the "original idea" on this topic.[16] He asserts that, "it is inconceivable to talk about national unity apart from the principle of national independence."[17] Kim Jong Il urges that, "All the Koreans in the north, south and abroad must unite closely under the banner of patriotism."[18] He claims, "successive south Korean authorities [i.e., previous presidential administrations in Seoul] have obstructed harmony between the north and the south with their anti-North confrontation policy. . . ."[19] Nevertheless, like Kim Dae Jung, Kim Jong Il advocates coexistence of each side's "different ideologies and systems."[20]

To confirm his faithfulness to the "great leader," Kim Jong Il ties his views to the cornerstone of Kim Il Sung's position as presented in the essay, *The Ten Point Programme of the Great Unity of the Whole Nation for the Reunification of the Country.* Kim Il Sung's essay cited above appeared at the beginning of former South Korean President Kim Yong Sam's administration, early in 1993. At an October 1993 meeting with U.S. Congressman Ackerman, then the chairman of the U.S. Congress' House Foreign Affairs Committee Sub-committee on East Asian and Pacific Affairs, Kim Il Sung autographed a copy of his essay on reunification. He asked the congressman to deliver the essay to Kim Yong Sam with the message that a North-South summit was in order. Unfortunately, Kim Yong Sam chose to ignore the invitation. It was not until the two Koreas were on the verge of war that Kim Yong Sam finally accepted Kim Il Sung's offer of a summit. Former U.S. President Carter conveyed the invitation to Kim Yong Sam as part of a deal to resolve the nuclear crisis. Kim Il Sung died before the meeting could take place. When Kim Yong Sam described the deceased Kim Il Sung as a "war criminal" in public remarks, Kim Il Sung's heir Kim Jong Il refused to meet the South Korean leader. For Kim Jong Il, participation in a summit with Kim Dae Jung is the fulfillment of his father's wishes, not a major new breakthrough in North-South dialogue.[21]

CONCLUSION—BACK TO THE FUTURE?

The Korean summit caused the world to sigh with relief, but forging a durable peace on the Korean peninsula remains more a dream than a reality. Over the past half century, there has been tremendous change in Northeast Asia. *Détente* between the superpowers has reduced their rivalry and thus eased tensions in Northeast Asia, specifically on the Korean peninsula. Russia's military commitment to North Korea is now significantly restrained relative to the past. China is more concerned with economic development that countering the military might of the United States and Japan.

The Korean War Armistice and the policy of deterrence remain in place, but not without alteration. Although the Military Armistice Commission is more or less dysfunctional and certainly no longer the sole channel of communication between the two Koreas, the Armistice backed by deterrence's balance of terror continues to prevent war. But now both are accompanied by North-South dialogue and U.S.-DPRK diplomatic contact. The Agreed Framework of 1994 has effectively prevented a nuclear arms race not only on the Korean peninsula, but also throughout East Asia. As a consequence of these changes and the pattern of increasing reliance on dialogue and diplomacy rather than just deterrence, the world is a much safer place.

On the Korean peninsula, there has been a fundamental shift of goals and balance of power. Both Koreas, for differing reasons, appear intent on pursuing coexistence rather than mutual destruction. South Korea, now a prosperous economic power in Northeast Asia, prefers peace to the risk of war that would only disrupt its prosperity. North Korea at the same time is equally intent upon survival. Weakened by its lost allies, particularly the Soviet Union, and subsequent economic decline, Pyongyang in recent years has been preoccupied with leadership succession and famine. For North Korea, its survival as a political entity requires that it pursue peace with South Korea.

All of this augers well for the long-term prospects for continuing coexistence and dialogue. But we must keep in mind the legacy of mutual mistrust that haunts both Korean leaders as they strive to bring their societies closer together. The dynamics of mistrust in Seoul and Pyongyang are certain to slow the pace of reconciliation, probably even disrupt it, as in 1992. Yet each round of dialogue replaces distrust with more trust. Time also favors resumption of dialogue and further progress toward reconciliation. The generation of Koreans who fought and killed one another in the Korean War is slowly being replaced by a less hostile and more conciliatory generation.

Having looked backward, we can now better see the future. The generation of Korean leaders who survived national division and civil war managed to initiate and improve a process of dialogue that has taken both Koreas half way to their shared goal of national reconciliation. The journey ahead remains equally long and arduous. The June summit, however, recharged Koreans' hope and determination to achieve national reconciliation. The goal remains distant, almost dreamlike. But the summit made the process real and exciting for the new generation of Korean leaders. Consequently, prospects will continue to improve for further reconciliation and durable peace in Northeast Asia.

Notes

1. U.S. Policy Toward New Korean Government," *Department of State Press Release 647,* August 12, 1948. Reproduced in George McCune, *Korea Today* (Cambridge: Harvard University Press, 1950), pp. 302–304.

2. Ibid., 306–308.

3. U.S. Department of State, *A Historical Summary of US-Korean Relations* (Washington, D.C.: U.S. Government Printing Office, 1962).

4. United Nations Command, *The Longest Armistice* (Seoul: Military Armistice Commission, 1962).

5. *A White Paper on South-North Dialogue in Korea* (Seoul: National Unification Board, 1988), p. 55.

6. Park Chung Hee, *Major Speeches of Korea's Park Chung Hee* (Seoul: Samhwa Publishing Co., 1974), pp. 23, 46.

7. One of the more readable and comprehensive discussions of recent South Korean politics and international relations since the Korean War can be found in Don Oberdorfer, *The Two Koreas, A Contemporary History* (Indianapolis: Basic Books, 1997). A comprehensive discussion of North Korea's response to South Korea, together with very helpful chronology and bibliography, is available in Doug Joong Kim, ed., *Foreign Relations of North Korea During Kim Il Sung's Last Days* (Seoul: Sejong Institute, 1994).

8. For an official rendering of the events between 1980 and 1987, see National Unification Board, *A White Paper on South-North Dialogue in Korea* (Seoul: National Unification Board, 1988). The author experienced much that occurred in South Korea between 1981 and 1987 while serving as the U.S. Embassy officer responsible for monitoring National Assembly and political party developments. He was present at the National Assembly when President Chun formerly launched his engagement policy toward the Communist bloc, and conveyed U.S. government advice to South Korean officials shortly after the KAL 007 incident and just before they met Soviet officials in Seoul, which was the first time the USSR sent its officials to Seoul. The author also conveyed U.S. government advice to ranking ruling party officials at the National Assembly shortly after the Rangoon Incident when retaliation was under discussion in the National Assembly. For a review of the general situation during the 1980s, see Oberdorfer, op.cit.

9. C. Kenneth Quinones, "From Containment to Engagement," in Daesook Suh and Chae-jin Lee, eds., *North Korea After Kim Il Sung* (Boulder, Colorado: Lymne Rienner Publishers, 1998), pp. 101–22.

10. *South-North Dialogue in Korea* (Seoul: International Cultural Society of Korea, 1989), p. 9. This small book contains English translations of President Noh's major statements on reconciliation and unification made in 1988 and 1989.

11. A growing library of books assesses the nuclear crisis on the Korean peninsula. For further reading see Chong Ok-im, *Pukhaek 588! Clinton Haengjongbu ui taeung gwa chollak* (Seoul: Seoul Press, 1995); Peter Hayes, *Pacific Powder Keg—American Nuclear Dilemmas in Korea* (Lexington and Toronto: Lexington Books, 1995); James Clay Moltz and Alexasndre Y. Mansourov, eds. *The North Korean Nuclear Program.* (New York: Routledge, 2000); C. Kenneth Quinones, *Hanbando unhyong* (Seoul: M&B Publishers,

2000), also available in a Japanese language version published by Chuokorensensha; Mitchell Reiss, *Bridled Ambition* (Washington, D.C.: Woodrow Wilson Center Press, 1995); and David Sigel, *Disarming Strangers* (Princeton: Princeton University Press, 1998).

12. For official discussions of the ROK's policy toward North Korea during the Kim Yong Sam Administration see Ministry of National Unification, *Peace and Cooperation—White Paper on Korean Unification* (Seoul, ROK Government, 1996); Office of South-North Dialogue, *South-North Dialogue in Korea*. No. 65 (Seoul: Ministry of Unification, 1998).

13. Kim Dae-jung, *Three-stage Approach to Korean Reunification* (Los Angeles: University of Southern California, 1997).

14. For a more extensive assessment of the June 15, 2000 Summit statement see Lee Jong-seok, "Achievements and Future Tasks of North-South Summitry," *Korea Focus* (July-August, 2000) Vol. 8, no. 4, 1–15. For the summit's particulars and atmospherics, see Choi Won-ki, *Nambuk chongsang huidam 600 il* (Seoul: Kimyongsa, 2000).

15. *Let Us Reunify the Country Independently and Peacefully Through the Great Unity of the Entire Nation*. (Pyongyang: Foreign Language Publishing House, 1998).

16. Ibid., p.4.

17. Ibid., p.10.

18. Ibid., p.11.

19. Ibid., p.13.

20. Ibid.

21. The author accompanied the congressman to Pyongyang and participated in the meeting with Kim Il Sung.

CHAPTER THREE

NORTH KOREA'S SECURITY STRATEGIES AND INITIATIVES TOWARD SOUTH KOREA[1]

L. GORDON FLAKE

The dramatic and unexpected image of first a handshake and then a hug between South Korean President Kim Dae Jung and North Korean leader Kim Jong Il, during the course of the historic inter-Korean summit in Pyongyang in June 2000, surprised the world and led to a growing presumption that fundamental change was afoot on the Korean peninsula. The successful conclusion of the summit, the emergence of a newly warm and cuddly Kim Jong Il, limited family exchanges, the two delegations marching together in the Sydney Olympics, and other recent developments would appear to indicate that North Korea has fundamentally altered its policy toward the South. At a minimum, both Koreas have extended an unprecedented level of mutual recognition. What remains unclear, however, is whether this diplomatic and charm offensive extends to security policy.

On the security front, the indications are far less conclusive. Military tensions have eased since naval clashes between Republic of Korea (ROK) and Democratic Republic of Korea (DPRK) forces in Korea's West Sea in 1999. The Demilitarized Zone (DMZ) has been remarkably quiet. Since the June summit, the DPRK has begun returning South Korean fishing vessels and crew captured in North Korean waters. There was even an historic meeting between both countries' Defense Ministers on Cheju Island in September 2000. At the same time, the North Korean military has conducted the highest level of military exercises since the late 1980s. There has been little or no progress on the proposed military "hot line" discussed during the June summit. And the Defense Ministers' talks appear unlikely to address key security issues anytime in the near future.

What then might be said about North Korea's security policy toward South Korea? The only safe conclusion is that, in view of the dramatic changes in other arenas, it may be in flux. From an analyst's perspective, the current situation of extreme fluidity is a particularly difficult time to craft any broad conclusions about North Korean policy or strategy. With the dramatic announcements and events of the past year, it would be unwise to rule out the potential for yet another dramatic breakthrough in the coming weeks or months.

Rather than attempt a definitive—and futile—prediction of North Korean intentions and actions in the coming weeks and months, this assessment instead examines recent developments closely, attempts to place such developments in an appropriate context, identifies possible touchstones that might be useful in assessing North Korea's strategy, and finally highlights some internal "brakes" that are likely to slow the pace of change of which North Korea is capable.

Defining the Question:
The Role of the United States

With the continuing U.S. military presence on the Korean peninsula and the strong alliance relationship between the United States and the Republic of Korea, it is questionable whether or not a North Korea security policy directed exclusively toward South Korea exists at all. Of course the burden of South Korea's defense lies primarily with the armed forces of the Republic of Korea since the United States maintains only approximately 37,000 troops on the peninsula. However, the forward deployment of many of those U.S. troops on the DMZ and their well-understood role as a "trip-wire" guaranteed to trigger full-scale U.S. involvement in any major conflagration, seem to indicate that, at least in terms of any major actions, it would be impossible for North Korea to pursue a separate security policy toward South Korea. As long as the United States maintains its role as a "protector" and as long the U.S.-ROK defense treaty is in effect, inter-Korean security issues can never be viewed in a vacuum. That said, there remains a realm of inter-Korean military interaction that lies below the more substantial conflicts that would of a necessity involve the United States. Furthermore, from an even broader perspective, North Korea's efforts to "drive a wedge" between the United States and the ROK and its repeated official insistence that U.S. forces be withdrawn from the peninsula are part of a security policy toward the South.

In the first two decades that followed the Korean War, nearly all interaction between North and South was conducted through the United
States, or more accurately, through the United Nations Command
(UNC) and the Military Armistice Commission (MAC) on the DMZ.
Only with dramatic shifts in the international arena (i.e., Nixon's trip to
China) were North and South compelled to begin direct dialogue in the
early 1970s. While the 1980s and 1990s saw further exchanges and further high level talks, the preponderance of the security dialogue remained focused on the DMZ. Some potentially momentous agreements
were reached during this period, but were never implemented. Throughout this process, the discussion of security issues was commonly used by
the DPRK to impugn the legitimacy of the ROK. The fact that the ROK
was not a signatory to the 1953 Truce Agreement[2] remains a North Korean argument today in its continued insistence that any peace agreement must be reached between the United States and the DPRK.
Perhaps the most common characterization and one of the most telling
of the relationship has been the North Korean use of the term "puppet"
to describe South Korea. This characterization has not necessarily
evolved with the times. In the 1990s, when the Kim Young Sam regime
in Seoul was considerably more recalcitrant than Washington in support
of the October 1994 Geneva Agreed Framework, DPRK news organs
and DPRK officials were heard to caution the United States, the alleged
puppet master, not to be swayed by the "South Korean puppets."

Those who are more skeptical of the prospects for real change in
DPRK policy are likely to see in recent developments a continuation of
this wedge-driving strategy. In this view, the recent rapprochement with
the South is ultimately targeted at the United States. By engaging the
South, the argument holds, North Korea hopes to undermine ROK willingness to support U.S. actions—particularly in the security arena. In late
1998 and early 1999, as U.S. concern over suspect underground facilities
at Kumchang-ri in North Korea and the DPRK's missile program
peaked, the Kim Dae Jung Administration continued to urge calm and to
doggedly pursue its Sunshine Policy of constructive engagement with
North Korea. However, with the September 1999 announcement of a
moratorium on North Korean missile tests and the U.S. intention to ease
economic sanctions on North Korea, and as the momentum has shifted
to inter-Korean relations, such tensions have eased. The improvement in
bilateral coordination is in large part due to the establishment of the Trilateral Coordination and Oversight Group (TCOG) initiated by former
Secretary of Defense William Perry in his role as Special Coordinator for
North Korea policy in the United States. Despite differing interests and
differing concerns, it is arguable that U.S.-ROK relations have never

been so close. Such closeness may still be tested by the most recent, and still unfolding, chapter in U.S.-DPRK relations. With the visit of General Jo Myong Rok to Washington, Secretary Albright's visit to Pyongyang, and preparations for a possible visit to North Korea by former President Clinton, concerns are being stoked anew in Seoul that the ROK is being excluded from the security dialogue on the peninsula.

The issue of the U.S. troop presence, despite numerous informal indications of flexibility on the issue from North Korean officials (President Kim Dae Jung has reported that in private conversations during the June 2000 summit even Kim Jong Il indicated a desire for a continued U.S. troop presence on the peninsula), remains the source of considerable debate regarding North Korean intentions. In all official forums, such as the Four Party Talks, North Korea continues to insist on the withdrawal of U.S. troops as a precondition for progress. As recently as the end of September 2000, the *Rodong Shinmun* called for the withdrawal of U.S. troops, describing the U.S. Forces Korea (USFK) as "the main force of disturbance of peace and safety on the Korean peninsula" and claiming there was no justification for the USFK to remain in the ROK.[3]

While developments remain so fluid as to defy any conclusive assessment, the recent flurry of diplomatic and economic exchanges between Seoul and Pyongyang do not yet seem to indicate that North Korea is prepared to pursue a dialogue on security issues directly with the South. North Korea continues to address key security issues (i.e., missiles, the DPRK nuclear program, and presumably even peace talks) to the United States. Ultimately, however, as Dr. Stephen Noerper notes in his assessment of the June summit, "Questions surrounding U.S. influence, the placement of security issues on future agendas, and rationale for U.S. theater or national missile defense will mount as North and South Korea move forward in their dialogue."[4] As such issues are raised, the challenge will be whether or not they can be solved, or even effectively addressed in the inter-Korean context. Issues such as North Korea's missile program, its nuclear program, and other weapons of mass destruction are all of concern beyond the Korean peninsula.

FROM A COLD SHOULDER TO A HUG:
THE ROAD TO TACIT RECOGNITION

Recent events on the Korean peninsula have given even the most ardent pessimist pause. Though largely symbolic, the images broadcast since the summit seem to suggest that the barriers to unification and reconciliation on the peninsula that were long presumed insurmountable no longer are. At a minimum, the "cold shoulder transformed to a hug" conveyed a historic degree of legitimacy and mutual recognition.

BATTLE FOR LEGITIMACY

From its very beginning the conflict between North and South has been more than a simple Cold War power struggle or a military-economic contest. It has been a fundamental struggle for national legitimacy. As both countries emerged from and addressed in different ways the humiliating legacy of Japanese occupation, both represent nascent Korean nationalism and have sought to define themselves as the "true Korea." The nature of this struggle goes far to explain why nearly fifty years after the end of direct fighting, the peninsula remains divided. As the winds of change have blown through the former socialist bloc over the past decade, this divide has also served to inhibit the pace of change in North Korea. Since North Korea's *raison d'être* hinged largely upon its being distinct from the South, any movement toward reform, opening, and a more capitalist form of government inherently threatened North Korea's very legitimacy.

Of course, this contest for legitimacy has also seen its share of direct conflict. South Korea can readily produce a litany[5] of North Korean aggressive acts over the past five decades: attempts on the life of President Park Chong Hee, tunnels under the DMZ, terrorists acts (such as the bomb attack in Rangoon in 1983 that killed much of the South Korean cabinet and the bombing of a Korean Airlines flight in 1987), and submarine incursions of the late 1990s. As recently as 1996 such actions were widely proclaimed in Seoul as evidence that North Korea had not given up its intent to communize the South by force.

There have also been remarkable diplomatic breakthroughs: the Red Cross talks in 1972, the family exchanges in 1987, the fielding of a single team to the 1991 world table tennis championships in Japan and the youth soccer championships in Portugal that same year, the unprecedented inter-Korean agreements of 1991 and 1992, and, of course, most recently, the inter-Korean summit. They were all heralded, at the time, as portending much more. Such past breakthroughs serve to put recent developments in context and, perhaps, to temper expectations. A cursory review of the impact the diplomatic initiatives of the past decades have had upon the peninsula's security environment makes it soberingly clear how little fruit has been borne by the process to date. In an excellent assessment of inter-Korean military relations, Dr. Ed Olsen summed up the security environment of the last decade noting that " . . . the two Korea's, which could have used the 1990s to free themselves from the legacy of the Cold War, have, instead reinforced its attributes."[6]

Previous diplomatic advances on the Korean peninsula have largely been prompted by shifts in the international environment and have not led to marked changes in military or security posture of either side. President Nixon's visit to China and the resulting improvement in relations between the United States and the PRC alarmed both Kim Il Sung and Park Chung Hee and led to a July 1972 Communiqué between North and South that emphasized that unification must be achieved through independent efforts without outside interference, but it did not take or even recommend steps to reduce tensions. As Russia and China normalized relations with South Korea in the early 1990s, Kim Il Sung was compelled to acquiesce to both North and South joining the United Nations separately. The inter-Korean Prime Minister-Level meeting, held in Pyongyang and Seoul in October and December 1991, culminated in what Don Oberdoerfer calls "the most important document adopted by the two sides since the North-South joint statement of July 4, 1972"[7]—the Agreement on Reconciliation, Nonaggression and Exchanges and Cooperation between the South and the North. If implemented, this agreement would have far-reaching implications for the security climate on the peninsula. However, amid rising tensions over the nuclear issue, a decade of economic decline, and other crises in North Korea, the agreement remains unimplemented. While the South clearly hopes to return to what is now called the "basic agreement," the North has shown little interest in revisiting the agreement.

Summit in Pyongyang!

It is in this environment that the June 2000 summit provided such a surprise. The April 2000 announcement that President Kim Dae Jung would travel to Pyongyang for a summit meeting with Kim Jong Il was hardly anticipated—inside or outside Korea. Kim Dae Jung's desire for a summit was well known; he proposed such a meeting during his inaugural address in 1999 and on several subsequent occasions. What was unexpected, of course, was Kim Jong Il's acceptance, and speculation immediately turned to his motives.

Absent of any major shifts in the international arena, North Korea appears likely to have been motivated at least in part by its own economic needs. One of the biggest challenges faced by Kim Jong Il since the death of his father in 1994 has been the continued contraction/"collapse" of the North Korean economy. Scott Snyder described one of the impacts of this "new situation" in his groundbreaking book on North Korean negotiating behavior: "Under current circumstances, North Korea has no choice but to pursue negotiations to gain the resources necessary to perpetuate regime survival."[8] Having failed to extract any real economic benefits from its six-year-old Framework Agreement with the United States and facing an increasingly recalcitrant Japan, North Korea may have felt that it had nowhere else to turn for the fast cash it needed to staunch its economic crisis.

In contrast to past summit proposals, this one key difference must be considered: the nature of the ROK leadership. President Kim Dae Jung's dogged pursuit of comprehensive engagement policy with the North—while initially and perhaps rightly viewed in Pyongyang as a Trojan horse—may have been perceived, ultimately as the least risky.

Regardless of North Korean motives, leading scholars seem to agree that the summit does represent a policy shift in North Korea toward the acceptance of coexistence that is significant. Chung-In Moon finds it notable that North and South "initiated the inter-Korean summit meeting without the help of third party intermediaries. This represents a radical departure from the past since the North had refused to have any official and direct contacts with the South Korean government." He continued, "At the present moment, it is not clear whether the North Korean motive is tactical or strategic, but it has become all the more clear that it is willing to change at least in inter-Korean relations."[9] Victor Cha added, "if anything, this meeting brings the two Koreas closer to mutually acknowledged coexistence rather than unification per se. In fact, the unification formulas referred to in the joint declaration are both premised less on integration and more on self-preservation, privileging one nation two systems as the primary point of reference."[10]

CURRENT SECURITY CONDITIONS

Has this potential shift toward a policy of mutual recognition and coexistence been expressed in the actions and security policies of the two Koreas? As of the writing of this paper, it is too early to tell. As of yet there seems to be little evidence that North Korea is abandoning its most recent slogan *Kang Song Dae Kuk*[11]—loosely interpreted, "strong and prosperous country" with the emphasis in Pyongyang placed upon the strong. With the highest level of military exercises in a decade being conducted by North Korea this year, this appears to be more than a mere slogan.

At the same time, it is possible to conclude that North Korea's ultimate strategy is to fastidiously avoid conflict while making itself so threatening as to ward off external threats. Some analysts have argued that North Korea knows it would lose a conflict with the ROK and the United States, and its posturing and threats are most likely intended to discourage hostile intent on the part of its enemies. To the more suspicious in the South, however, the key question remains whether or not North Korea has abandoned its goal of communizing the South by force. They are most likely to question whether or not recent North Korea initiatives mark a longer-term strategic shift or merely a short-term tactic during a period of weakness.

GREAT EXPECTATIONS:
PUTTING RECENT DEVELOPMENTS IN PERSPECTIVE

As recent diplomatic and economic developments have led to the presumption that there may be changes in North Korean security policy, a closer examination of such economic and diplomatic events is warranted. Recent developments would be undeniably significant if they were primarily a North Korean initiative. A summary review of the past year's events, however, seems to indicate that, while North Korea clearly has had to make some key decisions in the process, the bulk of the initiative emanated from Seoul, or more specifically from President Kim Dae Jung.

In addition to the historic June 2000 inter-Korean summit, in the 2000 year alone, North Korea has normalized relations with Italy, Australia, and the Philippines and appears poised to move ahead with a number of other nations. It has joined the Association for South East Asian Nations (ASEAN) Regional Forum and hosted the U.S. Secretary of State. As dramatic and unanticipated as these events may have been, do they show real change and the beginnings of fundamental reform in North Korea? While it is risky to make any definitive statements about a country that continues to surprise, there is arguably far less happening within North Korea than meets the eye. North Korea's actions and rhetoric have been unexpected, positive, and certainly a great improvement over the crisis atmosphere of recent years. However, thus far, there appears to be far more continuity than change in North Korea's actions.

While North Korea's recent diplomatic offensive is heartening, the DPRK has always sought broader international legitimacy, greater international relationships, and an expanded international donor base. During the Cold War its efforts were stifled by the bifurcation of the global system. Immediately after the Cold War, North Korea was very active in its diplomacy. It began normalization talks with Japan, held the highest level meetings to date with the United States and the ROK, and joined the United Nations. However, the cold reality of the post–Cold War 1990s intruded. The resumption of the joint U.S.-ROK Team Spirit exercises, the collapse of North Korea's trade relationships, the nuclear crisis, the decade-long period of economic contraction, the missile crisis, the underground facility crisis, the flooding, the famine, and, most importantly, the death of Kim Il Sung all shook the regime in North Korea and arguably led to a decade focused on domestic stability.

Only since 2000 has North Korea begun to reemerge—at least in part because it was able to find relative stability in an impasse with the United States. Since September 1999, the U.S.-DPRK front has been remarkably quiet. Up until the October 2000 visit to Washington, D.C. by General Jo Myong Rok and U.S. Secretary of State Madeline Albright's subsequent visit to Pyongyang, there appeared little basis for expecting a breakthrough in the waning days of the Clinton Administration. More importantly, however, the United States and the DPRK had stepped back from the near crisis atmosphere of 1998 and early 1999—when following the DPRK launching of a North Korean missile over Japan, there were revelations about a suspect underground facility, and the real possibility that the U.S. Congress might cut off support for the heavy fuel oil to be provided to North Korea by Korean Peninsula Energy Development Organization (KEDO). This crisis atmosphere made it appear that the Agreed Framework was in serious jeopardy. Remarkably, after nearly a decade of strong pressure on the United States at every turn, North Korea has apparently eased up. This was uncharacteristically docile for a nation that had blustered, threatened, and provoked during much of the last decade in an attempt to garner the attention of the United States and ostensibly to express displeasure with the slow pace of U.S. policy. Whether this was because it had given up on the Clinton Administration or was part of some broader strategy, the result was the same, a period of relative stability. Based on this stability in its relations with the United States, North Korea may have felt secure enough to pursue other options and other donors. In a more cynical view, stymied in its efforts to extract meaningful economic assistance from the United States, North Korea may have turned to more immediate sources of cash.

That is not to say that the situation on the Korean peninsula has not changed—it has. However, the real change has come from Seoul not Pyongyang. While media reports on recent developments tend to focus on what is new and what is unexpected—namely Kim Jong Il's acceptance of a summit, his public relations coup, and North Korea's diplomatic initiatives—this focus may unfortunately obscure what is really different on the peninsula.

There is no question that North Korea has changed more than expected and that such changes are symbolically important. However, it is Seoul's policy that has undergone a 180-degree course change. Under President Kim Dae Jung, South Korea appears finally to have rejected the zero sum mentality toward the North that has dominated inter-Korean relations for the last five decades. Not only has Seoul ceased its opposition to North Korean initiatives, but it is actively backing North Korea both internationally and on the peninsula. In some respects, South Korea has become North Korea's number one advocate with the world. South Korea played a key role in urging other nations to normalize ties with North Korea and openly campaigned for North Korean membership in the ASEAN Regional Forum (ARF). More importantly, South Korea has been making the key compromises. It was Kim Dae Jung's engagement policy that set the environment for the summit, it was Kim Dae Jung who proposed the summit, and it was Kim Dae Jung—the older of the two—who agreed to visit Pyongyang without the guarantee of a reciprocal visit to Seoul by Kim Jong Il. While it may indeed take "two hands to clap," it is obvious which hand is in motion. The one-sided nature of the economic relationship is even more obvious.

This is not said to discredit North Korean efforts. The symbolic concessions made by North Korea in accepting the summit, in hosting Kim Dae-Jung so graciously in Pyongyang, and in other initiatives, both internationally and on the peninsula are not insignificant. However, thus far, North Korean initiatives have been limited to the external and symbolic, and apparently have been calculated to limit exposure to and impact upon the broader North Korean populace. There is still little evidence of the fundamental economic, political, and societal reforms that must take place in North Korea before there can be any real integration of the two Koreas. Such is the very nature of the "internal brakes" that limit both the pace and the scope of real North Korea concessions. The DPRK's domestic stability still relies on control over information flows, population movement, and means of production.

Progress on security matters, particularly in the ROK-DPRK front has been far less dramatic. When President Kim Dae Jung suggested, upon his return from Pyongyang, that there was less cause for concern of a war on the peninsula, he was roundly criticized. Many in Seoul are still wary that while the atmosphere on the peninsula may have changed, the situation on the ground remains essentially unaltered. The ROK policy of constructive engagement with the North from the beginning has been based on a strong defense. Indeed, there is some debate as to whether or not this may have been a motivating factor for North Korea, particularly in the wake of the West Sea incident.

BELLWETHERS OF CHANGE:
GAUGING NORTH KOREAN INTENT

While there is always the possibility that there will be a major breakthrough on inter-Korean security issues, as of yet, there appear to be few indications of a current move in that direction. There are, however, a number of identifiable "signposts" or "bellwethers" that would likely indicate a more fundamental shift in North Korean policy.

SUMMIT FOLLOW-UP

The most timely, and perhaps the most likely, indication of a shift in North Korean security strategies toward the South would be progress on some of the more difficult issues raised in the inter-Korean summit last June. President Kim Dae Jung proposed creating a military-to-military hotline. The ROK hoped to discuss the creation of this military hotline, as well as mutual notification of the movements of military units and the possible exchange of observers to military exercises. However, such issues were deemed not appropriate for the first meeting between ROK Defense Minister Cho Seong-Tae and his DPRK counterpart Kim Il-Chol on Cheju Island in September 2000. Instead the discussions focused almost exclusively on economic issues.[12] Furthermore, the difficulty in arranging subsequent Defense Minister talks and the growing suspicion among critics in Seoul regarding the price paid for the talks in Cheju have led to growing skepticism regarding North Korean intentions.

Former German President Konrad Adenauer was reported to have said, "An infallible method of conciliating a tiger is to allow oneself to be devoured." While the Kim Dae Jung Administration has by no means let its guard down militarily, it clearly has been confident enough to make considerable concessions without requiring the same from the North. As a result, a key indicator of North Korean intent will be the realization of a reciprocal visit to Seoul by Kim Jong Il and other evidence of a North Korean willingness to give as well as receive—that is, compromise.

FOUR PARTY TALKS/PEACE TALKS

North Korea's attitude toward the now-dormant Four Party Peace Talks process is another important indicator of its intentions toward the South. In the October 12, 2000 Joint Communiqué between the United States and North Korea, released during the visit of General Jo Myong Rok to Washington, the Four Party Talks were only—perhaps grudgingly—included in a "variety of available means . . . to reduce tension on the Korean peninsula and formally end the Korean War . . ."[13] This was hardly an overwhelming endorsement of or commitment to the Four Party Talks process, the only process that has directly involved the ROK in discussions impacting upon the armistice and a hoped for peace treaty.

Such ambivalence toward the Four Party Talks is not new. Following the joint-proposal of the Four Party Talks by President Kim Young Sam and President Clinton in April 1996 on Cheju Island, North Korea took a full year and a half before agreeing to a "joint briefing" with both the United States and the ROK regarding the proposal. Even following the plenary and several subsequent sessions of the Four Party Talks, North Korea was not seen as serious about the process and was accused of using the meetings primarily to facilitate bilateral U.S.-DPRK discussions and as yet another venue to table request food aid and international assistance. If fact, it was largely the Four Party Talks process that gave rise to criticism in Washington that U.S. aid was merely part of an aid/food for talks deal with the North.

On a broader level, any discussion of a Peace Treaty with North Korea begins with detailed historical debates about South Korea not being a signatory to the Armistice. (In 1953 Syngman Rhee of South Korea refused to sign.) North Korea continues to insist that such issues must be discussed with the United States and that as South Korea is not a signatory to the Armistice, it has no place in such discussions. Whether or not North Korea ultimately drops this rhetoric, and recognizes that the current reality on the peninsula necessitates the involvement of South Korea in peace talks, will be an important touchstone of North Korea's security strategies. Such intentions have not been tested in the year 2000. The dramatic inter-Korean summit and subsequent talks of 2000 have avoided substantive discussion of security issues.

Should the Four Party Talks process resume, how North Korea responds, particularly when the ROK plays role as host and moderator, will be telling. One further indication will be the DPRK's demands regarding the withdrawal of U.S. troops from the peninsula. In previous sessions of the Four Party Talks process this demand was set by the DPRK as a precondition for progress and was widely seen as a blocking attempt indicative of the North's lack of commitment to the Four Party Talks process.

THE AGREED FRAMEWORK

Another indicator of North Korean intent is the 1994 Geneva Agreed Framework reached between the United States and the DPRK—or more specifically the construction of two light water nuclear reactors in North Korea by the international consortium KEDO as called for in the agreement. Those who followed the negotiations in 1994 will recall that the deal was nearly scuttled by the U.S. insistence that North-South dialogue be included in the language of the agreement, as an area of U.S. concern and as a prerequisite for the successful completion of the Light-Water Reactor (LWR) project. The Agreed Framework was initially very sensitive in Seoul as the ROK was for the first time "cut out" of direct talks between the United States and the DPRK. In addition, there were fears that the DPRK would use the process to de-legitimize the ROK. Emblematic of this was the early fight over the use of the term "South Korean model" to describe the LWR reactors that were to be provided the North.

Ultimately, however, KEDO has proven to be one of the rare success stories of the past decade. While there remains some debate regarding the wisdom of LWRs, given North Korea's current economic situation, KEDO is widely praised for its efforts. More relevant was South Korea's role in KEDO, and on the ground at the LWR site in North Korea, which has been unprecedented. How North Korea reacts to ever-greater numbers of South Korea laborers on the ground in North Korea and to the next phases of the KEDO project could be both telling and potentially confidence-building.

ADHERENCE TO PREVIOUS AGREEMENTS

Rather than looking for North Korea to propagate any new language or agreement affecting the security environment on the peninsula, many analysts in Seoul and Washington see North Korea's acceptance and fulfillment of its commitments in the 1991 basic agreement as the appropriate starting point. In particular, the 1991 accord already calls for the nonuse of force, implementation of confidence-building measures, large scale arms reductions, and continued observance of the armistice until mutual efforts to "transform the present state of the armistice into a solid state of peace" are accomplished.

MILITARY ARMISTICE COMMISSION

One important bellwether of North Korea's security policy toward the South has been its use of and attitudes toward the Military Armistice Commission (MAC). For decades after the end of the Korean War, the MAC functioned as the only viable channel of communication with South Korea, yet more often than not, it was used as a means of challenging South Korea's legitimacy. After some significant changes in the early 1990s (the division of Czechoslovakia and its withdrawal from the Commission, Poland's acquiescence to North Korean pressure to vacate its own seat, and finally China's own withdrawal in 1994), South Korea succeeded in placing one of its own generals on the Commission, only to have the Korean People's Army (KPA) declare the move illegal and declare the MAC null and void. In recent years, the MAC's role has declined in importance to inter-Korean contact as the ROK and the DPRK have utilized other channels.

The MAC and the UNC, however, remain the prominent players in a complex and arcane dialogue that likely speaks volumes regarding North Korean strategy. For example, does the recent DPRK insistence that the ROK secure written permission from the UNC for activities in the DMZ for rail and road links indicate a renewed DPRK respect for the UNC or an attempt to underscore the "inferior" position of the ROK in relation to the UNC? Or is it perhaps a face value desire to facilitate expanded economic contacts between North and South? Any answer at this early juncture is likely pure speculation as it may take an oracle to decipher North Korea's intent in this complex legalistic realm. However, DPRK initiatives in relation to the MAC and the UNC bear close observation.

UNIFICATION POLICY

Without delving into several decades of point-counter-point surrounding the complex dialogue on Seoul and Pyongyang's competing unification formulas, one key question remains: Has North Korea abandoned *Chokhwatongil* (unification through the communization of the South)? In some respects, it is unrealistic to expect any formal declaration of such. For North Korea to abandon its hope that the peninsula be united under its system would be tantamount to giving up—we would not expect the South to abandon its hope for a democratic and capitalist North. At the same time, the North's unification policies, and the emphasis given to certain elements, will likely shed light on the degree to which North Korea has internalized its apparent acceptance of peaceful coexistence.

During the course of the June 2000 summit meeting, Kim Jong Il reportedly continued to push the Koryo Confederal Democratic Republic.[14] Observers note that there has been little change in the North Korean position on this issue since Kim Il Sung proposed the formula in 1980. However, the DPRK has also expressed a willingness to discuss a loose form of confederation that would be implemented in a gradual process. The June 15, 2000 Joint Declaration issued during the summit acknowledges a " . . . common element in the South's proposal for a confederation and the North's proposal for a loose form of federation . . ." Perhaps this is a first step.

However, a key question that remains unanswered is whether or not Pyongyang's proposal still requires, as a first step, the withdrawal of U.S. troops from peninsula. In this regard, DPRK unification policy is functionally a vehicle for its security policy toward the South.

PROSPECTS:
HOW FAR CAN NORTH KOREA GO?

Ultimately, the prospects for a fundamental shift in North Korea's security policy may be determined by a set of limitations internal to the regime. The degree to which there can be real progress in inter-Korean relations, particularly security relations, will likely depend upon the capacity of the DPRK to change.

To those surprised by the flamboyant receptions given to President Kim Dae Jung and more recently, to Secretary Albright, one possible explanation for North Korea's exaggerated theatrics is that what Pyongyang cannot give on key issues, it can give in symbolism.

SOCIETAL OPENING/ REFORM

While the change that North Korea has undergone in the past decade is remarkable (who in 1990 could have predicted a summit in Pyongyang, an international appeal for food assistance, an acceptance of international monitors in North Korea, cooperation with the United States on the recovery of MIAs, and a myriad of other developments?), more remarkable still is how successful North Korea has been in avoiding anything resembling systemic change or reform.

The lack of systemic change within North Korea is itself likely the largest barrier to real *rapprochement* between North and South. As evidenced by the emotional, yet tightly controlled, resumption of visits by families separated by the Korean War, the North Korean system remains wary of outside exposure. In a society where the wielding of power still largely depends upon the regime's control over the flow of information, the movement of people, and the methods of production, change is an even greater threat than the security issues that dominate the headlines. This is the "Catch 22" that North Korea continues to face. After a decade of economic decline, it is increasingly apparent that to survive economically—at least in the long term—North Korea must reform, yet it is that very reform and opening that is most threatening in the short term.

GROWING DISPARITY

Another possible internal roadblock is the growing disparity between the two societies. After a decade of economic contraction in the North, it is easy to forget that at one point it was South Korea that was the economic basket case and North Korea the exemplar of development. (By most economist's estimates it was not until the late 1970s or even the early

1980s that the ROK finally overtook the DPRK in terms of per-capita GNP.) Unification proposals tabled in the 1970s and the 1980s sought to bridge a relatively narrow socioeconomic gap. Today, that gap is growing at an unprecedented and accelerating pace.

The youth of South Korea today are among the most internationally aware, Internet savvy, and cell-phone dependent in the world. At the same time, the next generations of North Koreans have, if anything, regressed. With the exception of the elite few, the population remains almost completely isolated from the world, much poorer than they were a decade ago, and now apparently stunted in their physical development by chronic food shortages and insufficient health care. This disparity is not limited to the rising generation; internationally, economically, militarily, by almost every measure there can be little meaningful comparison between North and South. This growing imbalance has led some to conclude that "North-South" dialogue is an anachronistic construct.

To date, however, this gap has been offset by a leadership in Seoul that has for the first time pursued a policy based on confidence. It is a policy that rejects the zero-sum mentality of the past and recognizes that it is often the stronger power that must compromise. However, there are already signs in Seoul that the body politic is increasingly uncomfortable with what are considered overly one-sided concessions on the part of the South and an apparent lack of reciprocity from the North. Should the South Korean economy worsen, such sentiment is likely to grow. More importantly, the sustainability of this more generous approach post-Kim Dae Jung is much more difficult to forecast. How North Korea responds to a less generous approach from Seoul, may ultimately be the clearest test of its intentions and strategy toward the South.

NEED FOR AN EXTERNAL ENEMY

North Korean society has been kept on an almost constant "war footing" for decades. It is, as of yet, uncertain how North Korea will be able to make the transition to an international environment without a clear "enemy" that can be used to mobilize the masses.

CONCLUSION

While there is no question that the current environment in North Korea is by far preferable to the series of crises that dominated the headlines through much of the last decade, until the process of fundamental reform begins in North Korea, or at least until the pace of such changes speeds up, expectations for a breakthrough on the peninsula should be tempered. North Korea has made significant strides and may indeed be in the process of laying the foundation for future reforms, but the road ahead remains long and the challenges many.

In an article addressing a surge in anti-American sentiment in the wake of the June 2000 summit, former ROK Foreign Minister Han Sung Joo concluded that "When the dust from Kim Jong Il's performance settles, people will recall that North Korea still poses a security threat with over a million troops, forward deployed, and an arsenal of missiles and chemical and biological weapons."[15]

Ultimately, when the dust from the summit and the many other diplomatic initiatives has settled, it will be the situation on the ground, or more specifically, on the DMZ that will speak most clearly regarding North Korea's security strategy toward the South.

NOTES

1. The opinions expressed in this paper are the views of the author and do not necessarily represent the views of The Mansfield Center for Pacific Affairs.

2. ROK President Syngman Rhee refused to sign the agreement.

3. Jong-ho Yoon, "NK Party Organ Again Calls for USFK Withdrawal." *Chosun Ilbo,* Seoul, September 27, 2000.

4. Stephen Noerper, "Looking Forward, Looking Back." *Comparative Connections,* Pacific Forum, CSIS, 2nd Quarter 2000: US-Korea Relations, www.csis.org/pacfor/cc/002Qus_skorea.html.

5. Of course, North Korea can also produce a similar litany from its own perspective, although in Pyongyang the blame has been directed more toward the United States.

6. Edward A. Olsen, "Inter-Korean Military Relations," in *Patterns of Inter-Korean Relations,* Bae-Ho Hahn and Chae-Jin Lee, eds. (Seoul: Sejong Institute, Seoul, 1999), p. 191.

7. Don Oberdoerfer, *The Two Koreas: A Contemporary History,* (Reading, MA: Addison-Wesley, 1997), p. 261.

8. Scott Snyder, *Negotiating on the Edge: North Korean Negotiating Behavior* (Washington, D.C.: United States Institute of Peace, 1999), p. 144.

9. Chung-In Moon, "The Summit Talk, Domestic Politics, and Its North Korean Policy in the Midrange," paper presented at the conference "The Korean peninsula: Paths to Reconciliation and Reunification," September 29, 2000 (The Sigur Center for Asian Studies, George Washington University), p. 14.

10. Victor Cha, "Let's Not Get Summit Slap-Happy in Korea," *Policy Forum Online,* Northeast Asia Peace and Security Network, The Nautilus Institute for Sustainable Development, June 27, 2000 (www.nautilus.org).

11. Edward Olsen finds precedence in the Japan's Meiji Era Slogan *fukoku Kyohe* (rich country/ strong army) "Inter-Korean Military Relations," in

Patterns of Inter-Korean Relations, Bae-Ho Hahn and Chae-Jin Lee, eds., (Seoul: Sejong Institute, 1999).

12. While in Cheju, Defense Ministers agreed to establish a joint management area of DMZ to carry out rail and highway projects. "Gov't to Build Cargo Depot Inside DMZ," *The Korea Herald,* Seoul, September 28, 2000.

13. US-DPRK Joint Communiqué, Washington, D.C., October 12, 2000, *Northeast Asia Peace and Security Network Special Report,* (www.nautilus.org).

14. Chung-In Moon, "The Summit Talk, Domestic Politics, and Its North Korean Policy in the Midrange," paper presented at the conference "The Korean Peninsula: Paths to Reconciliation and Reunification," September 29, 2000 (The Sigur Center for Asian Studies, George Washington University), p. 11.

15. Sung-Joo Han, "The Shifting Korean Ideological Divide." *Policy Forum Online,* The Nautilus Institute for Sustainable Development, Northeast Asia Peace and Security Network, www.nautilus.org, July 11, 2000.

PART TWO

U.S.-KOREAN
SECURITY RELATIONS

CHAPTER FOUR

THE FUTURE OF U.S. FORCES IN KOREA

SELIG S. HARRISON

The end of the Cold War and the North-South summit of June 2000 have provoked growing discussion in Korea and the United States concerning the future of the American military presence in the peninsula. President Kim Dae Jung of South Korea has urged a continued American presence even after unification to help stabilize a regional balance of power.[1] Former President Clinton has pledged to keep U.S. forces in Korea "as long as they are needed and the Korean people want them to remain."[2] Challenging this position, an Economic Strategy Institute study group has urged a phased, seven-year disengagement of all U.S. forces,[3] and a Cato Institute proposal has called for a U.S. withdrawal within four years.[4] North Korea, for its part, while committed to an eventual U.S. withdrawal, has indicated its readiness to negotiate an indefinite transitional arrangement during which American forces would shift from their present adversarial role, restricted to the defense of the South, to a new, more symmetrical role as a stabilizer and balancer dedicated to deterrence of an attack by either the South against the North or the North against the South. The North has linked its proposal for a change in the role of American forces to the replacement of the 1953 Korean War Armistice and to an agreement with the United States limiting or ending North Korean missile testing, production, and deployment.

This chapter will not duplicate the voluminous technical literature concerning the military balance in Korea. It will not seek to judge whether, and to what extent, a continued U.S. military presence might be necessary if the overall character of the U.S. role in the peninsula remains unchanged. My focus instead will be on the shift in the North

Korean attitude toward the future of U.S. forces and how this shift relates to the ongoing search for a reduction of military tensions being conducted both in bilateral U.S.-North Korean negotiations and in the Geneva Four Power Talks. Against this background, I will examine China's attitude toward the future of the American military presence, showing that Chinese opposition would make it difficult to maintain U.S. forces in the peninsula following unification even under optimistic assumptions concerning the nature of Sino-U.S. relations. I will then conclude by discussing two related arguments often advanced against a U.S. disengagement: that it will create a "power vacuum," and that Korea would react to the U.S. withdrawal by deploying nuclear weapons.

I.

Seeking to resolve tensions with North Korea, the Clinton Administration offered to normalize economic and political relations with Pyongyang if, and only if, it agrees to limit the range of its missiles to 300 kilometers (180 miles) and give up its nuclear option once and for all, going beyond the suspension of its nuclear program negotiated in its 1994 freeze agreement with Washington.

The underlying assumption of this U.S. approach, based on a 1999 policy review by former Defense Secretary William Perry, is that economic incentives and political recognition should be sufficient to reach a settlement with a regime so beset by economic problems. Yet as Perry himself has acknowledged, it is security concerns that have led North Korea to pursue its nuclear and missile capabilities. Interviewed on "The News Hour" on September 17, 1999, Perry declared that "while they [North Korea] have many reasons for wanting this missile program, their primary reason is security, is deterrence. Whom would they be deterring? They would be deterring the United States. We do not think of ourselves as a threat to North Korea, but I fully believe that they consider us a threat to them."

North Korea feels both economically and militarily vulnerable because it has lost its Cold War Soviet and Chinese subsidies, including food and petroleum; because Moscow has terminated its security treaty with Pyongyang; and, because Beijing has increasingly played the role of honest broker between North and South. As its economic problems have persisted, the North's ability to wage a protracted conflict has been progressively undermined. In North Korean eyes, the United States, South Korea, and Japan want the South to absorb the North, as West Germany absorbed East Germany. The presence of U.S. ground, air, and naval forces in the South is viewed as a Sword of Damocles, posing an ever-present threat that Washington and Seoul will provoke a new war as a pretext for occupying the North. Pyongyang contends that the 37,000-strong U.S. military presence in the South can no longer be justified as a defensive response to a global Communist menace.

This perception of a U.S. threat is reinforced by the fact that the Korean War has never formally come to an end, even though the fighting stopped in 1953. The Military Armistice Commission, set up as a temporary expedient to oversee the cease-fire, lingers on. So does the United Nations Command, which provided a genuinely multilateral umbrella for U.S. intervention in the conflict, but is now only a fig leaf for what is a unilateral U.S. security commitment to South Korea. Even the wartime U.S. economic sanctions imposed against North Korea are still in force, for the most part, though the United States has pledged to relax some of them in exchange for a temporary moratorium on North Korean missile testing negotiated with Pyongyang in 1998.

North Korea has more and more explicitly signaled that the United States would have to phase out all three of these vestiges of the Korean War as the price for a comprehensive, long-term missile agreement. In a formal proposal on June 16, 1998, Pyongyang offered to negotiate a missile agreement if Washington would agree to link it with a formal end to the war and a basic shift to a more balanced role as an honest broker between North and South. The keystone of this proposal, as I will elaborate, is a plan for a trilateral Mutual Security Assurance Commission (North Korea, South Korea, and the United States) that would replace the Military Armistice Commission and lead to the termination of the UN (United Nations) Command. Under this plan, U.S. forces would remain, but without the UN fig leaf, for an indefinite transition period, and a peace agreement between the United States and North Korea would declare that the Korean War is over.

The 1998 North Korean proposal, which has not been acknowledged publicly by the United States, stated that "the discontinuation of our missile development is a matter which can be discussed after a peace agreement is signed between the Democratic People's Republic of Korea and the United States, and the U.S. military threat completely removed."[5]

The key phrases in this little-noticed offer were "peace agreement," not "peace treaty," and the U.S. military "threat," not the U.S. military "presence"—both critical distinctions. Pyongyang wants to defer a formal treaty to circumvent a long-standing stalemate over who should sign it. The signatories to the 1953 armistice were North Korea, China, and a U.S. general acting on behalf of the UN Command. The United States wants a treaty limited to North Korea and South Korea, but Pyongyang points out that the South never signed the armistice, since then-President Syngman Rhee wanted to continue fighting.

Until recently, Pyongyang has called categorically for a U.S. withdrawal from the South, but North Korean Foreign Minister Paek Nam Sun declared in an address to the Council on Foreign Relations in New York on September 27, 1999, that the United States need only announce a "political decision" accepting the principle of an eventual withdrawal as part of a negotiated tension reduction process that could extend over an indefinite period.

II.

The new North Korean posture was reflected formally in the Geneva talks on March 18, 1998, when the North Korean delegate offered to replace a proposed agenda item, referring to the "withdrawal of U.S. forces," with another one referring to "the status of U.S. forces."[6] Washington and Seoul rejected this offer, insisting that discussions relating to U.S. forces can take place only after confidence-building and tension reduction measures at the 38th parallel have been negotiated. North Korea responded that this is putting the cart before the horse, since military adversaries still formally at war cannot risk the concessions necessary for a reduction of tensions.

Even before the concept of a "change of status" of U.S. forces was formally unveiled at the Geneva talks in 1998, North Korean leaders had outlined it in detail in meetings with me and with other visitors beginning in 1995 and have periodically pushed their plan for a trilateral commission to replace the Military Armistice Commission in meetings with U.S. and South Korean generals at Panmunjom.

The underlying premise of the North Korean concept is that the nuclear freeze agreement envisages a normalization of relations with the United States that is incompatible with the adversarial relationship enshrined in existing arrangements. As a precondition for diplomatic relations, North Korean leaders say, the United States must phase out the UN Command as the legal umbrella for the American presence in Korea and join with North Korea in replacing the Military Armistice Commission with "new peace arrangements."

The contents of the North Korean proposal were unveiled for the first time during a four-hour meeting I had on September 28, 1995, with General Ri Chan Bok, the North Korean representative at Panmunjom, and later were presented formally by General Ri to a visiting State Department official, Kenneth Quinones, on July 18, 1996.

In my meeting with General Ri, I pressed him to explain precisely what the North had in mind when it spoke of "new peace arrangements." First, he said, the armed forces of the United States and North Korea would set up what might be called a North Korea-United States Mutual Security Assurance Commission. It would consist solely of military officers. Immediately following its establishment, another commission, the North Korea-South Korea Joint Military Commission, negotiated in 1992 but never instituted, would begin to operate in parallel with the North Korea-United States commission.

The functional role of both commissions would be to prevent incidents in the demilitarized zone (DMZ) that could threaten the peace and to develop arms control and confidence-building arrangements. General Ri said explicitly that the North would not object to the presence of U.S. forces in Korea if the armistice and the UN Command were replaced:

> The Americans think that if they join in establishing the new peace mechanism that we will raise the question of withdrawing troops from the Korean peninsula. But it's clear from the Asian strategy of the (United States) that the U.S. army will not pull out tomorrow. It will take a long time. Accordingly, we will set up a new peace mechanism on the basis of a mutual understanding that U.S. forces will continue to be stationed in Korea indefinitely.

The purpose of the "new peace arrangements," first Deputy Foreign Minister Kang Sok Ju told me on September 29, would be to stabilize the North-South status quo militarily. "The new structure," Kang said, "will help to prevent any threat to the peace, whether from the South against the North or the North against the South."

One of the key officials I met during my 1995 visit said that "Korea is surrounded by big powers—Russia, China, and Japan. We must think of the impact of the withdrawal of U.S. troops on the balance of power in the region." Another said that "if U.S. troops pull out of Korea, Japan will rearm immediately. We will formally ask you to withdraw your troops, but we don't mean it."

I told General Ri that I did not think the United States would terminate the UN Command as the basis for the American presence unless tensions at the 38th parallel were first reduced. I proposed a mutual pullback of offensive forces or, at the very least, significant reductions in those forces. I also emphasized that the North-South military commission would have to go into effect simultaneously with the proposed United States-North Korea commission and that the two bodies should be coordinated closely by a trilateral steering committee. Since the United States could not speak for South Korea, I said, the U.S.-North Korea commission should not deal with North-South issues and should confine itself to issues involving U.S. forces. General Ri's answer was that the North is willing to negotiate a compromise on the modalities of a new structure and to consider arms control measures. But these issues, he said, should be discussed initially between North Korean and U.S. generals.

In our 1995 discussion, General Ri insisted on a bilateral mutual security commission consisting only of U.S. and North Korean generals. His only gesture to the South was that the Joint North-South Military Commission would be reactivated concurrently. However, when I told him in our conversation on May 6, 1998, that such a commission would have to be trilateral in order to be considered seriously by the United States, he replied that "if you propose this, we will very favorably consider it." When I asked why the North itself did not propose the inclusion of the South, he said that "it is not for us to bow down to you, pleading for your cooperation." General Ri made clear that the South could be a full member of the commission, not merely an observer.

Asked whether the U.S.-South Korean mutual security treaty could remain in force under the proposed "new peace arrangements," he replied "definitely, yes." I then observed "we the U.S. and the South can do this because you do not want the issue of your mutual security treaty with China to be raised, isn't that right?" He smiled, commenting that "these are longer-range issues that can be considered in time."

In mid-1995, to counter North Korean pressures for direct talks with the United States on replacing the Armistice, South Korea began to float trial balloons, suggesting a four-power peace conference including China. North Korea initially resisted Chinese participation in the four-power talks, reflecting an overall strategy designed to offset the power of neighboring China, Japan, and Russia with a U.S.-focused diplomacy. Significantly, with respect to China, while ready to accept Beijing as a signatory to an eventual peace treaty or treaties, North Korea has not proposed the inclusion of its giant neighbor in the projected trilateral commission. Beijing does not belong in the commission, Pyongyang argues, because it has not had forces in Korea since 1958, in contrast to the United States, which still has 37,000 troops in the South and would have operational control over South Korean forces in time of war.

The fact that the United States retains wartime operational control over South Korean forces explains why the North insists that some form of U.S.-North Korean dialogue be built into any new peacekeeping arrangements. The only way to avoid this demand would be for the United States to relinquish operational control to the South. This significant change in U.S. policy was advocated in 1996 by retired major general Lim Dong Won, who directed negotiations with the North during the Roh Tae Woo period and has served as National Security Adviser, Director of the National Intelligence Service, and Unification Minister during the Kim Dae Jung government.

"Only with the reversion of operational control will North Korea respect and fear the South," Lim declared. "Unless the operational control is returned to us, the North will continue to confine its approaches to the United States alone and sidestep or bypass the South."[7] But the South Korean government suspects that the surrender of operational control might presage a U.S. withdrawal, and the United States, for its part, fears that the South might drag the United States into a needless conflict unless it is kept on a tight leash.

III.

The creation of a new trilateral Mutual Security Commission, accompanied by activation of the Joint North-South Military Commission, would create a format for negotiations on confidence-building and tension reduction measures in which North Korea has said it would be prepared to participate. The nature of the trade-offs in such negotiations is beyond the scope of this paper. Broadly speaking, the United States would focus on ending or limiting the North Korean missile and nuclear threat and on getting Pyongyang to pull back the forward deployed forces that threaten Seoul, especially its artillery and multiple-rocket launchers. In return for such North Korean concessions, Washington and Seoul would have to be prepared for reciprocal concessions, including the possible pullback of U.S. ground forces to Pusan, as proposed in past North Korean armed control scenarios, and for the eventual withdrawal of some or all of them from the peninsula. North Korea also would be likely to seek the relocation or removal of U.S. Air Force units stationed in Korea. Pyongyang argues that U.S. air power gives the South its critical military advantage over the North—a capacity for "leapfrogging" the North's defenses that can only be offset by forward deployments.

That the North does not ask the United States to break its security treaty link with the South is significant. This means that American forces could return if necessary. However, the United States could logically seek to accompany a disengagement of its forces with a regional neutralization agreement in which China, Russia, and Japan would join in pledging not to introduce military forces into the peninsula. The United States would terminate its treaty with Seoul; Beijing, its treaty with Pyongyang; and Russia would pledge not to reactivate its former security commitment.

If the North Korean missile threat to the United States is as serious as the United States says it is, the disengagement of U.S. forces in large part could be justified as necessary to remove the missile threat. However, there are other reasons why disengagement linked to tension reduction would serve U.S. interests.

One is that the present form of the U.S. presence reinforces North-South tensions. The economic subsidy provided by U.S. forces and U.S. bases enables the South to have a maximum of security with a minimum of sacrifice. The South's upper- and middle-income minority, in particular, has acquired a vested interest in the status quo. So long as the South has the U.S. military presence as an economic cushion, it is under no compulsion to explore a *modus vivendi* with the North. Former ambassador to South Korea, William Porter, who pressed Seoul unsuccessfully during his tenure (1967–71) to increase its modest financial support of the American presence, summed up the situation graphically during a conversation with me in Seoul on April 16, 1970. "They have attached themselves to the big fat udder of Uncle Sam," Porter said, "and naturally they don't want to let go."

Opponents of disengagement have argued that the South would react to a U.S. withdrawal by accelerating its defense buildup, and that its accompanying anxieties would foreclose meaningful dialogue with the North. But this line of analysis is not borne out by the South's approach to North-South dialogue in recent years. For example, far from considering mutual force reductions, as proposed by the North, the South has been moving in the opposite direction, expanding its defense budgets and its military-industrial complex. An open-ended American presence is more likely to result in continued tension than would a U.S. departure preceded by ample notice and serious mediation efforts. It is only in the absence of U.S. forces that Seoul would have to face up to post–Cold War realities, choosing between the sacrifices required to match the level of defense strength now provided by the United States and an accommodation with the North based on a loose confederation and the coexistence of differing systems.

IV.

In the final analysis, the most powerful reason why disengagement would serve U.S. interests is that the continued presence of U.S. forces following unification would provoke serious tensions with China.

Significantly, while Beijing has shifted to a more symmetrical posture in its dealings with the two Koreas, its new posture remains conspicuously asymmetrical in one critical aspect. China continues to maintain its 1961 treaty commitment to intervene militarily in the event of an attack against North Korea. Article Two of the Chinese-North Korean

"Mutual Aid and Cooperation Friendship Treaty" declares that "the two signatory nations guarantee to adopt immediately all necessary measures to oppose any country or coalition of countries that might attack either nation." Each signatory, the treaty adds, "must spare no effort to supply the other with military or any other support." Abrogation of the treaty is not easy. The right to abrogate can be invoked only at specified five-year intervals, and each party must then give advance notice of one year. The Beijing-Pyongyang treaty constitutes a more binding and unqualified commitment than the U.S.-South Korean mutual security treaty, which conditions U.S. intervention on consultations with Congress. The Soviet Union also had a security treaty with Pyongyang, with a binding intervention clause, but in 2000, the Russian Federation said that this clause was "inoperative," and a revised treaty, adopted in 1999, provided only for "consultation" in the event of external threats to the security of either country.

Despite its treaty obligations, Beijing has signaled with increasing clarity that its central objective in Korea is to encourage a relaxation of North-South tensions, promote stability, and avoid involvement in another Korean War that would divert energy and resources from its economic priorities. Banning Garrett and Bonnie Glaser, in a systematic 1995 survey of Chinese elite perceptions of policy options in Korea, found that "Chinese leaders would be likely to consider military intervention only if they perceived Chinese security to be directly threatened or if the war had begun as a clear-cut case of unprovoked aggression by Seoul or the United States. Under other circumstances, they would probably reject any intervention to save the North Korean regime in a conflict with the South."[8]

Garrett and Glaser concluded that China would have "few ideological concerns" about the loss of a Communist ally through Korean unification. The consensus of analysts was that North Korea is "unlikely" to collapse during the next decade and that reunification will eventually take place through a gradual and peaceful process. What worried these analysts was not the prospect of unification as such. Rather, their anxieties centered on the possibility that unification will occur in a destabilizing fashion and, above all, on what they see as a genuine danger, that it will lead to diminished Chinese influence in the peninsula relative to that of other powers.

When Garrett returned to interview ten key Korea specialists in Beijing in 1998, their assessment of basic Chinese interests largely echoed what he had heard three years earlier. In 1998, however, he found new apprehensions that the United States might ignite a war in Korea by overreacting to North Korea's missile development and greatly exaggerating the danger of a covert nuclear weapons program. "The Chinese are alarmed," he wrote, "by the prospect of military conflict on the Korean peninsula, worried that the U.S. might be too eager to threaten and use force to resolve its differences with the DPRK, and uncertain how China would react to the use of force by the United States."[9]

My own intensive exchanges with Chinese officials and analysts concerning Korea, including conversations during 1999, parallel and extend the findings of Garrett and Glaser. While reserving judgement on U.S. intentions in Korea and carefully avoiding threats of Chinese retaliation in the event of U.S. involvement in another Korean War, Chinese diplomats pointedly warn that it would be difficult for the United States to contain military operations within North Korea in such a war, since U.S. and South Korean forces would be tempted to engage in "hot pursuit" of North Korean forces and refugees fleeing across the Chinese border.

North Korea is important to China, mainly as a buffer against a U.S., Japanese, or Russian military presence in Korea. By the same token, China would not be opposed to the unification of Korea if it occurs peacefully and if a unified Korea can maintain a neutral foreign policy and defense posture in which foreign military forces are excluded from the peninsula.

The principal focus of Chinese concern is that the United States will seek to carry over its military alliance with South Korea to a unified Korea. In the absence of the American military presence, most Chinese observers believe, a neutral, unified Korea, while free-wheeling and jealous of its independence, would be closer to China than to any other power, psychologically bound not only by their historic ties but also by shared fears of Japanese expansionism. A formal military alliance would not be necessary, in the Chinese perspective, because Korea and China share deep fears of Japanese expansionism that could quickly be translated into joint action in the event of a military crisis. Conversely, the purpose of a U.S. military presence in Korea, linked to a U.S. alliance with Japan, would be to bring Korea into a regional U.S. strategy designed to contain Chinese influence.

Tao Bingwei, the leading North Korea specialist in the Chinese Foreign Ministry, has openly expressed Chinese suspicions that the emerging U.S. relationship with Pyongyang is the first step in a long-term U.S. plan to preempt Chinese influence in Korea. Warning Washington not to use North Korea as an anti-China beachhead, he said obliquely but pointedly at an international conference in 1996 that "if one country should attempt to use its development of relations with the DPRK as a means to promote certain strategies of its own, it will inevitably add complex new factors to the solution of the Korean issue."[10]

Advocates of a post-unification U.S. military presence in Korea often misrepresent the Chinese position, suggesting that China would be content to see U.S. forces remain in Korea indefinitely. "After the normalization of Sino-American relations," wrote Professor Yang Li-wen of Beijing University, "there emerged an argument in the United States that China 'tacitly approved' or even 'welcomed' the continued stationing of U.S. troops in South Korea in order to oppose the Soviet Union. This is a serious distortion of China's Korea policy and quite contrary to facts." In reality, Yang said, China wants the United States to withdraw its troops from Korea "as soon as possible" because their presence "prolongs the division of Korea and will lead to the perpetual U.S. mastery of South Korea."[11] This view has frequently been echoed by other Chinese spokesmen. The *Beijing Review* has called regularly for a U.S. withdrawal "at the earliest possible date," and Ye Ruan, a key Foreign Ministry official, declared shortly after the collapse of the Soviet Union that "the United States should speed up its force withdrawal from Korea in the light of new circumstances."[12]

As these statements indicate, it is a gross overstatement to say that China has "welcomed" or even "tacitly approved" the U.S. military presence in Korea. At the same time, a distinction should be made between the way that China views the American presence in the context of a divided Korea and the way it would view a post-unification presence. With Korea divided, Chinese officials say privately, a precipitate U.S. withdrawal could be destabilizing. Thus, many Chinese analysts have soft pedaled demands for a rapid withdrawal in recent years, suggesting instead a phased disengagement process linked to North and South Korean force reductions and redeployments. Once Korea is unified, however, Chinese officials and analysts agree, the United States could no longer argue that its forces are needed to keep the peace, and the only plausible rationale for their continued presence would be the containment of China.

Some American advocates of a continued U.S. military presence acknowledge that China would prefer to have a complete withdrawal of U.S. forces following unification but argue that Beijing could be induced to accept a partial withdrawal. Thus, Morton H. Halperin writes that many Chinese express a readiness to acquiesce to a U.S. presence if American forces and bases remain south of the 38th parallel.[13] The late Paul H. Kreisberg cited conversations indicating that Beijing would insist on the removal of all ground forces, but would not object to a continued security treaty link that would permit the reintroduction of U.S. forces in specified circumstances.[14] By contrast, Robert Scalapino finds it "very unlikely that China would accept willingly an American military presence on its border. After nearly 50 years, the Korean War would have been lost. Perhaps a Korean-American security agreement could be achieved without ground forces in the area—but even an adjustment of this nature would likely cause complications with China."[15]

My own conclusion after exhaustive discussions on this issue with Chinese officials over the years is that post-unification U.S. military links of any kind with Korea would become a bitterly divisive issue in Sino-U.S. relations unless these links were part of an anti-Japanese alignment with Seoul and Beijing. In Chinese eyes, the argument that such links would help to "stabilize" Northeast Asia is a thinly-veiled rationale for a strategy actually designed to prevent the regional hegemony that China expects by virtue of its size and power.

V.

Many advocates of a post-unification U.S. military presence argue that without U.S. nuclear protection, Korea would have to develop its own nuclear weapons or seek Chinese nuclear protection. It is possible that Korea will develop nuclear weapons, in my view, but this is unlikely unless Japan goes nuclear. The security of Korea clearly lies in minimizing tensions with Tokyo, and a U.S. disengagement, as such, would not alter this basic reality. Similarly, a military alliance with China of any kind would make little sense in Korean terms because it would only strengthen Japanese hawks.

As I have elaborated elsewhere,[16] if it is possible to head off a nuclear arms race between Japan and Korea, the most promising way to do so would be for Korea to press for a series of declaratory regional denuclearization agreements that would set the stage for the long-term pursuit of a broader regional nuclear-free zone agreement with verification machinery. One such declaratory agreement would bar the manufacture, use of, or deployment of nuclear weapons in Korea by North and South Korea, the United States, China, Russia, and Japan. Another would commit Korea, the United States, China, and Russia not to use nuclear weapons against Japan in return for a formal Japanese commitment not to develop nuclear weapons.

As the price for forswearing nuclear weapons, Japan would no doubt insist on significant steps to honor Article Six of the Nuclear Nonproliferation Treaty (NPT). In Article Six, the existing nuclear powers pledged to phase out their own nuclear weapons in return for the commitment by non-nuclear NPT signatories to remain non-nuclear. Japan pressed for steps to implement Article Six at the 1995 NPT Review Conference and would be likely to pursue this issue in earnest once again before surrendering its nuclear option.

Fears of a nuclear-armed Korea are linked to the belief that U.S. disengagement would create a "power vacuum," prompting China, Japan, and Russia to compete for dominance in Korea as they did from 1894 to 1905. But the critical difference between then and now is that Korea at the turn of the century was not yet politically sensitized and mobilized. Still largely a feudal, rural society with a limited educational infrastructure, it had not developed a broadly-based nationalist consciousness and was not yet seeking to assert its identity in the community of nation-states. The powerful spirit of Korean nationalism, aroused by four decades of Japanese colonialism and five decades of division, has introduced a new and decisive element into the situation. Nationalism will make any form of unified regime much less vulnerable to foreign manipulation than the politically quiescent and economically underdeveloped Korea of a century ago. Once the division is ended, in short, there will be no power vacuum for outsiders to fill.

The assumption that Japan, China, and Russia would not respect a military neutralization of Korea reveals both a misreading of history and a blindness to the changes that have taken place in Northeast Asia during the past century.

In contrast to the European experience, the unification of Korea would not be perceived by its neighbors as inherently threatening. Germany in the first flush of its unification during the nineteenth century was expansionist, but in the case of East Asia, Japan was the expansionist power and Korea the victim of its colonial oppression. Moreover, Korea became the focus of external contention a century ago precisely because at that time a power vacuum did exist in Seoul, where the Yi dynasty was collapsing. The vulnerability of Korea coincided with a decline of Chinese power that tempted a newly assertive Japan to move into the vacuum. By contrast, there is no such power imbalance between China and Japan today. Neither would risk a military confrontation over Korea except in the face of the gravest provocation, and it would be much more difficult for either of them to manipulate internal factional divisions in a unified Korea than it was in the late nineteenth century. A militarily neutral Korea would be respected by each of its immediate neighbors, in short, if it is also respected by the United States and other extra-regional powers.

NOTES

1. Personal interview with President Kim, Seoul, May 4, 1999. See also the statement by Minister of Foreign Affairs and Trade Joung Binn Lee that "the American forces will be needed here even after the establishment of

a peace regime on the Korean peninsula." (U.S. Department of State, Office of the Spokesman, June 23, 2000, Press Conference of Secretary of State Madeleine Albright and Minister of Foreign Affairs and Trade Joung Binn Lee).

2. Seoul, April 10, 1994.

3. Clyde Prestowitz and Selig S. Harrison, eds., *Asia after the "Miracle"* (Washington, D.C.: Economic Strategy Institute, 1998), pp. 66–68.

4. Doug Bandow, *Tripwire* (Washington, D.C.: Cato Institute, Washington, 1996) p. 35.

5. Korean Central News Agency, Pyongyang, June 16, 1998, Foreign Broadcast Information Service Document ID FTS 19980616000035.

6. The verbatim text of the relevant portion of the March 18th session was made available by the Office of the National Security Advisor, Republic of Korea.

7. "Challenges to Korean Security," an address at a conference on "The Path to Reunification," sponsored by the Kim Dae Jung Peace Foundation, Seoul, June 10, 1996.

8. "How China Views Korea and its Future," *Asian Survey*, Vol. XXXV, no. 6, June 1995, p. 544. See also Report on a Study Mission to Beijing, June 10, 1995, p. 4.

9. "Chinese Views of the North Korean Situation and U.S. Korea Policy: Key Findings," a discussion outline prepared for a Brookings Institution seminar on January 14, 1999, based on discussions in Beijing from December 8 to 11, 1998.

10. "North Korea Today," an address at a conference on "The Path to Reunification" sponsored by the Kim Dae Jung Peace Foundation, Seoul, June 11, 1996.

11. "The United States and Korea," *Beijing Review*, September 5, 1987, p. 7.

12. "Arms Control Prospects in Asia," a paper prepared for a conference on Asia After the Soviet Union, at the Carnegie Endowment for International Peace, Washington, September 12, 1992, p. 5.

13. "U.S. Security Objectives After Korean Reunification," a paper prepared for a conference on Northeast Asia After the Cold War, sponsored by the Century Foundation, May 10, 1998, p. 3.

14. "Korea and Asia in the 21st Century," a paper prepared for a conference on Asia in the 21st Century, sponsored by the Naval War College, March 19, 1997, p. 10.

15. "Korean Security After Unification," a paper prepared for a conference on "Security Challenges in U.S. Asia Policy," sponsored by the East-West Center, November 1, 1996, p. 8.

16. *Japan's Nuclear Future* (Washington, D.C.: Carnegie Endowment for International Peace, 1996), pp. 35–40.

CHAPTER FIVE

NORTH KOREA'S DEFENSIVE POWER AND U.S.-NORTH KOREA RELATIONS*

KYUNG-AE PARK

Over the years, the United States has attempted to exert an influence on North Korea to contain the latter's potential threat to the security of East Asia in general and South Korea in particular. In an effort to exhibit its power over North Korea—its ability to get North Korea to do things the latter otherwise would not do—the United States has sometimes threatened the use of force, as it did at the height of the nuclear crisis in 1994. When the United States approved the dispatch of substantial military reinforcements to South Korea in the early summer of 1994, it was widely believed that the Korean peninsula was at the brink of another war. However, the intention of the United States to resort to military force was vigorously protested by South Korea and its neighboring countries. To South Korea, another war would devastate not only the North but also the South itself. When the situation did not warrant the use of force, the United States adopted another strategy—engagement. In spite of condemnations from hardliners that appeasement would merely encourage North Korea's bad behavior, the Clinton Administration calculated that "well-placed concessions could have a powerful controlling effect on a country that needs the world and that has something to give by following the rules of international society."[1] This strategy of conflict avoidance resulted in the bilateral Agreed Framework of 1994, which eventually led to the formation of a multilateral organization to implement the agreement, the Korean Peninsula Energy Development Organization (KEDO). Although North Korea often threatened to scuttle the agreement, accusing the United States of delaying the delivery of heavy oil and the funding for light-water reactors, the two sides continue to abide by the agreement. In line with the U.S. engagement policy toward North Korea, the South Korean president, Kim Dae Jung, adopted the reconciliatory Sunshine Policy toward North Korea. China and Japan also followed suit by participating in such multilateral efforts to engage North Korea as the Four Party Talks and the KEDO, respectively. More recently, South Korea, the United States, and Japan have dramatically improved relations with North Korea. North Korea's positive response to South Korean overtures led to the landmark summit meeting between the two in June 2000. Following this first-ever inter-Korean summit meeting, the North Korean leader, Kim Jong Il, dispatched his first special envoy, General Jo Myong Rok, to the United States in October 2000, and the former U.S. Secretary of State, Madeleine Albright, made an immediate return visit to Pyongyang. Since April 2000, Japan also has engaged in bilateral talks with North Korea toward the goal of diplomatic normalization.

Nevertheless, a series of developments regarding North Korea's nuclear and missile issues since August 1998 have continued to set off alarms in the United States, Japan, and South Korea: North Korea's launch of an allegedly new rocket missile (*Taepodong I*)—which revealed a much more advanced missile program than the United States had expected; the discovery of its suspected underground nuclear facilities in Kumchang-ri; and North Korea's alleged intention to test-fire a new long-range missile (*Taepodong II*) unless a missile deal is made with the United States. The *Taepodong I* missile is believed to have the capacity to reach South Korea and Japan. The suspected underground facilities could have put the Agreed Framework in danger of collapse had it not been for the U.S.-North Korea bilateral agreement reached in March 1999. The *Taepodong II* missile is believed to be capable of delivering a several-hundred-kilogram payload anywhere in the United States. These incidents resulted in a stalemate between North Korea and the United States and heightened tensions in East Asia. South Korea started talks with the United States to gain approval on its bid to develop long-range missiles to extend its missile range, and Japan has approved the new U.S.-Japan defense cooperation guidelines and cooperative research in the Theater Missile Defense with the United States.

There is no conclusive evidence that North Korea has already deployed the new *Taepodong* missile, but if it were deployed it would result in the precipitation of a major security crisis in the region. Likewise, although the investigation of the Kumchang-ri site did not find any nuclear facilities, if other suspected sites were to be detected, it could implode the Agreed Framework, marking a significant setback in U.S.-

North Korea bilateral relations and in easing tensions on the Korean peninsula. After her visit to North Korea, Albright emphasized that it is "absolutely essential" for North Korea to disclose details of its nuclear capabilities for further cementing of bilateral relations, and this is certainly the stance of the new Bush Administration. North Korea has put a moratorium on further missile launches since the Berlin agreement of September 1999 in return for the lifting of economic and political sanctions by the United States. Also, the Albright visit to North Korea resumed the bilateral missile talks, easing concerns over the issue. Nevertheless, the missile issue continually threatens U.S.-North Korea relations in the absence of tangible progress on curbing the research, testing, development, and export of North Korean missiles. In addition, North Korea reportedly possesses chemical and biological weapons, which could cause further strain in Washington's relations with Pyongyang.

This study will examine nuclear and missile tensions in U.S.-North Korea relations and analyze North Korea's defensive power, that is, its ability to resist U.S. influence. It will first examine the development of tensions arising from North Korea's alleged missile launch, underground nuclear facilities, and continuing missile threat. It will then analyze various sources of North Korea's defensive capability, in an attempt to probe how the missile and nuclear tensions are intertwined with North Korea's defensive power and why U.S. deterrence policy would not be an effective way of managing nuclear and missile conflicts with North Korea.

CONTROVERSY OVER NORTH KOREA'S NUCLEAR FACILITIES AND MISSILE DEVELOPMENT

In the middle of August 1998, U.S. spy satellites detected a huge underground complex in North Korea suspected to be nuclear facilities under construction. Upon its discovery, Washington concluded that it might be North Korea's effort to revive its frozen nuclear program. The United States immediately insisted on access to those facilities and the House of Representatives Appropriations Committee voted to drop U.S.$35 million in funding for North Korea's heavy oil from a foreign aid bill. The U.S. Congress subsequently gave the Clinton Administration a deadline of June 1, 1999 to inspect the suspected site.

In the midst of the controversy over the underground facilities, another challenge came when North Korea was reported to have test-fired a ballistic missile over Japanese territory on August 31, 1998. It alarmed the United States because at risk were not only the countries surrounding Korea but also nations within the range of those countries that might eventually purchase North Korean missiles. The United States has made it clear that the North Korean missile program is a serious threat to the East Asian region and will irreparably harm efforts to improve their bilateral relations. It has continued to press North Korea to cease all development, testing, deployment, and export of missiles and missile technology.

The report on North Korea's missile test over Japanese territory exasperated Japan. Its immediate response was that it would break off diplomatic talks with North Korea, refuse to give any food aid, suspend contributions to the KEDO, and ban all chartered flights between Japan and North Korea. Then ruling Liberal Democratic Party (LDP) secretary-general, Yoshiro Mori, did not hesitate to say, "If the firing was intentional, it's quite fair to say that a war could have broken out."[2] The Japanese flared up because of the mere fact that a booster flew over Japan, regardless of whether it was a missile or a satellite as North Korea insisted. Since then, Japan has continuously raised suspicions about North Korea: Japanese newspapers reported that North Korea has three suspected nuclear weapons development facilities and has begun construction on at least five underground ballistic missile launch sites near its borders with China and South Korea.[3]

South Korea condemned North Korea's missile launch, arguing that it was a serious security threat to the region as it demonstrated North Korea's ability to deliver a missile, whether it was a ballistic missile or a satellite. The responses from China and Russia were less harsh. The Chinese Foreign Ministry simply stated that it had no prior knowledge of North Korea's plan to test-fire a ballistic missile, and urged all relevant parties to negotiate in order to safeguard peace and stability. Russia asked North Korea for an explanation of the test, but clearly stated, "It is our principled stance that we want a normal, neighborly relationship with North Korea."[4]

North Korea responded to these charges with great anger and a threat to wipe out "American imperialists, Japanese reactionaries, and South Korean puppets." Claiming that the Kumchang-ri underground facility is for civilian economic use, it warned that U.S. allegations were "as good as a declaration of war." It demanded the United States compensate for "slander, insult and defamation" if the U.S. charges were proved groundless through a visit to the site. Its demand for $300 million or other economic benefits and food aid equivalent to that amount is claimed "very just because once [North Koreans] open an object, which is very sensitive in view of [their] national security . . . [they] cannot use it for its original purpose."[5]

According to North Korea, the August rocket launch was its satellite *Kwangmyongsong No. 1*, and a satellite launch is an internationally recognized right of a sovereign state. It accused the United States of taking an unnecessarily hard-line stance on the missile and nuclear issues in order to use it as an excuse to start a war. It went on to say that if the "U.S. imperialists provoke a war," North Koreans will not miss the opportunity and will answer it with an annihilating blow.[6] Mass anti-U.S. rallies were held in Pyongyang with a stern message that the United States should know North Korea's warning was not a bluff. Vice Defense Minister Jong Chang Yol warned, "If [the United States] finally unleashes a war, our People's Army will blow up the U.S. territory as a whole. . . . The U.S. imperialist aggressors should be mindful that this planet will never exist without Korea."[7] North Korea then publicly announced its preparedness for another medium-range missile launch on 1998 Christmas Day: "It was foolish for the United States to expect any change in our attitude. We are fully ready to launch an artificial satellite again when we think it is necessary."[8] This was to show that the U.S. and its allies' warnings did not frighten North Korea. A Chinese reporter stationed in Pyongyang confirmed that North Korea was then in a state of war readiness against anticipated U.S. air strikes on the Kumchang-ri facility and a subsequent all-out war.[9]

North Korea's attack on Japan was particularly severe. Following its criticism of the United States, the North Korean Foreign Ministry stated, "what is more intolerable is Japan's behavior."[10] According to North Korea, the Japanese authorities were "lonely insisting that the satellite launch was that of a ballistic missile" and were "running amuck alone even embarrassing their fellows."[11] Accusing Japan of using the rocket launch as a "pretext to revive militarism," North Korea declared that bilateral relations had reached the point of "heading to the dangerous threshold of war." Japan is accused of using the missile issue to create favorable public opinion for the revised U.S.-Japan defense cooperation guidelines and the development of the Theater Missile Defense system. North Korea sternly warned that whether its artificial satellites would be used for a military purpose or not entirely depends on the attitude of Japan, the United States, and South Korea, all of which it denounced for engaging in a "criminal triangular military alliance."

Following the alleged missile launch, there had been widespread reports about North Korea's plan for a second launch in the fall of 1999, which caused further tension between the United States and North Korea. As another North Korean launch could trigger a missile race in East Asia, it was perceived as a grave threat to U.S. interests. North Korea's expected launch of a missile alarmed Japan and South Korea again. *Yomiuri Shimbun* reported that about 60 percent of the Japanese feared a direct attack on Japan by North Korea.[12] South Korea began to pressure the United States for an agreement to increase the range of its military missiles from 180 km to 500 km and to nullify the limit on the range of commercial launch vehicles.[13]

As tensions were rising in U.S.-North Korea relations and around the Korean peninsula, the United States initiated talks with North Korea on these issues. In March 1999, both sides successfully defused the nuclear site crisis, at least for the present, by agreeing on U.S. visits to the suspected site at Kumchang-ri in return for a political reward as well as economic aid promised by the United States. However, suspicions about other alleged nuclear facilities still remain as the agreement deals only with the Kumchang-ri site.

Talks also began on North Korea's missile test and the Berlin Agreement in September 1999 brought about North Korea's pledge not to test-fire a long-range missile for the duration of the high-level talks with the United States. In order to derive North Korea's cooperation, the United States lifted some economic sanctions, administered under the Trading with the Enemy Act, the Defense Production Act, and the Department of Commerce's Export Administration Regulations. In response to this, North Korea announced a temporary ban on its missile tests to help create an atmosphere favorable for bilateral talks. Another negotiation effort in July 2000 over this issue ended in a stalemate, however, as both reiterated their stance: North Korea sought compensation for suspending its exports of missile technology and the United States refused to pay. North Korea also rejected U.S. demands to curb its missile development program, arguing that missile development is part of its right to self-defense. The second Berlin meeting, in January 2000, led to the agreement on the first high-level North Korean visit to the United States, reciprocating U.S. Presidential Special Envoy William Perry's visit to Pyongyang in May 1999. The subsequent visit of the North Korean special envoy to the United States and Albright's following visit marked a milestone in U.S.-North Korea relations. After the exchange of visits, the two countries moved closer toward easing concerns over the issue as North Korea proposed to give up its long-range missiles in exchange for the launching of its satellites by other countries. Nevertheless, the missile talks in November 2000 stalled again, and major issues remain to be resolved.

In regards to resolving the impasse between the United States and North Korea, many policymakers in the United States have advocated a power politics position. Former Representative Bob Livingston argued that the United States ought to stop talking to North Korea and withdraw from the Agreed Framework. He said, "I see this [missile launch] as a pretty good excuse just to get out of the [Agreed Framework]."[14] Another Congressman, Benjamin Gilman, former Chairman of the House International Relations Committee, echoed Livingston, saying, "It is time for the [Clinton] Administration to reappraise our policy toward North Korea. It's evident our current policies have been ineffective in engaging the North Korean machine and reducing military tensions on the Korean Peninsula."[15] He went on to say, "For the first time in our history, we are within missile range of an arguably irrational rogue regime. Regrettably, we cannot defend against that threat."[16] They contend that the absence of a strategy based on power politics by the United States and its allies will only maintain high tension. Senator Craig Thomas, former chairman of the Senate Foreign Relations Subcommittee on East Asian and Pacific Affairs, expressed his strong doubt in North Korea's goodwill to solve the problem: "I don't think there is any reason to trust them. You have a government that is more like a cult, and that is obviously going downhill economically."[17] The agreement on the Kumchang-ri site and the Berlin Agreement were criticized as U.S. buyouts of North Korea's belligerence. The House Republicans also raised their doubts about the Perry report, which suggests a comprehensive package peace proposal to establish diplomatic relations with North Korea. Overall, the engagement policy was attacked as appeasement, bribery, and a one-sided love affair. With the new Republican administration, the attack has been more intense.

This hard-line stance by policymakers derives from the traditional power approach, which is grounded in the belief that the powerful can make the less powerful act against the latter's will. It is my contention, however, that although North Korea is much less powerful than the United States, the power politics approach is of limited use in analyzing U.S.-North Korea relations. It will be demonstrated in the following section, by analyzing various sources of North Korea's ability to resist U.S. demands, that North Korea is able to defend its interests even against the only superpower, the United States.

NORTH KOREA'S DEFENSIVE POWER

In accordance with traditional power politics, relations between countries with power asymmetries are often characterized by impositions from the stronger nation. In this case, any noncompliance by the weaker is expected to meet with a sanction by the stronger party. However, a small number of studies have pointed to a paradoxical phenomenon of the "power of the weak," suggesting that weak powers are able to exercise substantial influence in the international system and manipulate and lead a great power against its will. In analyzing the power of weak states, most of these studies—which were conducted during the Cold War era—focused their analyses on structural/systemic factors, especially the matter of bipolarity and the degree of great power competition.[18] They analyzed the power of the weak mostly within alliances, such as the influence of the weak on their great power allies under a tight or loose bipolar system. In assessing weak allied states' influence, the relationship between the superpowers was also regarded as a dynamic factor, and many studies explored whether weak state power increased or decreased as tensions between the superpowers arose. Weak state power was mainly accounted for by external factors such as polarity and great power relations, while internal domestic factors received little attention. Although critics of neorealism have recently shown the salience of domestic constraints on state behavior, they have based their studies primarily on great powers. Due to this great power bias, studies have been largely silent on the domestic elements of weak states.[19]

In the post–Cold War era, however, the matter of bipolarity or superpower tension in assessing weak state power is no longer relevant. Furthermore, in analyzing a country that is not yet integrated into the international interdependence web, such as North Korea, domestic variables are of greater importance. The following section examines the domestic factors that help Pyongyang increase its capacity to withstand pressure from Washington and compensate for the asymmetry of power between the two systems. These factors contribute to enhancing North Korea's "defensive power" to resist U.S. "offensive power." "Offensive power" refers to influence capability, or the ability to affect the environment, while "defensive power," correspondingly, is the ability to avoid being influenced by other states, that is, the ability to resist the offensive capabilities of the environment.[20]

THREAT TO ITS SURVIVAL

The rapidly changing security environment since the late 1980s has been filled with frightening developments for North Korea. The demise of socialism and normalization of the relationship between North Korea's former allies, Russia and China, and South Korea have been widely viewed as a prelude to North Korea's collapse. When Moscow informed Pyongyang of its decision to establish diplomatic ties with Seoul, then-Foreign Minister Kim Young Nam warned that North Korea had no choice but to facilitate the development of necessary weapons, indicating a possible development of nuclear weapons. North Korea perceived a grave danger to its security and survival, and the new developments around the world and on the Korean peninsula aroused its fear and a sense of crisis. Since early 2000, North Korea has made diplomatic offensives. It has established diplomatic relations with several countries, including Italy, Great Britain, Canada, the Netherlands, Australia, and the Philippines. These initiatives reflect North Korea's efforts to overcome the perceived danger to its security and survival.

For the United States, the nuclear and missile problem with North Korea is explained as part of its global strategy to prevent their proliferation. It is also part of American efforts to reduce military conflict in the post–Cold War era. Although it is a matter of major significance in the U.S. global strategy, it is not a matter of life and death for the United States. The American stakes in the Korean nuclear and missile standoff are high, but by no means the highest. After all, the United States, preoccupied with deterring the proliferation effect and preserving the Nuclear Nonproliferation Treaty (NPT) regime, agreed to settle the problem in 1994 by freezing the present nuclear activities of North Korea. It gave up its initial condition of any negotiation, namely, nuclear transparency, including North Korea's past nuclear activities. Despite the CIA's estimate that there was a "better than even" chance that North Korea had already developed one or two bombs, the United States left these intact for five years at least.

On the other hand, North Korean stakes in the nuclear and missile issues with the United States are directly linked to its own survival. North Korea has always been excessively concerned with the American military threat. North Korea has believed that the United States, having brought down socialism in the former Soviet Union and Eastern Europe, is also determined to overthrow its own government in collusion with South Korea. Washington's uncompromising position on keeping its troops in South Korea further bolsters North Korea's perceived threat. North Korea's 1999 New Year joint editorial[21] called for making the year a "turning point in building a powerful nation," emphasizing both a militarily and economically powerful socialist state. This indicates that its survival under security threats and economic difficulties is given first priority. For North Korea, avoiding transparency in missile and nuclear issues is a desperate need as it could contribute to building a militarily powerful state or at least to being perceived as a militarily powerful state. In this sense, North Korea has a compelling reason to resist U.S. demands for inspection of alleged missile and nuclear underground sites, unless it receives some economic compensation and thus increases its ability to survive economic disarray. For state survival, concessions in military areas need to be compensated to increase economic survivability. Otherwise, giving in to U.S. demands and giving up whatever leverage North Korea might have in nuclear and missile issues would be putting both military and economic survival in grave danger.

Moreover, considering that missiles and nuclear weapons have great economic value and are thus indispensable for its economic survival as well, North Korea has every reason not to give them up, especially through mere pressure from the United States and other countries. The North Korean economy continued to decline during the 1990s, with the result that fewer than 20 percent of its factories were in operation. Kim Jong Il's second secret trip to China within eight months, in January 2001, for a tour of Shanghai's financial district demonstrates how serious North Korean economic disarray is. It is not surprising that North Korea has demanded monetary compensation whenever nuclear and missile problems have been raised, in return for an inspection of their alleged sites or for ending their exports. According to the U.S. CIA, North Korea has become the world's largest missile exporter, earning about $580 million between 1987 and 1992. North Korea itself acknowledged the value of missile exports for foreign exchange: "Starting with the food problem, we must solve our economic problems alone . . . by aggressively progressing in the global advanced technology market which includes commercial satellite launches."[22] Missile and nuclear weapon issues are aimed at boosting its survival as they have multifaceted merits, not only militarily, but also economically.

In short, North Korea's fear of military insecurity and economic failure have led it to perceive the nuclear and missile issues as struggles about the very existence of the nation. When the issues are perceived to be mainly about its survival rather than as something to do with U.S. efforts to prevent nuclear and missile proliferation, North Korea has compelling reasons to resist U.S. demands. As noted by A. George, the relations between stronger and weaker states are often characterized by asymmetry of motivation.[23] This motivational asymmetry can compensate for the inferiority of a weaker state in power capabilities when that state has stronger motivational power, which is closely related to the stakes in a dispute. North Korea's perceived stakes in the nuclear and missile issues are much higher than the stakes for the United States, and this motivational power of North Korea greatly enhances its resistance and exercise of defensive power.

JUCHE IDEOLOGY

Juche (self-reliance) ideology in North Korea is the central guideline for both domestic and foreign policies. The core concepts of *Juche,* independence and sovereignty, have been the manifest goal of North Korea's foreign policy.[24] North Koreans commonly believe that the *Juche* ideology successfully protected the country from the uneasiness of Sino-Soviet tension and shielded Pyongyang from the strong winds of "revisionism" that swept other socialist countries. Concerning the winds of reform sweeping across Eastern Europe in the 1980s, Kim Il Sung emphasized that North Korean socialism, in conformity with *Juche* ideology, was quite "unique" and completely different from the socialism in Eastern Europe which lacked leadership and a leading ideology:

> All other socialist countries have adopted old forms of socialism or have adopted mechanically other countries' socialist formula to their countries without having a correct leadership and a leading ideology even though they are quite different in social character and social situation. Consequently, the socialist construction there will not be successful.[25]

Lack of nationalistic ideology rather than the superiority of capitalist countries was blamed for the demise of socialism.[26] Socialism in North Korea, Kim maintained, "remains completely unchanged to the wonder and admiration of the entire world."[27] Accusing Moscow of colluding with South Korea on the occasion of establishment of full diplomatic relations between the two, *Rodong Shinmun* emphasized that this was an era of *independence*. It contended that no matter how serious the twists and turns might be, the North Korean people would live their own way to the end.[28]

What is important in North Korea's foreign policy with respect to the promotion of *Juche* is the principle of anti-foreign intervention, which is clearly prescribed in the Constitution itself. Article Three states that "the DPRK is against imperialist aggressors, and it is a revolutionary regime which embodies the spirit of national *independence* [emphasis added] . . ." As such, the regime is built on the grounds of national self-determination and anti-imperialism. Under this *Juche* doctrine, North Korea has pursued a policy of military self-defense, economic self-sufficiency, and ideological nationalism. Apparently, the pursuit of *Juche* in all walks of life has not always been congruent with harsh reality, and North Korea has shown a remarkable resilience over the years as we can see in its appeal for food aid to the international community. Nevertheless, Pyongyang has extolled independence as a major tool in foreign policy. In the first editorial of *Rodong Shinmun* on foreign policy after the death of Kim Il Sung on July 8, 1994, it was reaffirmed that "the ideology of independence is a basic cornerstone of our republic's foreign policies and activities."[29]

In light of this ideological conviction, it would be difficult for the United States to compel North Korea to comply with its demands regarding missile and nuclear sites. Being promoted as the Mecca of the "immortal idea" of *Juche,* it is unthinkable for North Korea to give in to any intervention and pressure from the "imperialist" it has denounced since the country's inception. It is one thing to talk and negotiate with the "imperialist" in a situation where both will lose some and gain some; it is another to yield to its pressure. The United States should expect full and firm resistance from a country where independence and sovereignty are hallmarks of foreign policy. U.S. demands to open up alleged missile and nuclear sites and to end these programs run completely against Pyongyang's self-defense principle. North Korea makes it clear that its missile program is part of its right to self-defense. According to *Juche,* "the implementation of self-defense is a military guarantee for the political independence and economic self-sufficiency . . ."[30] North Korea's official stand on this matter is unambiguous and straightforward:

> A country incapable of defending itself by its own strength has no say. When one relies on others in national defense, he is bound to study their faces and moods and cannot say freely what is on his mind. Any sensible man can easily find such cases in the events taking place in the international arena today.[31]

It is only in this context that we can understand North Korean military generals' condemnations of the U.S. stance toward the suspected Kumchang-ri nuclear site. They reiterated a threatening rhetoric, notwithstanding that it is unusual for them to make a public statement.[32] Undoubtedly, all countries have some ideology of self-reliance, sovereignty, and independence. However, no other country has adopted self-reliance as *the* ruling ideology. In North Korea, *Juche* is linked to politics, economics, social life, and even to the very existence of Kim Jong Il's leadership and his legitimacy. In this situation, North Korea has no choice but to withstand U.S. pressures. *Juche* provides the rationale for Pyongyang to exert defensive power over the United States.

RIVALRY WITH SOUTH KOREA

Ever since the division of Korea and the ensuing inception of two separate regimes on the peninsula, the two have engaged in a fierce competition to be recognized as the only legitimate state on the peninsula. The failure of reunification through the Korean War triggered a "legitimacy war" between the two, in which they attempted to undercut each other in every possible way. The current reconciliatory moves by both Koreas do not suddenly end the deep-rooted system competition. Five decades after the division, it became clear that Pyongyang had lost the race to Seoul. Diplomatically, South Korea put Pyongyang off balance with its successful *Nordpolitik,* earning recognition from North Korea's former allies while Pyongyang became increasingly isolated in the international community until it initiated the recent diplomatic offensives. Also, the military balance on the peninsula has changed over the years in favor of South Korea, which still maintains a strong military alliance with the United States, while North Korea can no longer rely on China or Russia for the supply of weapons and military equipment. The economic arena undoubtedly marked the most dramatic losing battle for North Korea.

Nevertheless, North Korea believes itself to have an edge on the South in one area that has attracted many South Korean students and intellectuals over the years, especially in the 1980s—national sovereignty based on the *Juche* ideology. *Juche* promotes the belief that North Korea represents a sovereign polity embodying a national spirit. In contrast, it depicts South Korea as a country militarily, economically, and politically dependent on "imperialist powers." To Pyongyang, the governments in South Korea have not been in any position to declare political sovereignty and to appeal to the nationalist sentiment of the people: American troops are still stationed on South Korea's soil, in contrast to Chinese troops' withdrawal from the North as early as 1958; South Korea normalized relations with the former colonial power, Japan, as early as 1965, in spite of public uproar and student demonstrations; and South Korean governments have made no resistance against American interventions in domestic political affairs in order to gain Washington's support.

North Korea has exploited this edge in its reunification policy as well. Its fundamental reunification strategy and its various demands for maintaining a meaningful inter-Korean dialogue have been remarkably consistent over the years.[33] As far as Pyongyang is concerned, reunification should be achieved independently, free from any foreign intervention. Pyongyang never forgets to remind South Korea of the fact that the principle of independence for reunification was embodied in the historic North-South Joint Communiqué of July 4, 1972, and reaffirmed in the 1991 inter-Korean Agreement on Reconciliation, Nonaggression, Exchanges, and Cooperation. This principle was declared again in the June 15 agreement of the historic inter-Korean summit meeting in 2000.

North Korea's tenacious and fervent emphasis on *Juche* in reunification met with sympathy among South Korean youth, students, and dissidents in the late 1980s. With the democratization movement, South Korean students and intellectuals began to voice their aspirations for reunification, which even included a demand to pursue reunification on North Korean terms. These radical student activists and dissidents earned "high respect" as "patriotic democrats"[34] by Kim

Il Sung, who lost no time in capitalizing on the dissident movement and anti-Americanism in the South. Democratization in South Korea created confusion and instability, which led to the ascent of radical anti-government groups sympathetic to the North. It also boosted anti-Americanism in South Korea. The anti-Americanists viewed the presence of U.S. troops in South Korea as a national disgrace and a humiliation, as well as the primary factor prohibiting national unification. They also viewed the U.S.-ROK Combined Forces Command (CFC) as a national disgrace. Formed in 1978, the CFC put over 600,000 personnel from both the United States and South Korea (about 80 percent of the Korean army) under the direct command of an American four-star general until 1994.[35] In fact, even the former UN commander in South Korea, General Richard Stilwell, called it "the most remarkable concession of sovereignty in the entire world."[36] Many nationalistic student activists were involved in a nation-wide organization, *Jusapa* (*Juche* ideology group), which believed in *Juche* and aimed at eliminating foreign powers from South Korea.

Ever since the fierce competition between the two Koreas began, North Korea has been at a disadvantage. Nevertheless, Pyongyang could secure a comparative advantage in asserting ideological sovereignty and independence. Although South Koreans' attraction to *Juche* has recently been on the wane,[37] viewed from North Korea's perspective, this is the only area where it could possibly beat the South in the race. Even today, if South Koreans were assured of non-violence by North Korea and somehow led to believe that North Korea's missiles or nuclear facilities were to be raised only in the context of U.S.-North Korea relations, many South Koreans would not hesitate to support North Korea's unbending attitude toward the United States. North Korea's ability to exert defensive influence on the United States in the missile and nuclear problems should be understood in this context. No matter how strongly the United States pressured North Korea, Pyongyang could not afford to submit. Its submission would mean giving up the only comparative edge it possibly has over the South, and consequently would signify a complete defeat in the competition.

Furthermore, the consequences of being bullied into submission by the United States and having to give up the nuclear and missile programs, without being able to extract any deal, would not be limited to the missile and nuclear issues. It would have a far-reaching impact on the reunification strategy based on independence, and on the united front strategy that aims at mobilizing North Korean sympathizers in the South. A North Korean cave-in to the United States would disappoint South Koreans who are sympathetic to its independent policies. For North Korea, losing them would be directly linked to losing ground for its united front strategy. In this sense, helplessly complying with the United States has multiple implications for North Korea beyond the missile and nuclear issues. In view of the rivalry with South Korea, therefore, there is every reason to expect North Korea's refusal to submit to U.S. pressure, and to expect its response of tough resistance.

CONSOLIDATION OF THE NEW REGIME

North Korea revised its constitution in September 1998, making the late Kim Il Sung "eternal President" and Kim Jong Il chairman of the National Defense Commission, which emerged as the nation's most powerful organ. As the chief of the Commission and as General Secretary, Kim Jong Il is in full control of North Korea. The eternal authority of his father also backs his leadership. However, now that the official succession process is completed, the new regime has to prove its leadership in order to maintain the regime's legitimacy. Kim Jong Il's ideological basis of legitimacy is provided by his status as the executor of the *Juche* idea. Yet, he will ultimately have to satisfy the people with his leadership performance. Being aware of this task, North Korea claimed the rocket launch, for example, as Kim Jong Il's achievement that gives "pride and delight to the nation" and as "one more fruit of the independent national economy and technology" under the "wise leadership" of Kim.[38] Its launch on August 31, 1988, a few days before the adoption of the new constitution, was in part intended to boost people's morale ahead of the formation of the new regime.

In the diplomatic area, results of the negotiations in the missile and nuclear issues would coincide with the building of Kim Jong Il's leadership. In this situation, giving in to U.S. pressure would be an unthinkable option for Pyongyang. It would damage not only Kim's performance-based legitimacy but also his ideological-base of legitimacy as the "realizer" of *Juche*. His leadership-building through credible performance in the foreign policy area becomes even more important considering the fact that his performance in the economic area is constrained by the inherent dilemma he faces. On the one hand, he is bound to protect ideological purity to maintain his ideological-base of legitimacy, which can be done most effectively under a tightly closed and controlled system; on the other hand, the economic performance-base of his legitimacy would be enhanced in a more open system.[39] Thus, he is in a system that has "generic vulnerability"[40] built into it. In this dilemma, Kim's achievement in the foreign policy area could somewhat offset constraints in the area of economic performance. In this regard, he would be credited for any success in making Washington comply with North Korea's demands and in squeezing any concessions from the stronger. The necessity of Kim Jong Il's leadership-building thus enhances North Korea's ability to resist the United States and increases its capacity to exert defensive power over Washington.

BEING "SMALL"

Several studies have attached importance to the smaller international environment of a small state as an advantage over a big state. While big states' international environment of interest is global, that of small states' is mainly regional, and this means that the number of foreign policy problems that a small state has to deal with is smaller than that of a big state. Therefore, a small state can concentrate on a smaller number of issues, enhancing the possibility of making a more coherent policy.[41] As one scholar puts it: "[i]n relations between great and small states it will often be more useful to inquire about intensity of interest than to define interest in terms of power."[42] Keohane echoes the same point:

> Weakness does not entail only liabilities; for the small power, it also creates certain bargaining assets. Typically, the smaller the state, the more it can take large-scale patterns of international politics for granted, since nothing it does can possibly affect them very much . . . [a small state] is able to concentrate on a narrow range of vital interests and ignore almost everything else. At the same time, it can disregard or heavily discount the effects of its actions on the stability of international politics in general.[43]

The asymmetry in attention and the cohesion of concentration between North Korea and the United States is beneficial to Pyongyang in its missile and nuclear dealings. These issues are the only major foreign policy issues that North Korea has to cope with, while they are only two of many vital foreign policy issues for the United States. In addition, by virtue of being the only superpower in the post–Cold War era, the United States has to take many considerations into account in choosing its course of action, including the impact of its policies on other major countries in East Asia, the NPT, the Missile Technology Control regime, and other small states, which could be the next North Korea. As such, it has to consider divergent interests of and pressures from other countries, which could pose various constraints to U.S. policy. The KEDO is a case in point. Differences of opinion among members led one KEDO official to say, "it is at least as hard getting consensus among KEDO participants on nonproliferation strategy as it is getting agreement with the DPRK."[44] China's deviant position on North Korea's underground construction site is another case. China argued that the United States had no right to demand an inspection based only on suspicions: "no country in the international community is entitled, or authorized, to have such a right."[45] Divergent views on North Korea's rocket launch were also evident. While Japan and the United States were linking North Korea's launch of another missile with the collapse of the Agreed Framework and the KEDO project, China maintained that the missile issue was irrelevant to the latter. Meanwhile, South Korea urged the United States and Japan to take a softer stance toward North Korea, contending that closer U.S.-North Korea ties would improve Seoul's relations with Pyongyang.[46] According to U.S. officials, South Korean officials downplayed the discovery of North Korea's underground facilitates because they feared undermining President Kim's Sunshine Policy toward North Korea.[47] When Japan did not endorse its financial commitment to the KEDO, South Korea pushed it to separate that issue from North Korea's alleged missile test. Although all of these countries broadly share consistent interests on the Korean peninsula, there are differences in priorities, which put pressure on the United States and constrain its policy toward North Korea.

Having limited relations with other states and only a limited range of foreign policy, North Korea can concentrate on its own interests. Free from any pressure to consult with other countries, North Korea can maintain a higher intensity of interest and can thus be prepared to pay a higher price to attain its objectives. Its higher intensity of interest improves its bargaining position and serves as a source of strength and influence it can exercise over the United States.

U.S. POLICY TOWARD NORTH KOREA

If North Korea is expected to exert its defensive power by resisting U.S. offensive power, it would be difficult for the latter to get North Korea to act the way it wants in resolving the missile and nuclear crisis. If coercion were not likely to solve the problem, the next best policy would be to further engage North Korea. Engagement should continue to be the most viable policy option for the United States. An engaged North Korea would be much more conducive to stability in Northeast Asia than a desperate North Korea because the latter might be more willing to accept risks if pushed further into a corner. As one unofficial spokesman for North Korea admits, if the Agreed Framework falls apart, North Korea's only option will be to go nuclear and do it publicly by targeting nuclear warheads at the United States and Japan and by selling nuclear weapons to other countries.[48] Avoiding a desperate North Korea should entail more extensive engagement by the United States and other regional actors in East Asia, in line with the détente mood between the two Koreas.

Most of all, the United States should be more faithful in implementing various agreements with North Korea, including the nuclear reactor project agreed to in 1994, to build confidence in bilateral relations. The former U.S. Secretary of State Madeleine Albright acknowledged in August 1998 that judging from all indications, North Korea was living up to its part of the Agreed Framework. Even after the alleged nuclear underground facilities were discovered, a U.S. official said that North Korea had not yet technically violated the accord because "there is no evidence that it has begun pouring cement for a new reactor or a reprocessing plant that would convert nuclear waste into bomb-grade plutonium."[49] On the other hand, the United States fell behind in its promised oil shipments, and the light-water reactor project is already a few years behind the scheduled 2003 target date. The United States admitted this, saying that North Korea "clearly can complain as long as we have failed to meet that obligation . . ."[50] This has given North Korea an opportunity to threaten to scrap the agreement. When the United States fails to fulfill its obligations under the accord and at the same time turns a deaf ear to North Korea's repeated threats to abandon the agreement, it is only natural for North Korea to be frustrated and to doubt U.S. intentions regarding the accord. This will only strengthen the position of hard-liners in North Korea who question the deal as a U.S. lever to buy time after freezing North Korea's nuclear program. In their view, the United States has no intention of implementing it, as they have not seen the promised benefits such as diplomatic recognition, complete lifting of sanctions including counter-terrorism control on North Korea, and provision of two light-water reactors; they think the United States will only drag out the implementation process, waiting for North Korea's collapse. They believe that the United States agreed to the Framework Agreement on the unfounded assumption that North Korea would extinguish in the near future, as one senior Defense Department official said in 1995: "Five years from now, North Korea is not going to be there."[51] The perception that the United States is reneging on its obligations will only invite North Korea's frustration, distrust, and eventually the development of other bargaining cards, such as missiles, to get U.S. attention. In fact, after North Korea tested its *Rodong* missile in May 1993, it ceased other tests when the United States detected North Korea's preparations and asked it to stop in the spring of 1994 and again in October 1996.[52] In light of this, the 1998 test reflects North Korea's frustration over the lack of progress in bilateral relations. Further engagement of North Korea requires keeping promises on already existing agreements.

In addition, the missiles issue should be dealt with separately from the nuclear problem. The United States and Japan have warned that if North Korea launches another missile, the KEDO could be in jeopardy. However, the Geneva Agreement does not cover missiles. Linking the two is dangerous because this could bring the already agreed-upon nuclear issue back to the starting point. Among the bilateral issues, the United States and North Korea have shown most progress in the recovery of the remains of U.S. military men killed during the Korean War. This is mainly due to the strategy of resisting linkages among issues. A U.S. official stated, " . . . [W]e steadfastly resist being tied to talks on missiles and nuclear facilities and to food aid. This separation of issues has allowed our work in North Korea to continue virtually uninterrupted for three years in spite of other crises that have arisen."[53] North Korea has demonstrated that it is capable of separating issues and negotiating with skill if the terms of negotiation are acceptable. The United States should separate negotiation on missiles instead of putting both missile and nuclear issues in danger by linking them. While these measures can be initiated through U.S.-North Korea bilateral negotiations they should be followed by multilateral efforts, as was the case in the development of the KEDO. The United States should enlist active support of other regional actors to form a multilateral consensus on "cooperative threat reduction."

In conclusion, the United States is far more powerful than North Korea, and the latter, being a weaker state, is not usually able to twist the arm of the former. Weak states have great constraints placed on their influence over other states. Nevertheless, the traditional power approach falls short in accounting for North Korea's role and influence in the nuclear and missile crises with the United States. America's superior military and economic power does not guarantee North Korea's compliance with U.S. interests. If North Korea is determined to exercise its defensive power, refusing to comply with U.S. pressure, it will intensify tensions between the two. The engagement policy will be much more effective and feasible in reducing tensions in U.S.-North Korea relations than policies based on power politics. Rapprochement between the United States and North Korea will happen only if the United States devises more extensive engagement policies.

NOTES

* This chapter has appeared in *Pacific Affairs*, vol. 73, no. 4, Winter 2000–2001, pp. 535–553.

1. Ralph B. A. Dimuccio, "The Study of Appeasement in International Relations: Polemics, Paradigms, and Problems," *Journal of Peace Research*, vol. 35, no. 2, March 1998, p. 253.

2. *Northeast Asia Peace and Security Network Daily Report,* September 1, 1998.
3. Kyodo News Agency, December 19, 1998 and *Yomiuri Shinmun,* January 8, 1999.
4. *Northeast Asia Peace and Security Network Daily Report,* September 2, 1998.
5. Ibid., January 11, 1999.
6. DPRK Press Release, Permanent Mission to the United Nations, no.66, December 3, 1998.
7. *Northeast Asia Peace and Security Network Daily Report,* December 3, 1998.
8. *New York Times,* December 26, 1998.
9. *Northeast Asia Peace and Security Network Daily Report,* December 14, 1998.
10. DPRK Press Release, Permanent Mission to the United Nations, no. 60, August 5, 1998.
11. Ibid., no. 62, September 16, 1998.
12. *New York Times,* August 15, 1999.
13. South Korea declared a new policy in January 2001 to increase the range to 300 km, with an accord reached with the United States.
14. *Northeast Asia Peace and Security Network Daily Report,* September 1, 1998.
15. Ibid., September 2, 1998.
16. *The Washington Times,* October 28, 1999.
17. *New York Times,* December 6, 1998.
18. For studies on these factors, see Ulf Lindell and Stefan Persson, "The Paradox of Weak State Power," *Cooperation and Conflict,* vol.21, no.2, June 1986; and Kjell Goldmann, "Tension Between the Strong, and the Power of the Weak: Is the Relation Positive or Negative?" in Kjell Goldmann and Gunnar Sjostedt, eds., *Power, Capabilities, Interdependence* (London: Sage, 1979).
19. However, there are a few exceptions to this. They include Miriam Fendius Elman, "The Foreign Policies of Small States; Challenging Neorealism in Its Own Backyard," *British Journal of Political Science,* vol. 25, no. 2, April 1995, pp. 176–77; Michael N. Barnett and Jack S. Levy, "Domestic Sources of Alliances and Alignment: The Case of Egypt, 1962–73," *International Organization,* vol. 45, no. 3, Summer 1991; and Steven David, "Explaining Third World Alignment," *World Politics,* vol. 43, no. 2, January 1991.
20. Hans Mouritzen, "Tension Between the Strong, and the Strategies of the Weak," *Journal of Peace Research,* vol. 28, no. 2, May 1991, p. 219.
21. Joint editorial was published by *Rodong Sinmun,* the organ of the central committee of the Workers' Party of Korea, *Joson Inmingun,* the organ of the Ministry of the People's Armed Forces, and *Chongnyon Jonwi,* the organ of the central committee of the Kim Il Sung Socialist Youth League.
22. *Northeast Asia Peace and Security Network Daily Report,* September 15, 1998.
23. A. George, *Bridging the Gap: Theory and Practice in Foreign Policy* (Washington, D.C.: United States Institute of Peace Press, 1993), p. 111.
24. See B. C. Koh, *The Foreign Policy Systems of North and South Korea* (Berkeley, CA: University of California Press, 1984), chapters 5 and 11.

25. *North Korea News*, December 24, 1990.
26. A private conversation with a professor of the Academy of *Juche* Science, North Korea, during my visit there in November 1995.
27. *Pyongyang Times*, January 1, 1991.
28. *Rodong Shinmun*, October 5, 1990.
29. Ibid., September 8, 1994.
30. Chang Ha Kim, *The Immortal Juche Idea* (Pyongyang: Foreign Language Publishing House, 1984), p. 324.
31. Ibid., p. 325.
32. For example, see *Northeast Asia Peace and Security Network Daily Report* for statements by a spokesman for the General Staff of the Korean People's Army on December 2, 1998, by Vice Defense Minister Jong Chang Yol on December 3, 1998, and by Army General Officer O Kum Chol on December 8, 1998.
33. About changes and continuities in North Korea's unification strategies, see Kyung-Ae Park and Sung-Chull Lee, "Changes and Prospects in Inter-Korean Relations," *Asian Survey*, vol. 32, no. 5, May 1992.
34. New Year's Message, *Pyongyang Times*, January 1, 1988.
35. As of December 1, 1994, the peacetime operational control of the South Korean combat forces was transferred to the chairman of the ROK Joint Chiefs of Staff from the commander of the CFC, a U.S. general. The control will revert to the CFC commander in time of war.
36. *Far Eastern Economic Review*, May 12, 1988, p. 21.
37. Nevertheless, South Korean students have continually held protests to demand the withdrawal of U.S. troops from South Korea.
38. *DPRK Press Release*, Permanent Mission to the United Nations, no. 60, September 5, 1998.
39. For the two bases of legitimacy as they apply to North Korea, see Han S. Park and Kyung-Ae Park, *China and North Korea: Politics of Integration and Modernization* (Hong Kong: Asian Research Service, 1990).
40. Larry Diamond, "Beyond Authoritarianism and Totalitarianism: Strategies for Democratization," *Washington Quarterly*, vol. 12, no. 1, Winter 1989, p. 150.
41. About the difficulties of a big state with general interests, see David Vital, *The Making of British Foreign Policy* (London: George Allen and Unwin, 1968).
42. Erling Bjol, "The Power of the Weak," *Cooperation and Conflict*, no. 3, 1968, p. 11.
43. Robert Keohane, "The Big Influence of Small Allies," *Foreign Policy*, vol. 1, Spring 1971, pp. 162–63.
44. *Northeast Asia Peace and Security Network Daily Report*, January 12, 1999.
45. An interview with Wu Dawei, China's ambassador to South Korea, *Korea Herald*, January 7, 1999.
46. For a statement by South Korea's Foreign Minister, see *Northeast Asia Peace and Security Network Daily Report*, January 11, 1999.

47. *New York Times,* August 17, 1998.
48. Ibid., January 3, 1999.
49. Ibid., August 17, 1998.
50. *Northeast Asia Peace and Security Network Daily Report,* December 8, 1998.
51. *Washington Post,* December 15, 1995.
52. Leon Sigal, "For Sale: North Korea's Missile Program," *Northeast Asia Peace and Security Network Policy Forum Online,* no. 22, November 11, 1998.
53. *The International Herald Tribune,* December 10, 1998.

CHAPTER SIX

U.S.-NORTH KOREAN BILATERAL RELATIONS AND SOUTH KOREAN SECURITY

BRUCE CUMINGS

Millennial fever gripped everyone as the days counted down to the year 2000. How much more so for the Korean people: for them, the twentieth century was not a good one. After nearly a half-century of brutal imperial occupation by Japan, the country was divided after the Pacific War ended, wracked by a vicious civil war, and then returned to its contentious antebellum condition of national division and military confrontation. Many Koreans thought that this century of troubles would come to an end after the Berlin Wall fell in 1989, which appeared to remove the ideological polarities and bloc politics that characterized the Cold War, perhaps clearing the way for a long-awaited reunification. But as the century came to a close and we got a decade-long perspective on 1989, unification had barely come closer and cold war was barely further away than it was a decade ago. But there has been modest improvement on both counts, because of several important diplomatic initiatives and the changes that a major humanitarian crisis have forced on North Korea. Indeed Korea, for all its problems, may be a place where a humanitarian crisis and a democratic transition in the Republic of Korea can be the prelude to settling this long-lasting, seemingly interminable civil conflict as well.

Since the death of Kim Il Sung in 1994, North Korea has been visited with two years of flood (1995 and 1996), a summer of drought (1997), and a resulting famine that has claimed or currently threatens the lives of two million people. This is a textbook example of the calamities that are supposed to attend the end of the Confucian dynastic cycle, and North

Korean citizens must wonder how much more suffering Mother Nature will mete out before she is done. Kim's son, Kim Jong Il, waited out the three-year traditional mourning period for the first son of the king before assuming his father's titles; he became Secretary of the Worker's Party in 1997, and he inherited the position of maximum leader at the 50th anniversary of the regime's founding on September 9, 1998.[1]

Among the many crises that North Korea has suffered in the past decade, the years-long famine seems to be the worst. Andrew Natsios, the vice president of World Vision, has argued for several years that North Korea has lost 500,000 to one million of its citizens to famine, and if full information were at hand, the total might be closer to two million, that is, nearly 10 percent of the population.[2] An unscientific survey in August 1997 of about 400 Koreans living in China and crossing the border into North Korea frequently came up with an estimate that 15 percent of the population in towns along northern border had died. In orphanages, from which have come many of the televised images of this famine, the figure was 22 percent; in poor mining towns in the far north, about 9 percent.[3]

It is not clear that such figures would apply to the whole country. Regional differentiation is great in North Korea, with 10 percent of the population living in the highly centralized and much privileged capital. Foreign travelers have not witnessed starvation conditions in Pyongyang, and visitors to other parts of the country sometimes can't find it, either. For example, an international delegation that visited the upper East coast in August 1997, to break ground for the light-water reactors envisioned in the October 1994 nuclear framework agreement, did not see much evidence even of malnutrition, let alone famine. The Democratic People's Republic of Korea (DPRK) is a class society, regardless of its claims to have eliminated classes, and families who have homes in villages and small cities have small plots of land at their disposal, every inch of which is under cultivation. Foreigners who have visited homes with private gardens have found that such residents did not need government rations and had enough to eat.

If Mother Nature shares much of the blame for North Korea's recent travails, most experts also believe that even in the best weather conditions, the North's agricultural problems are irremediable, short of major reform. The collapse of the Soviet Bloc left the DPRK's export markets in a lurch, exports that had been exchanged at favorable rates for petroleum. A rapid decline in petroleum imports in the 1990s, in turn, hurt the national transportation network and the huge chemical industry, which provided so much fertilizer to farms. In spite of its image in the United States as an East Asian Albania, North Korea is an industrial society and the absence of critical fuels and industrial inputs has stymied the economy. For several years now, industry may have been running at less than 50 percent of capacity. Pyongyang's problems seem fairly straightforward: if it could find ways to export goods to the world market to earn the foreign exchange needed to import food, oil, and other essentials, it would not only stabilize but probably prosper. But the leadership has not taken the fundamental decisions necessary to do this, and so its reform process has been piecemeal and haphazard.

The North Korean administrative system is also to blame. Bureaucratic lineages and hierarchies often exist as independent kingdoms, leading to much difficulty in communicating and coordinating with each other. The military leaders have clearly been at odds with those in the Foreign Ministry in recent years, something that foreign diplomats have witnessed on occasion, but the problem goes much beyond that. Generational conflict (between an increasingly small but still influential revolutionary old guard and people in their 40s to 60s), relative bureaucratic autonomy, the practice of provincial self-reliance, a vast party apparatus organizing upwards of one-third of the adult population, the privileged position of the military (gaining 25 percent or more of the annual budget), the death of the only leader the country ever had, and the piling on of externally-generated crises have all resulted in a kind of immobilism in the 1990s.

Decisions are pushed upward through the hierarchy, and at the top no one seems capable of making the hard decision to push the country on a truly new course. North Korea is neither muddling through toward some sort of post-communism, the way other socialist states did after 1989, nor is it reforming like China and Vietnam. The leadership seems deeply frightened by the consequences of opening up the economy, preferring instead to open tiny coastal enclaves (like the Najin-Sonbong export zone in the Northeast). This fear can be seen in widely featured articles in June 1999, about the dangers of "reform and opening," "pluralism," "protest," and the like, and the necessity to set up a "mosquito net" to keep out "liberal," "capitalist," and "decadent" influences.[4] On the one hand, this spate of articles (which said nothing new) probably was designed to please hardliners in the regime. On the other hand, the reference to a "mosquito net" is particularly interesting because 20 years ago Deng Xiaoping used the same metaphor to explain how China could open up its economy while retaining Communist political control and keeping out capitalist "contamination." Still, for all the troubles that came in the 1990s, there are few signs that any of them have threatened the stability of the top leadership. It is more at the local level that the system is breaking down.

A Korean visitor who recently traveled by car from Pyongyang to the Northeastern city of Hamhung, for example, told me that he had seen a large barter market operating every day along the riverbank in Hamhung. Hard currency, especially dollars, was in wide if informal use, and highly valued of course. He thought that the historically centralized, planned delivery of goods and services by the state had almost completely broken down at the local levels, with many people telling him that government food rations had not been delivered for months.

Foreign relief experts say that food brought into the country is not diverted to the privileged military. It is more a matter of locally-produced food stocks going to the elite in Pyongyang and to the vast military, which enrolls 5 percent of the entire population. Otherwise foreign observers speak of an egalitarian sharing of existing food stocks combined with a triage policy, where the young, the elderly, and the infirm are the first to suffer. The government is helping where it can, denying where it must, and keeping the essential pillar of its power—the military—sufficiently fed.

Unfortunately, the post–Cold War world is almost inured to such humanitarian disasters. Twenty-five nations were scourged by war, human displacement, hunger, and disease in 1993–1995, increasing to 60 to 65 in the last several years. One expert wrote that "humanitarian emergencies are primarily imbedded in intra-state crises," with stalemates in civil wars playing a big role; unresolved conflicts, like those in Afghanistan and Angola, merely bring death and destruction in their wake, with no fundamental resolution of the problem.[5] The Korean War is the most stalemated conflict in the world, unmoving since 1953, and amid all the other problems that have characterized this conflict, we have a major famine in North Korea. Unlike other humanitarian emergencies around the world, however, this one has provided little evidence of a collapse of state power, except for the breakdowns at the local level, discussed above. There have been few significant changes in the leadership since Kim died. There have been defections, many of them hyped in the South Korean press and the world media, but only one—that of Hwang Jang Yop in February 1997—was truly significant, and although the regime was embarrassed and demoralized by Hwang's departure, he had never been a central powerholder, and the core leadership still appears unshaken.

Another curiosity in the current crisis is that North Korea suffers as if it were Somalia or Ethiopia, but has a much more developed and modern economy. The DPRK historically had a powerful industrial economy and remains relatively urbanized, with less than 30 percent of the population working in agriculture. Until recent years international agencies found that life expectancy rates, child welfare, inoculation rates, and general public health conditions were all quite high in North Korea, comparatively speaking. Unlike other places afflicted by humanitarian disasters, this is not a peripheral, penetrated state with a weak government and a strong society. North Korea has had effective sovereignty, high state capacity, and has long ranked high in measures of effective statehood. In short, unlike many other nations with humanitarian disasters, serious reform could happen here once key decisions were taken, because this is a country that can mobilize everyone for centrally-determined tasks. With its well-educated and disciplined workforce, North Korea could effectively exploit a comparative advantage in labor cost in world markets. Indeed, for years major South Korean firms have hoped to marry their skills with North Korean labor (and several have actually done so, like the Daewoo textile factory in Nampo, the port of Pyongyang).

In some ways a comparison of North Korea's problems and other humanitarian emergencies is artificial, or forced, because no other place in the world has the anachronistic and special characteristics that distinguish the Korean peninsula. The Cold War continues here, as does the Korean War, in a fragile peace held by an armistice and fortified by the world's largest military confrontation. Nearly two million heavily armed troops confront each other on the peninsula, we often hear; what we do not hear enough about, however, is how close they came to war, and how recently.

In the middle of 1994, the United States nearly plunged into a conflict that the local American Commander General Gary Luck estimated would kill a million people, including upwards of 100,000 American soldiers, not to mention costing more than $100 billion (about double the total cost for the Persian Gulf War). Yet this near-war, like so much else about Korea, is mostly unknown to the American people. Don Oberdorfer's recent book[6] contains a detailed account of the frightening crisis over North Korea's nuclear program, which lasted from mid-May to late June 1994. Based on much new inside information garnered from interviews in Washington and around the world, this harrowing account also makes clear that it is high time to reevaluate the half-century long American troop presence in Korea. With the Cold War over and the Soviet Union gone, the American people should have a choice about whether they want their sons and daughters to be chewed up in another Korean War. As things stand today, with 37,000 Americans still manning the ramparts of a little-known "family quarrel," as Oberdorfer aptly calls it, that choice has already been made.

For more than a year, beginning in August 1998, the American people were treated to another media barrage about North Korean perfidy. Indeed, it appeared that a new war might blow up in the spring of 1999—not in Kosovo, but in Korea. The ostensible causes were Pyongyang's intransigence about opening up a mountain redoubt[7] that U.S. intelligence officials said was a surreptitious site of continuing nuclear weapons activity (a possibility thought to have disappeared with the 1994 agreement that mothballed the graphite reactor at Yongbyon). This mini-crisis began with a key intelligence leak, leading to David Sanger's sensational *New York Times* article (August 17, 1998), revealing alleged nuclear activity inside a mountain northwest of Pyongyang. Readers were led to believe that the site had just been discovered, when in fact it had been the object of American surveillance for at least six years.[8] Nor were readers told that fully 8,200 underground installations exist in the North,[9] many of them connected to the security of a country that has never been able to control the prying eyes of satellites and U-2 aircraft.[10] Readers of the North Korean press at the time, however, learned that it would agree to an American inspection of the facility—for a price of $300 million, since the site would be useless to its security after the inspection.[11] At length Pyongyang finally derailed this particular crisis on March 16, 1999, when it made an unprecedented concession to allow multiple American inspections of the underground facility, and agreed to continue negotiations about its missiles.[12]

Two weeks after Sanger's story appeared, a hailstorm of alarmist press reports claimed that Pyongyang had sent a two-stage missile arcing over Japan, leading to virtual panic in Tokyo—as if the missile had barely cleared the treetops. North Korea's press, however, had spoken for weeks of little else but preparations for the celebration of the 50th anniversary of the regime. Shortly Pyongyang announced that its *three*-stage *rocket* had put a satellite in orbit—beeping out the "Song of Kim Il Sung." Weeks later the U.S. intelligence community concluded that it was indeed an anniversary fireworks display, but that the satellite had failed to reach orbit.[13]

This was a major intelligence failure, needlessly inflaming Japanese opinion about a rocket that entered the stratosphere over the northern tip of the Honshu Island (Tokyo relies on Washington for monitoring missile firings). But that did nothing to stop hardliners from plying their friends with privileged information. By mid-autumn rightwing Republicans were again highly critical of Clinton's North Korea policies, and moderate insiders in Washington were convinced that they were trying to kill the 1994 agreement. Soon the Pentagon leaked a new U.S. war plan that would take advantage of prevalent North Korean infirmities to wipe out the entire regime, should the North attack: to "abolish North Korea as a state and . . . 'reorganize' it under South Korean control." "We will kill them all," a Pentagon insider told veteran East Asia correspondent Richard Halloran.[14] Predictably, Pyongyang retorted with unprecedented propaganda broadsides about taking any new war directly to U.S. territory—and erasing us instead.[15] That kind of fiery rhetoric, combined with the rocket launch, succeeded only in vastly enhancing the chances that Japan will finally agree to deploy the theater missile defense system that the United States has been pushing on Tokyo for 15 years. It was a perfect illustration of the tit-for-tat minuet between their hardliners and ours, to justify their budgets.

A Way Out?

In spite of this volatile confrontation, the limited history since 1989 suggests grounds for optimism about the seemingly endless Korean conflict. The crisis over the North's nuclear problem lasted for three years and nearly led to war, but the final result was good: a comprehensive diplomatic agreement in October 1994 to freeze the North's nuclear facilities, build light-water reactors that will help its deficient energy regime, and open relations between Pyongyang and Washington. In 1997, the North finally agreed to Four Power Talks to end the Korean War; the minicrisis of 1998–99 also ended with an unprecedented inspection agreement, followed by a major step forward in American policy toward the North, under the leadership of former Defense Secretary William Perry. North Korean immobilism, which seems so fearsome whether inside the country or in the interminable negotiations over almost any diplomatic issue, has not stood in the way of significant change. In recent years North Korea has actually changed quite a lot, above all in its basic strategic orientation: long determined to get the United States out of Korea, it now appears to want us to stay involved, to deal with changed international circumstances since 1989 and to help the country through its current, unpredictable transition.[16] This dramatic possibility is a key to understanding how ongoing diplomacy might finally dissolve the extraordinary tensions that have inhabited Korea for half a century.

If the 1994 framework agreement froze the North's nuclear program and represented the first time since the Korean War that any serious problem on the peninsula had been solved through diplomacy, the Four Power Talks that have been ongoing for the past four years represent the first time since 1953 that any serious attempt has been made to replace the armistice with a lasting peace. In adopting this four-way modality, North Korea erased its longstanding policy of refusing to negotiate with the South about the armistice (Seoul never signed the 1953 armistice, leaving an opening that the North exploited ever since), the United States finally became serious about negotiating a peace (which it had not been at the designated peace conference at Geneva in 1954[17] or at any time since), China offered its own participation and good offices (which it usually was reluctant to do unless Pyongyang first approved), and the South showed its own constructive attitude by proposing the talks in the first place, at the time of Bill Clinton's 1996 visit to Korea. The Four Power Talks are terribly important because they envision an outcome in which the huge and intense military confrontation in Korea could be replaced by a comprehensive peace mechanism, with full guarantees for all sides. No one yet knows the shape of a completed agreement, and there is little public news of progress in the ongoing talks.

The Four Power Talks are very involved and still secret of course, but it would appear that Pyongyang's new search for a "peace agreement" with Washington and Seoul is a euphemism for dropping its longstanding desire for a peace *treaty*. An "agreement" would also provide a cover allowing the maintenance of American forces on the peninsula, and would not require ratification by the U.S. Senate. The process would include—and would necessitate—confidence-building measures such as drawing down force deployments and bringing back many forward-deployed troops from the DMZ. Undoubtedly the North also would expect a large package of aid from the United States as part of such an agreement. But this is the key thing that observers should keep their eye on in the so-called "Four Power Talks"—and not Pyongyang's public demands for the withdrawal of U.S. troops.

In spite of a phalanx of noisy Beltway opposition, the high-level media din about the North Korean threat (even to the point that Pyongyang might unleash the smallpox virus on its enemies[18]), and the apparent absence of much progress in the Four Power Talks thus far, mid-level State Department officials have patiently negotiated one agreement after another with Pyongyang, in a long series of talks on various problems. They also began a six-month-long review of Korea policy in the fall of 1998, which markedly changed the direction of U.S. policy and culminated in the Perry mission to Pyongyang in June 1998. Dr. Perry finally issued a public version of his report (and this policy review) in October 1999, the essence of which is a policy of engagement predicated on the coexistence of two Koreas for another considerable period of time, progressive lifting of the 50-year-old American embargo against the North, a deepening of diplomatic relations, and a substantial aid package for the North. The North, for its part, agreed to continue to observe the 1994 agreement, to suspend missile testing, and to continue talks with the United States about ending its missile program, including sales of missiles to the Middle East.

The North has sought to couple these talks with the food problem, linking any further progress to increased external aid. The United States has routinely denied a direct relationship between the two. Of course the two problems are linked, but American diplomats don't wish to appear to be in the position of playing politics with the lives of famine victims. In effect, though, substantial American food aid has flowed into North Korea in the past several years, various kinds of talks continue—and so there is an informal linkage. (The agreement on inspection of the underground site was in effect a trade-off for $500 million in food aid over the next two years.)

The way to deal with this question, in my view, is to give food aid and indeed aid of all types to the north, in the near term when it can make a difference, without preconditions as to progress in the Four Power Talks, the missile-control talks, or other forums. There has already been plenty of progress on the critical nuclear issue; we can reward Pyongyang for mothballing its billion-dollar investment in the Yongbyon reactor and reigning in its dangerous missile program. We can win many friends and influence many people by joining with our allies, South Korea and Japan above all, in a package of aid for the DPRK: a big bundle of aid, in the billions of dollars.

Pyongyang does best with its back to the wall; it is a world champion of clever resistance and resurgence in such a situation.[19] It is on completely unfamiliar terrain, however, when foreigners bearing gifts knock at the door. Such an aid package is the one thing that will silence the hardliners in the regime and bolster reformers, and the downside risks (diversion to the military, etc.) are all tolerable, given the North's current inability to wage anything but a suicidal war. In other words, the ongoing humanitarian emergency and the needs of the North Korean economy provide a major opportunity to transform the existing situation on the Korean peninsula, to bring North Korea into the world economy and then watch that system contain, corral, and ultimately transform Pyongyang's insurgent and recalcitrant posture.

Such a package would also *save* a lot of money: according to figures in Oberdorfer's *Two Koreas,* the United States spends upwards of 20 to 30 billion dollars a year to maintain its Korea commitment, and it does so long after the purpose of this commitment—to contain Soviet and Chinese communism—evaporated. United Nations agencies have called for food and other assistance to North Korea in the tens of millions of dollars, and China, the United States, and other countries have already provided food aid that runs to hundreds of millions. But the amount needed is much larger today. The few billion dollars necessary to put the North Korean economy back on its feet and to buy out its missile program sounds very expensive, but the United States has spent similar amounts in retiring the nuclear weapons of Central Asian states like Kazakhstan—and such an amount is little more than chickenfeed when compared to the annual American expenditure over the past half-century for all things Korean, let alone the minimum of $100 billion that a new war would cost. In that sense, a few more billion dollars are literally drops in the bucket.

If the United States were to spend just $1 billion per year on food and other kinds of assistance to the North, that would be a very good investment in orienting Pyongyang away from confrontation and toward engagement with the United States and the outside world. Helping the regime to open up trade and investment opportunities and moving rapidly toward the diplomatic relations called for in the 1994 accord, would help to bring North Korea out of isolation and support reform elements in the regime. Above all, unlike the endless and seemingly irremediable humanitarian crises and civil wars in places like Afghanistan, Somalia, Rwanda, Angola, Bosnia, and Kosovo, in North Korea this program might actually work to defuse the problem. With the collapse of the Soviet Union, the quick rise to power of China, and a still unpredictable transition in the power relations of Northeast Asia occasioned by the end of the Cold War, this is a golden opportunity for the United States to make a new friend, solve an old problem, and prepare for a twenty-first century that is likely to be much kinder to the Korean people.

If this all sounds unrealistic, consider that the Republic of Korea, facing a far greater threat to its existence than does the United States, has made much more far-reaching changes in its policies toward the North since Kim Dae Jung was elected in December 1997. With his persistent and patient Sunshine Policy, President Kim has done more to change policy toward the North than any South Korean or American president going back to the end of the Korean War, and he has not allowed provocations by hardliners in Pyongyang to derail his new initiatives. It was Kim Dae Jung who first urged former President Clinton to lift the 50-year-old economic embargo on North Korea (during a visit to Washington in June 1998), arguing that as long as the embargo continued one could hardly expect the regime to change its economic policies and open up. At the time his efforts met indifference from the White House, and ill-concealed contempt from national security managers. But now his policy is American policy.

The main reason to push for a large aid package is that the alternatives are all worse. The favored scenario of hardliners in Washington and Seoul, a DPRK collapse, has not happened, and will not happen—and it *should* not happen. North Korea was supposed to have collapsed abruptly back in 1989, certainly after the Soviet Union disappeared in 1991, above all after its founding father died in 1994. And how could it possibly survive in the face of the nuclear crisis, new war scares, flood, drought, and famine (1994–1998)? But the DPRK has not collapsed, and its leaders have warned many times that for the world to hope for its collapse is to hope for the next Korean War.[20] The political obstacles to a major American effort on behalf of the DPRK are many, we can all instantly imagine them: critics will say this is weak-kneed appeasement,[21] the CIA will leak old stories about the North's war plans, South Korean hardliners will accuse us of abandoning them and will make life difficult for President Kim and his Sunshine Policy, and hardliners in the North will be tempted to take the money and run. With well-constructed safeguards on the uses of this aid, however, and a clear statement of its purpose, this would work. Ultimately, a peace settlement combined with a big aid package will open the path to reconciliation and reunion: the recompense that the twenty-first century will unquestionably bestow upon the Korean people, sooner or later. Why not make it sooner?

Large-scale aid to the North, not to mention reconciliation, reunification and the essential magnanimity needed to bring it about, all seem so difficult to imagine because such virtues cut against the grain of Korea's history in the past 50 years. History teaches us how easy it is to get into a war—indeed it happened overnight in June 1950—and how hard it is to get out: 51 years, and counting. Who would have imagined, when American troops first marched into Seoul in September 1945, that one of the most destructive wars of this century would occur five years later and that 55 years later, we still are not out of it, it could still happen again?

NOTES

1. Kim chose not to become titular head of state, however, in spite of Pyongyang's press stating that he would; the former Foreign Minister, Kim Yong Nam, is now President of the DPRK. Much speculation ensued that Kim Jong Il did this so he would not have to greet foreign heads of state.
2. *Chicago Tribune,* September 17, 1997.
3. Korean Buddhist Savior Movement, figures provided to me on September 13, 1997.
4. See the June 1, 1999 articles in *Nodong shinmun* and *Kulloja.*
5. Raimo Vayrynen, *The Age of Humanitarian Emergencies* (Helsinki: United Nations University, World Institute for Development Economics Research, 1996), pp. v, 2–5.
6. *The Two Koreas* (New York: Addison-Wesley, 1997). See also Cumings, "Time to End the Korean War," *The Atlantic Monthly,* February 1997.
7. A facility built into the side of a mountain in Kumchang-ri, about 60 miles northwest of Pyongyang.
8. Don Oberdorfer told me this at a conference in Washington in September 1998.

9. *Chungang ilbo* (Central Daily), Seoul, December 8, 1998.

10 U-2s are still used in the Korean theater.

11. Korean Central News Agency, September 3, 1998.

12 *The New York Times*, March 17, 1999.

13. Tracing the missile's path and the number of stages that fired off required pouring over radar tapes, which took several weeks; the announcement that it was, indeed, a satellite throw was buried in the media.

14. Richard Halloran, *Far Eastern Economic Review*, December 3, 1998; Halloran quoted the second statement in his November 14, 1998 story posted on the "Global Beat" Internet site.

15. Korean Central News Agency, December 3, 1998.

16. Selig Harrison interviewed a North Korean general who told him that whereas the North may call publicly for the withdrawal of American troops, in reality the troops should stay—to help deal with a strong Japan, among other things. See Harrison, "Promoting a Soft Landing in Korea," *Foreign Policy*, no. 106, Spring 1997.

17. In 1986, I interviewed one of the American negotiators at Geneva in 1954, the late U. Alexis Johnson, who explained to me how he had prepared for a peace conference; the result of which, he knew well in advance, would be no diplomatic progress whatsoever, let alone a peace treaty.

18. *New York Times*, April 22, 1999.

19. For example, when huge foreign armies occupied its territory in the fall of 1950. On that episode see Cumings, *Origins of the Korean War*, vol. 2 (Princeton, NJ: Princeton University Press, 1990), chapters 20 and 21.

20. Perhaps the most dramatic statement came in March 1996, on the heels of CIA Director John Deutsch's testimony in Congress that it is not a question of whether North Korea will collapse, but when. Within 48 hours Vice Marshal Kim Kwang Jin declared that "the point now is not whether a war will break out in the Korean peninsula . . . but when it will be unleashed." See International Affairs Bureau of Chongryun, *Korea Report*, no. 308 (Tokyo, March 1996).

21. At the time of the October framework agreement in 1994, Bob Dole attacked the Clinton administration for "propping up an odious regime that is closer to full collapse than at any time in the past forty years." Quoted in Harrison, "Soft Landing."

PART THREE

The Dynamics among Major Powers and Korean Security

CHAPTER SEVEN

THE RISE OF U.S.-CHINA RIVALRY AND ITS IMPLICATIONS FOR THE KOREAN PENINSULA[1]

SCOTT SNYDER

It has been conventional wisdom that good relations between the United States and the People's Republic of China (PRC) are a necessary condition for reconciliation on the Korean peninsula. The fact that the United States and the PRC share the objective of maintaining stability in Korea has also been used in recent years as a rhetorical justification for strategic U.S.-PRC cooperation. But the Korean peninsula may also become an object of strategic competition in the future, particularly if the U.S.-PRC relationship itself becomes primarily a competitive one. Indeed, most analysts believe that shared U.S.-PRC short-term objectives of maintaining stability on the Korean peninsula will inevitably diverge at the moment of Korean reunification, bringing American and Chinese strategic interests into direct conflict with each other and once again inducing a historically familiar pattern of great power competition over Korea. After exploring recent trends in China's relationship with the two Koreas and the role Korea has played as part of the U.S.-China relationship in recent years, this chapter will explore the extent to which a downturn in the U.S.-PRC relationship may become a source of future instability in Korea, the extent to which it is possible to isolate or distance security questions on the Korean peninsula from the broader regional security environment, and the possible sources and implications of U.S.-PRC tensions and their likely impact on the situation in Korea.

Post—Cold War Overview of Chinese Policy
toward the Korean Peninsula

Any examination of the role of the Korean peninsula as an object of potential competition or cooperation in the U.S.-PRC relationship must start with an acknowledgement that the post–Cold War context has already brought significant changes to China's own thinking about how it relates to the Korean peninsula. The ties "forged in blood" as a result of China's intervention on behalf of the DPRK to save it and Kim Il Sung from defeat in the winter of 1951 have faded, and the personal ties among top leaders that characterized the Sino-DPRK relationship are no longer operative now that both Kim Il Sung and Deng Xiaoping have left the scene, although Kim Jong Il's "secret" visit to Beijing on May 29–31, 2000, brought full attendance from Chinese Communist Party leaders.[2] Strains in the old "lips and teeth" relationship came to the surface in the late 1980s as former Republic of Korea (ROK) President Roh Tae Woo's *Nordpolitik*, or Northern Policy, wooed Chinese leaders to recognize the potential for exponential growth in PRC-ROK economic ties. The complementarity between the two economies and the aggressively entrepreneurial style of Korean industrialists—always pushing for new markets and larger market shares—were factors that expanded trade flows from tens of millions of dollars in the late 1980s to over $3 billion by 1992. One result of this steadily increasing economic interaction was the formal establishment of ties between Seoul and Beijing in August of 1992, a decision which marked a practical shift by Beijing from a fraternal policy of "lips and teeth" to one of "equidistance" between Seoul and Pyongyang.

Beijing implemented its equidistance policy in the early 1990s through attempts to balance political interactions between Seoul and Pyongyang. Both North and South Korea were treated in equivalent fashion on issues of politics and public symbolism, including overt use of the Chinese media to reinforce the political message of equidistance by providing equal space to events related to North and South Korea. One evidence of the equidistance policy's limiting effect on ROK-PRC relations was that Beijing was chronically unable or unwilling to deliver many of the political benefits (i.e., leverage over North Korea) Seoul initially sought through its Northern Diplomacy. An exception was the delivery of North Korean defector Hwang Jang Yop to Seoul via the Philippines following his February 1996 request for asylum at Seoul's embassy in Beijing. Meanwhile, the burgeoning Sino-South Korean economic relationship continued to proceed apace during the 1990s, with two-way trade reaching approximately $30 billion in 2000 and South

Korean investors among the most active foreign players in Liaoning and Shandong provinces.[3] Simultaneously, Chinese attempts to put the economic relationship with the DPRK on a market-oriented track were resisted. The PRC essentially failed to wean North Korea from "friendship prices" for oil, despite active efforts to do so in the early 1990s; China has consistently been a leading provider of humanitarian assistance and primary trading partner for the North throughout the 1990s.

The third stage in the development of a post–Cold War PRC policy toward the Korean peninsula has been the transition from equidistance to stability as the PRC's fundamental objective. The emphasis on stability—including an unequivocal embrace of the status quo or divided nature of the Korean peninsula—has been most evident during the course of North Korea's food crisis of 1995–1997, but the roots of Chinese support for stability on the Korean peninsula as a fundamental policy objective lie in China's response to the Korean nuclear crisis and support for a negotiated settlement with North Korea that eventually culminated in the U.S.-DPRK Geneva Agreed Framework of 1994. In fact, the PRC had always urged the United States to go further with North Korea, advocating that the United States should fulfill the concept of "cross-recognition" (i.e., U.S. and Japanese normalization with the DPRK to balance the Chinese and Soviet moves toward normalization with the South and indirectly preserve balance between both sides of a divided Korea). The North Korean nuclear crisis, with attendant risks of renewed confrontation that would inevitably influence China's economic development agenda, was the first step toward a Chinese policy that disregarded considerations of equidistance in favor of a policy that focused on China's essential interest in reducing the level of confrontation between the two Koreas without inducing a sudden change in the status quo on the Korean peninsula; that is, Korean unification, even if the emphasis on stability meant choosing the side of Seoul over that of Pyongyang.

The North Korean food crisis—with accompanying flows of refugees from North Korea into Northeastern China—appears to have crystallized thinking regarding China's own stakes and interests on the Korean peninsula. First, China has an ongoing interest in preservation of the status quo, including prevention of North Korea's economic or political collapse to the extent possible. China's lavish delivery of assistance to North Korea through both official and private channels had a significant strategic component. It lessened flows of refugees to Chinese territory, it delayed a possible North Korean collapse, and it enhanced China's own economic influence inside North Korea. China's humanitarian contributions to North Korea are reported to have represented one-quarter to one-third of China's overall budgeted foreign assistance.[4]

Second, Chinese leaders have recognized that the ultimate balance of power to shape the future on the Korean peninsula has already shifted to Seoul. This recognition is demonstrated by the increasingly active high-level ties among Chinese and Korean leaders, including regularized cabinet-level exchanges and a deepening of dialogue on matters of mutual interest: Jiang Zemin spent a week in Seoul as a guest of then-president Kim Young Sam in 1996; the face of China's "fourth generation" leadership, Hu Jintao, has spent time in Korea; defense minister level exchanges commenced in 1999; and, Premier Zhu Rongji became the last member of China's core leadership to visit South Korea in October 2000.[5]

Third, China has had more active participation in international diplomacy involving the Korean peninsula both through its own initiative and through widespread recognition, particularly in Seoul, where as a practical matter China's views can not be ignored in the process of seeking a comprehensive settlement of Korean issues.[6] China's participation in the Four Party Talks process, despite initial North Korean statements that appeared to favor exclusion of the PRC from such a process, reflects China's historical involvement in and proximity to Korea, and Chinese contributions through this forum have generally been seen as positive. In fact, Chinese positions on a number of issues in the Four Party forum— including the need to maintain the armistice as an interim mechanism in the face of North Korean efforts to dismantle the Military Armistice Commission and Chinese willingness to criticize North Korea for actions that may destabilize the regional security environment—reflect China's large stake and interest in Korean peninsula stability.

KOREA AS AN ISSUE IN
THE U.S.-PRC RELATIONSHIP

The process of adaptation to a new security environment in Northeast Asia has involved half-steps and hedging strategies among all the parties in the region. It is natural that this would be the case since the cold war confrontation on the Korean peninsula itself remains unresolved at the same time that the Cold War has ended globally. Under these conditions, all parties are doing what they can to position themselves in preparation for an as-yet-undefined new security environment in Northeast Asia.[7] The United States and China have also been feeling their way along in a new, post–Cold war environment in which the fundamental strategic rationale for establishing the relationship in the early 1970s dissolved along with the Soviet Union itself.

Although the pattern in U.S. attitudes toward China has been one of oscillation between either euphoria and over-expectation or disappointment and confrontation, such swings have been made more complex by the lack of a strategic anchor (such as opposition to the Soviet threat during the Cold War) as a lens through which to assess the relationship in the 1990s. The extremes have remained stark and the oscillations rapid and unpredictable. For instance, former President Clinton initially linked China's human rights performance to continued Most Favored Nation (MFN) trade status in 1993 and subsequently reversed course one year later. National Security Advisor Tony Lake nearly categorized China as a rogue state in 1994, but his successor Sandy Berger has avidly pursued a "strategic partnership" including an exchange of summits between Presidents Clinton and Jiang Zemin in 1997 and 1998.[8] However, a substantive, in-depth strategic dialogue on key regional issues has been slow in coming, and the accidental bombing of the PRC Embassy in Belgrade assured that any prospective "strategic partnership" with Beijing would be very slow in becoming a reality, if indeed such a vision for the relationship is even plausible. The one bright spot in the relationship has been the identification of China's World Trade Organization (WTO) entry—despite difficulties in other areas of the relationship—as one area where cooperation was clearly in the mutual interest of Washington and Beijing.

Stability on the Korean peninsula is one area in which U.S. and PRC short-term interests have converged over time, and it is one of the obvious areas in which a dialogue regarding respective strategic interests is necessary and desirable. However, it is also true that as a relative priority in U.S.-China relations, regional stability on the Korean peninsula has consistently, as a practical matter, ranked behind Taiwan, China's admission to the WTO, nonproliferation, the bilateral trade imbalance, and possibly human rights.

Despite the relatively low priority of Korea as an issue in U.S.-PRC relations, the United States and China share common interests in preserving stability and preserving nuclear nonproliferation on the Korean peninsula that may aptly be called the "three no's" of policy toward the Korean peninsula: no nukes, no war, and no collapse of North Korea. In fact, the North Korean nuclear crisis of 1993–94 provided an initial opportunity to move the Korean peninsula onto the agenda of U.S.-PRC dialogue, particularly as the United States sought China's help in urging North Korea not to abandon the Nuclear Nonproliferation Treaty (NPT). China clearly is a key player in any effort to meet North Korea's nuclear challenge, but the overall relationship at that time was poor enough that consultation was sporadic at best. Both sides began the practice of publicly acknowledging shared interests in regional stability, but public statements on this topic equaled or exceeded the level of official consultation taking place at that time. Although the PRC did receive credit for weighing in with North Korea (and the United States) to urge a negotiated settlement of the nuclear crisis, there was relatively little official policy coordination or even dialogue. In fact, China's lack of cooperation in the abortive U.S. sanctions drive in the United Nations in early June of 1994 may be seen as one factor that could have become a real sticking point in the U.S.-PRC relationship had the drive for sanctions actually been implemented. Indeed, it wasn't until initiation of the Four Party Talks, discussed below, that U.S.-China official working-level consultations developed effectively.[9]

The second shared U.S.-PRC "no" in policy toward the Korean peninsula is "no war." Neither the United States nor the PRC would be interested in seeing renewed military aggression that would lead to military conflict between North and South Korea, and China has indicated that it would not intervene in a conflict on the Korean peninsula instigated by North Korea. However, in the event of military conflict instigated by South Korea or third parties, China has not renounced its treaty obligations to fight with North Korea. Likewise, the United States would come to the defense of South Korea in the event of an attack by the North, but would be extraordinarily reluctant to become involved in hostilities that might develop under other circumstances. In fact, concern developed at the highest levels within the U.S. government regarding South Korean intentions at the height of the aftermath of the North Korean submarine incursion in September of 1996, at which time there were reports of contingency planning in Seoul that included plans for military operations north of the Demilitarized Zone (DMZ). President Kim Young Sam's demands for a North Korean apology for the incident were noticeably milder following a November 1996 meeting between Presidents Clinton and Kim Young Sam on the sidelines of the Asia-Pacific Economic Cooperation (APEC) conference in Manila, no doubt in part as a result of a firm message delivered to President Kim that stability would take priority over destabilizing rhetoric or other actions in response to the submarine incident.

Finally, the United States and China have taken actions which, if examined together, suggest that neither party favors any destabilizing collapse of North Korea, which would involve spillover and instability beyond North Korea's borders. (In fact, no government is eager to see North Korea's collapse at this time.) One of China's policy objectives in responding to North Korea's food crisis from 1995–1997, as stated above, had been to maintain stability in North Korea, and U.S. desires for a "soft landing" for North Korea were parallel with Chinese interests in stability. Despite a sharp policy debate over whether or not U.S. aid to North

Korea was intended to "prop up" an evil regime, there is no question that China's assistance was intended to do so, a fact that was not lost on many policy makers in Seoul who were anxiously awaiting the crash of North Korea's "broken airplane," as described by former President Kim Young Sam. Although Chinese and American humanitarian policies toward North Korea are not coordinated, they have been complementary, with the United States and China playing the leading role in providing humanitarian assistance to North Korea during the past few years.[10]

EMERGENCE OF CHINESE COOPERATION AND RECENT KOREAN PENINSULA DEVELOPMENTS

Although PRC exhortations on behalf of a negotiated solution to the North Korean nuclear crisis represented a form of cooperation with the United States to deter North Korea from challenging the NPT, the development of close U.S.-PRC consultations among senior level officials did not take place until the summer of 1997 when Assistant Foreign Minister Wang Yi and Acting Assistant Secretary of State for East Asia and the Pacific Charles Kartman held an official meeting on the Korea issue. At the same time, the United States and South Korea were having "explanatory" talks with North Korea to convince the North to accept the April 1996 joint U.S.-ROK Four Party Talks proposal of Presidents Bill Clinton and Kim Young Sam.

One of the most constructive benefits of the Four Party process, once it was finally inaugurated in December of 1997, was to provide an opportunity for in-depth interaction involving Chinese, Americans, and Koreans to forward a practical agenda for resolving the Korean conflict, even if such discussions made absolutely no progress whatsoever with the North Koreans. In fact, one of the clearest results of the Four Party Talks has been to underscore just how isolated North Korean officials are in pursuing some of the more impractical facets of their agenda. The Four Party Talks process has also underscored the complementarity of U.S. and PRC short-term interests, which have coincided and allowed for some very constructive cooperation despite the relative contention and politically sensitive nature of other issues in the relationship. At the same time, the Four Party Talks have revealed subtle long-term divergences in U.S. and Chinese policies toward the Korean peninsula, respectively, most notably regarding the future scope and level of U.S. troop presence on the peninsula.

For the PRC, however, the opportunity for participation in the Four Party dialogue, despite a relatively passive initial approach to the process, far outweighs the downside of either exclusion from discussion regarding the outcome of events on the Korean peninsula or the renewal of tensions and even possible military conflict or heightened competition with the United States for influence in Korea. The initiation of the Four Party Talks also coincided with the PRC's heightened awareness of the strategic importance and potential impact of instability on the Korean peninsula that developed as a result of North Korea's food crisis in 1996. The level of attention and expertise in China on both North and South Korea has risen considerably in recent years as a result of the Korean peninsula's possible influence on China's strategic interests.

If anything, North Korea's missile launch in August of 1998 has also heightened China's awareness of how negative events on the Korean peninsula may affect China's security interests. The major impact of North Korea's missile launch has been to serve as a catalyst for the joint development of Theater Missile Defense (TMD) between the United States and Japan, a project that the PRC has opposed primarily for its potential applications if such a system were extended to include Taiwan.[11] North Korea's negative contribution to China's security interests was not appreciated in Beijing, and there have been reports from South Korea that China played an instrumental role in impressing upon North Korean leaders the importance of avoiding a second launch by agreeing to a missile moratorium in September of 1999. However, it is difficult to know whether the North Koreans may have been successful in extracting additional assistance from China as part of any PRC-DPRK negotiation that might have influenced North Korea's decision to suspend its missile development program for the duration of missile negotiations with the United States.

Another factor that has complicated U.S.-PRC cooperation on Korean issues has been the negative impact on the overall relationship of the U.S. bombing of the PRC Embassy in Belgrade during the Kosovo conflict. Despite China's vested interests in short-term cooperation with the United States on Korea, the negative impact of Chinese perceptions that the United States is trying to extend its hegemony or pursue humanitarian interests that might eventually come into direct confrontation with China's emphasis on sovereignty is a factor that dampens support for strategic cooperation with the United States on regional issues such as the Korean peninsula. It is interesting to note that, despite the bombing, a decision was made relatively quickly thereafter that official discussions on Korea would *not* be affected despite the Chinese decision to suspend its dialogue with the United States on military issues, nonproliferation, and human rights in the immediate aftermath of the embassy bombing. China's own strategic interests in continuing consultation on the Korean peninsula outweighed the risks of being excluded from involvement in sensitive issues related to the future of the Korean peninsula.

Chinese scholars have continued to maintain a cautiously skeptical view of U.S. intentions on the Korean peninsula, particularly in the aftermath of the May 1999 PRC Embassy bombing. Although China has encouraged normalization of relations between the United States and North Korea as a step toward stabilization of tensions and reduction of confrontation, Chinese scholars are well aware of the limits of Chinese leverage over North Korea and may be concerned that Washington sometimes seems to have greater opportunities than Beijing to influence Pyongyang while maintaining a close alliance relationship with Seoul. Others are banking on discord between Washington and Seoul as an opportunity to eventually weaken U.S. influence on the Korean peninsula. Although the promotion of dialogue and reconciliation between North and South Korea is in Beijing's interests, there is considerable distrust regarding Washington's motives in encouraging such a process and some Chinese analysts are worried that the process might develop at the expense of China's own national security interests. China's support for Four Party Talks is at least partially motivated by a desire not to be left out of the process since developments between the two Koreas will directly affect China's own security interests.

U.S.-PRC STRATEGIC COMPETITION AND THE STRATEGIC DILEMMAS POSED FOR CHINA'S POLICY TOWARD KOREA

Republican President George W. Bush, in his first major foreign policy speech of the 2000 campaign, said he regards China not as a "strategic partner," but as a "strategic competitor."[12] Aside from the question of the extent to which a political campaign speech is a good guideline for how presidential candidates would actually pursue policies if elected, the suggestion that the U.S.-PRC relationship is likely to continue to be a rocky one, defined at least as much by conflict as by cooperation, is not unrealistic. In fact, some analysts would suggest that the U.S.-PRC relationship has been dominated by conflict since the Belgrade embassy bombing, WTO agreements notwithstanding. In a world where the United States and China may increasingly face each other toe-to-toe, what are the implications for policy toward the Korean peninsula, particularly if the long-term divergence of interests between the U.S. and PRC on the Korean peninsula is the lens through which policy makers assess strategy and tactics?

The primary flash point for potential U.S.-PRC competition continues to be on the issue of Taiwan, but the policy relationships between cross-straits relations and policy toward the Korean peninsula have historically been linked from the very beginning. For instance, Mao's decision to intervene in Korea meant delaying any plans for achieving the conquest of Taiwan, however impossible such an operation might have been. The two Koreas have also tried to play both sides of the strait against each other, usually to ill effect. The ramifications of South Korea's unceremonious dumping of Taipei in favor of Beijing in 1991 are being felt even today in the still awkward relationship between South Korea and Taiwan. And North Korea has tried to woo investments from Taiwan as a bargaining tool against Beijing, with little success and to ill effect in Pyongyang's own relationship with Beijing. These games are set to continue at a low level for some time, and the two Koreas could find themselves once again in the thick of things if indeed there were a severe escalation of tensions between Beijing and the United States involving the Taiwan issue.

In fact, Kosovo and the North Korean missile test together have posed some real dilemmas for China's own choices in its policy toward the Korean peninsula and toward the United States that would only grow starker in the context of increased competition or conflict in the U.S.-PRC relationship. The first dilemma is how to respond to the U.S.-Japan decision in favor of joint development of TMD as a response to North Korea's missile development program. Based on their own dismissal of North Korea's missile development capabilities, Chinese analysts are quick to presume that North Korea is a proxy for China. This is an assumption that is clearly false if one looks only at TMD, but may have some salience if one considers some rationales for pushing forward on National Missile Defense efforts designed to respond to Inter-Continental Ballistic Missiles (ICBMs). For China, the key question is how to interpret the current debate over Japan's own national identity and appropriate capabilities and scope of military action (a debate that North Korea's missile test was primary in fueling) without taking actions that might indirectly undermine the U.S.-Japan alliance, the dissolution of which would immediately trigger Chinese concerns about an independent, militarily powerful Japan.

The other dilemma for China is how to deal with North Korea itself. The debate in China over how to deal with North Korea in the short-term is very much parallel to the U.S. debate over how to avoid extortionary demands while getting results from the North, the primary difference between the U.S. and Chinese structural position being that China is already a "friend" of North Korea while the United States remains an "enemy" of the North. This debate is now complicated by a more fundamental debate over U.S. strategic intentions, and there is concern that China may attempt to utilize its relationship with North Korea tactically in an attempt to induce U.S. cooperation on areas it identifies as a high priority. Chinese concerns over how and whether the Clinton Doctrine may be applied (assuaged somewhat by the Australian-led intervention in East Timor and collective inaction of the international community on Chechnya) continue to have a strongly negative effect on the prospects for international cooperation with the United States, all the more so because the Chinese leadership has made a fundamental decision that the U.S.-PRC relationship, up to now, has been too important economically to put at risk through increased tensions between Washington and Beijing. The primary assumption that the United States is simply too important to China's future to engage in a confrontational relationship—in contrast to the relatively high number of festering issues and problems in the relationship—could have a positive impact on Chinese cooperation with the United States inside the leadership, but the fundamental premise of the United States as a potential partner is increasingly under challenge in both Beijing and Washington, the PRC's WTO entry notwithstanding.

China's more active posture toward the Korean peninsula in recent months and years reflects both its own legitimate strategic interests and a greater sense of wariness—in the context of a clearly limited near-term U.S.-China relationship—regarding the extent to which China's long-term interests may be affected negatively by a strong U.S. influence on the Korean peninsula that might extend even to Pyongyang. Beijing is the informal link in the chain of shared interests currently encircling Pyongyang that will ultimately determine whether North Korea will respond positively to U.S., South Korean, and Japanese engagement policies. One result of increased U.S.-PRC competition will be the heightened temptation on the part of Beijing to take actions that are not coordinated with the general direction of U.S.-Japan-ROK engagement with North Korea laid out in the Perry process. Such a course by Beijing would be a welcome development for North Korea, which would then seek to play off the major powers (these days the United States and China) against each other to see what the market will bear. If the purpose of China's deepening leadership contacts with Kim Jong Il is as a vehicle for challenging U.S. strategic interests, a renewed crisis would make Korea a central object of U.S.-China competition.

The question of which direction a unified Korea leans diplomatically would engender competition for a close relationship with Seoul between China and the United States. In particular, China will want to maintain a friendly relationship with a unified Korea that shares a common border, and the United States may hope to maintain its troop presence and alliance relationship with its Korean ally. (A continuing U.S. presence in post-reunification Korea may be perceived negatively by a rising China with its own version of a Monroe Doctrine for former tributary states and near neighbors.) The objective of the United States in such a situation should be to manage the alliance relationship in such a way that there is no question who is the more reliable and closer partner to South Korea. If the conflict of interest engenders premature competition for influence in Korea between the United States and China, many Korean issues may be more difficult to resolve.

SOUTH KOREA'S STRATEGIC OBJECTIVE: AVOIDING HAVING TO CHOOSE AMONG FRIENDS

As the economic relationship between China and South Korea grows, the concrete costs of possible tension or confrontation between the United States and China become more worrisome. South Korea's stakes in the avoidance of a confrontation that would split the region will continue to grow in tandem with the economic relationships between Chinese and South Korean private sectors. South Korea's private sector would be hard-pressed to give up those tangible economic benefits for the sake of coming into line with possible U.S. political demands in times of tension or confrontation. The possibility of being forced to choose between China and the United States in the event of confrontation or discord between Beijing and Seoul is increasingly viewed in the category of worst-case scenarios to be avoided at all costs. For South Korea, the primary objective is to avoid being caught in any crossfire between Beijing and Washington while enhancing political and economic relations and strategic influence with Beijing in ways that will also assure a stable and gradual process leading ultimately to Korean reunification.

One concept that has been entertained by some South Korean specialists is the idea that Seoul may play the role of "internal" balancer, perhaps quietly mediating difficult issues between Washington and Beijing during times of high tension to ensure that the situation does not get out of hand. However, the effective pursuit of such a role might involve the necessity of making precisely those hard choices that any South Korean leadership may most seek to avoid. It also presumes that the task and objective of the United States in the use of its influence is to provide "external" balance, but the balance is precisely what would be at stake if the United States and China were to develop a confrontational relationship.

Another possible objective of South Korea's foreign policy as it considers responses to a possible downturn in Sino-U.S. relations might be to seek to insulate its core foreign policy objectives from the most negative effects of such a downturn. For instance, the widespread assumption that good U.S.-China relations are necessary for progress to be made in reducing inter-Korean tensions raises the question of how to delink major power relations from the inter-Korean relationship, particularly if one assumes continued difficulty in the relationship between Washington and Beijing. During the Cold War such a task was impossible and even Korea's historical geographic location as the flash point or vortex of major power confrontation suggests the challenging nature of such an exercise.

NOTES

1. The author would like to acknowledge the research assistance of Mr. Moon Chun Sang in preparing this chapter.

2. Hae-bom Jee, "Kim Jong-il's China Visit Confirmed," *Choson Ilbo* (English Edition), June 1, 2000, http://www.chosun.com/w21data/html/news/200006/200006010456.html

3. Victor D. Cha, "Engaging China: Seoul-Beijing Détente and Korean Security," *Survival,* vol. 41, no. 1, Spring 1999.

4. Author interview with Chinese researcher on North Korea, Beijing, July 1999.

5. Scott Snyder, "Upgrading Communication Channels, Messages Are Getting Clearer," *Comparative Connections,* Pacific Forum CSIS E-journal, First Quarter 2000, http://www.csis.org/pacfor/cc/001Qchina_skorea.html

6. Doo-Bok Park, "Forum: Kim Jong Il's Visit to China and the North-South Summit," *Munwha Ilbo* (in Korean), June 5, 2000, p. 6.

7. Robert A. Manning and James Przystup, "Asia's Transition Diplomacy: Hedging Against Futureshock," *Survival,* vol. 41, no. 3, Autumn 1999.

8. James Mann, *About Face: A History of America's Curious Relationship with China, from Nixon to Clinton* (New York: Alfred A. Knopf, December 1998).

9. Leon V. Sigal, *Disarming Strangers: Nuclear Diplomacy With North Korea* (Princeton, NJ: Princeton University Press, 1998).

10. See Scott Snyder "North Korea's Decline and China's Strategic Dilemmas," United States Institute of Peace Special Report, October 1997, http://222.usip.org/oc/sr/snyder/China-NK-pt1.html.

11. John Pomfret, "Beijing Presses Its Case Against Missile Shield; Official Warns U.S. on Ties with Asia," *Washington Post,* March 8, 1999.

12. Kelley Shannon, "George Bush on China," *Los Angeles Times,* May 16, 2000, http://www.issues2000.org/More_George_W_Bush_China.htm.

CHAPTER EIGHT

U.S.-JAPAN SECURITY COOPERATION AND THE TWO KOREAS

B. C. KOH

INTRODUCTION

U.S.-Japan security cooperation is closely intertwined with the two Korean states. The United States, Japan, and the Republic of Korea (ROK) are *de facto* allies thanks to Washington's bilateral military alliances with both Tokyo and Seoul. The Democratic People's Republic of Korea (DPRK) enters the equation as the principal source of threat to the security of all three. The North Korean threat, perceived or real, increased measurably in the early 1990s with the emergence of the nuclear issue—that is, Pyongyang's suspected nuclear weapons development program and its intransigence via-à-vis the International Atomic Energy Agency (IAEA), the United States, South Korea, and Japan.

North Korea's firing of a three-stage rocket over Japan in August 1998, in particular, laid bare the latter's vulnerability to the former's ballistic missiles, which seemed capable of reaching any and all targets in Japan. All this has led to a conspicuous escalation of trilateral consultations among the United States, Japan, and the ROK, in addition to galvanizing Japan to strengthen both its own defense capability and bilateral security cooperation with the United States.

When the United States and Japan revised the guidelines on their defense cooperation in 1997, they specifically dealt with contingencies in "areas surrounding Japan." Even though the Korean Peninsula was not specifically mentioned, there could be little doubt that it was very much on the minds of the two allies when they focused their attention on "situations in areas surrounding Japan."

This chapter proposes to explore these developments and issues. First, it will examine the ways in which the U.S.-Japan alliance has affected or been affected by developments on the Korean Peninsula. Following will be a closer look at the North Korea factor—that is, threats posed by Pyongyang's nuclear and missile development programs and their impact on the U.S.-Japan alliance. A brief discussion of bilateral security cooperation between Tokyo and Seoul will follow. Finally, it will propose a speculative prognosis.

THE U.S.-JAPAN ALLIANCE

It is noteworthy that the U.S.-Japan alliance was forged against the backdrop of the Korean War. When U.S. President Harry S. Truman and Japanese Prime Minister Yoshda Shigeru signed the Japan-United States Security Treaty in San Francisco in September 1951, the Korean Peninsula was embroiled in a fratricidal civil war that had escalated to a veritable international war, with 17 states under the United Nations Command led by General Douglas MacArthur on one side and China and North Korea on the opposite side. Still under the Allied, that is, U.S. occupation, Japan was both an indirect participant in the war as the principal logistical base of the UN forces and a major beneficiary of the conflict in economic terms.

By the time the United States and the ROK signed a mutual defense treaty in October 1953, Japan had regained independence but its indirect linkage with South Korea remained unabated. By their common strategic links with the United States, Japan and South Korea arguably had become "quasi-allies," even before establishing diplomatic relations.[1]

The conclusion of a new Treaty of Mutual Cooperation and Security between Japan and the United States in 1960 preceded the Japan-ROK normalization by five years.[2] The treaty, along with the stationing of U.S. troops in Japan, nonetheless solidified Tokyo's indirect security links with Seoul, which also continued to rely on both its mutual defense treaty with Washington and the presence of U.S. troops on its soil. Significantly, the 1960 treaty explicitly recognizes the dual mission of U.S. forces deployed in Japan. Article VI thus stipulates: "For the purpose of contributing to the security of Japan *and the maintenance of international peace and security in the Far East,* the United States of America is granted the use by its land, air and naval forces of facilities and areas in Japan." (italics added)

Neither the 1960 U.S.-Japan security treaty nor the 1953 U.S.-ROK mutual defense treaty, however, envisions automatic involvement of the United States in the event of an external attack against its allies. According to Article V of the U.S.-Japan treaty, "Each Party recognizes that an armed attack against either Party in the territories under the administration of Japan would be dangerous to its own peace and safety and declares that it would act to meet the common danger *in accordance with its constitutional provisions and processes.*" (italics added)

The U.S.-ROK mutual defense treaty not only contains the same restrictive language but is subject to an "understanding" attached by the U.S. Senate, when it gave "advice and consent" to the treaty, that only a genuine external attack will activate its provisions; that is, should South Korea initiate attack against the North, the United States would not be obligated to provide assistance even in accordance with its constitutional processes.[3] The presence of U.S. troops in both Japan and South Korea, however, increases the probability of automatic involvement in any conflict, for the troops serve a "trip-wire" function.

True to its name, the U.S.-ROK pact is a *mutual* defense treaty, which imposes obligations on *both* parties to provide assistance in the event of an external attack against either. Owing to the constraints of Article IX of the Japanese constitution, however, the U.S.-Japan treaty precludes the possibility of Japan's participation in the defense of the United States. The article contains a renunciation of war "as a sovereign right of the nation" and a stipulation that "land, sea, and air forces as well as other war potential will never be maintained." However, with the encouragement of the United States, the *de facto* drafter of Japan's postwar constitution, Japan has asserted its "inherent right of self-defense," which, in its view, permits it to possess the "minimum level of armed strength" needed to exercise that right. The justification of the Self-Defense Forces along these lines places severe constraints on Japan's ability to deploy its troops abroad.[4]

Japan's defense policy, of which the U.S.-Japan alliance is the centerpiece, is keenly sensitive to developments on the Korean Peninsula. The National Defense Program Outline (*Boei keikaku no taiko*) adopted by Japan's National Defense Council (*Kokubo Kaigi*) and Cabinet in October 1976 thus cites the persistence of tensions on the Korean Peninsula as an important contextual factor shaping the program.[5] In revising the program following the end of the Cold War, the National Defense Council and the Cabinet took note not only of "new kinds of dangers, such as the proliferation of weapons of mass destruction, including nuclear arms and missiles," but also of "continuing tensions on the Korean Peninsula." The revised program, adopted in December 1995, underscored the importance of the "close cooperative relationship between Japan and the United States, based on the Japan-U.S. security arrangements" in creating a "stable security environment." The Japan-U.S. alliance made clear that it was a *sine qua non* not only for the security of Japan but for the stability of the region and of the world as a whole.[6] A noteworthy event in the evolution of U.S.-Japan security relations was the publication of the U.S.-Japan Joint Declaration on Security by former President Clinton and Prime Minister Hashimoto in Tokyo on April 17, 1996. While noting that "since the end of the Cold War, the possibility of global armed conflict has receded," the two leaders nonetheless stressed that "instability and uncertainty persist in the [Asia-Pacific] region." In their words, "Tensions continue on the Korean Peninsula. There are still heavy concentration of military force, including nuclear arsenals. Unresolved territorial disputes, potential regional conflicts, and the proliferation of weapons of mass destruction and their means of delivery all constitute sources of instability."[7]

Agreeing that "continued U.S. military presence is . . . essential [not only for the defense of Japan but also] for preserving peace and stability in the Asia-Pacific region," the two leaders decided to "initiate a review of the 1978 Guidelines for Japan-U.S. Defense Cooperation to build upon the close working relationship already established between Japan and the United States." They "agreed on the necessity to promote bilateral policy coordination, including studies on bilateral cooperation in dealing with situations that may emerge in the areas surrounding Japan and which will have an important influence on the peace and security of Japan."[8]

The two leaders underscored the "vital importance" of "stability on the Korean Peninsula" to their countries, pledging "every effort in this regard, in close cooperation with the Republic of Korea." Finally, they cited the "North Korean nuclear problem" as one of the issues on which Japan and the United States would cooperate in the United Nations and the Asia Pacific Economic Cooperation (APEC) forum with the aim of helping to "build the kind of world that promotes our shared interests and values."[9]

The revised Guidelines for U.S.-Japan Defense Cooperation approved by the U.S.-Japan Security Consultative Committee (SCC) in September 1997 contained a lengthy section on "situations in areas surrounding Japan." Whereas the 1978 guidelines had devoted only two paragraphs to "U.S.-Japan cooperation in the case of situations in the Far East outside of Japan which will have an important influence on the security of Japan," the 1997 guidelines' section on "cooperation in situations in areas surrounding Japan that will have an important influence on Japan's peace and security" was nearly four pages long.[10]

The 1997 guidelines stress that "the concept, situations in areas surrounding Japan, is not geographical but situational." The governments of the United States and Japan, it states, "will make every effort, including diplomatic measures, to prevent such situations from occurring." When the two governments "reach a common assessment of the state of each situation, they will effectively coordinate their activities."

The types of contingencies in which the United States and Japan may either act unilaterally or engage in bilateral cooperation include the following: (1) relief activities and measures to deal with refugees, (2) search and rescue operations, (3) noncombatant evacuation operations, and (4) activities for ensuring the effectiveness of economic sanctions for the maintenance of international peace and security. The revised guidelines also commit Japan to provide U.S. forces engaged in operations in areas surrounding Japan with "additional facilities and areas in a timely and appropriate manner, and ensure the temporary use by U.S. Forces of [Japan] Self-Defense Forces facilities and civilian airports and ports." Additionally, "Japan will provide rear area support to those U.S. Forces that are conducting operations for the purposes of achieving the objectives of the U.S.-Japan Security Treaty." Although such support "will be provided primarily in Japanese territory," it "may also be provided on the high seas and international airspace around Japan which are distinguished from areas where combat operations are being conducted." Finally, Japan's "Self-Defense Forces will conduct such activities as intelligence gathering, surveillance and minesweeping, to protect lives and property and to ensure navigational safety," while "U.S. Forces will conduct operations to restore the peace and security affected by situations in areas surrounding Japan."

How the new guidelines would be implemented in the event that the "situations" they envision materialized, however, remained to be spelled out in implementing legislation. The Japanese Diet thus enacted three bills into law in May 1999—one dealing with "situations in areas surrounding Japan" (*shohen jitai-ho*), another revising the Self-Defense Forces law to allow the Maritime Self-Defense Forces ships to rescue Japanese nationals abroad (*kaisei Jieitai-ho*), and a third pertaining to the revised Japan-U.S. Acquisition and Cross-Servicing Agreement (*kaisei Nichi-bei buppin yakumu sogo teikyo kyotei*).[11]

The elevation of the revised guidelines from a set of principles to actual guides to action, with the necessary legal, institutional, and procedural apparatus in place, evoked varying reactions from Washington, Seoul, and Pyongyang. The reactions, it should be noted, preceded the completion of the full legislative cycle on the three bills in the Japanese Diet, for their adoption by the House of Representatives (HR) on April 27, 1999, a month before the House of Councilors (HC) followed suit, was tantamount to Diet approval. Prime Minister Obuchi Keizo had worked hard to ensure that the HR would act before his departure for

Washington for a summit meeting with former President Clinton. In their joint press conference in Washington on May 3, 1999 Clinton said: "We in America are gratified that the Lower House of Japan's Diet now has approved a new set of U.S.-Japan guidelines to allow us to respond with flexibility and speed to any regional crisis in Asia."[12]

Seoul's reaction was somewhat guarded. Officially, it expressed the hope for continuing "transparency" and "close consultations." Unofficially, one could hear words of caution underscoring the dual nature of what had happened. On the one hand, the passage of the laws that would facilitate the implementation of the guidelines was a welcome development, for it would strengthen the capability of the United States, Japan, and South Korea to cope with military threat emanating from North Korea. On the other hand, the development might signal the construction of a "foothold" enabling Japan to project its military power to the Asia-Pacific region.[13]

Predictably, Pyongyang reacted with a harsh denunciation of Japan's "aggressive" designs. A *Nodong sinmun* commentary, which reflects Pyongyang's official position, asserted that the passage of the guidelines-related bills had shown how "frightening" the "ambitions of the Japanese reactionaries" were. Under the pretext of "cooperation" with the U.S. forces and Japanese security, it said, Japan's "Self-Defense Forces" had now completed all preparations for embarking on "overt aggression abroad." Arguing that the "first target" of such aggression was "our Republic," the North Korean daily warned that the DPRK "will never condone the reckless moves by the Japanese reactionaries, in collaboration with the U.S. imperialists, to crush us to death."[14]

In sum, the U.S.-Japan alliance has not only survived the end of the Cold War but been fortified. Although the number of U.S. troops deployed in Japan has declined from 52,000 during the Cold War years to about 47,000 in the post–Cold War era, the readiness of both U.S. Forces and Japan's Self-Defense Forces for contingencies and, particularly, their ability to work together have markedly grown. As the Japanese Ministry of Foreign Affairs puts it, the end of the Cold War, while diminishing measurably the chances for large-scale wars, has not banished threats to security in the "Asia-Pacific region encompassing our country." "In addition to the continued existence of large military forces, including nuclear weapons," such problems as "North Korea's nuclear weapons development" and "territorial disputes in South China Sea" plague the region, fueling instability and uncertainty.[15] Let us now turn to the question of why North Korea has become such a salient factor in Japan's security calculus and hence in Japan-U.S. security cooperation.

THE NORTH KOREA FACTOR

The turning point in Japan's perception of the North Korean threat came in 1993, when Pyongyang's missile capability and suspected nuclear weapons development program jolted Tokyo. The nuclear issue had actually become salient in 1990, and Japan had urged North Korea to defuse the perceived threat during the abortive normalization talks that took place between January 1991 and November 1992. With the DPRK's conclusion of a safeguards agreement with the International Atomic Energy Agency (IAEA) in April 1992 and the initiation of IAEA inspections of North Korea's declared nuclear facilities in the following month, however, the nuclear issue appeared to be on its way toward resolution.[16]

In March 1993, however, faced with the IAEA's demand for a "special inspection" of two undeclared sites in Yongbyon, the nuclear complex located about 60 miles north of Pyongyang, North Korea served notice that it would withdraw from the Treaty for the Nonproliferation of Nuclear Weapons (NPT) after three months in accordance with the treaty's provisions on withdrawal. This raised the possibility that the North might soon resume its nuclear weapons program.[17]

While efforts were under way to resolve the crisis through diplomatic negotiations between the United States and the DPRK, a new type of threat to Japan's security burst on the scene. In the latter part of May, North Korea test-fired a rocket into the Sea of Japan (or the East Sea). Japan's Defense Agency concluded that the rocket was *Nodong 1* missile, which would put "more than a half" of Japan within its range, estimated at 1,000 km (621 miles).[18] The possibility, no matter how remote, that the North might be able to combine its nuclear and missile power—that is, to develop capability to load nuclear weapons on its intermediate-range ballistic missiles—must have alarmed or, even, frightened Japan's defense planners.

When the nuclear crisis was defused with the signing of the Agreed Framework between the United States and the DPRK in Geneva in October 1994, Japan became a founding member, along with the United States and the ROK, of the Korean Peninsula Energy Development Organization (KEDO), the international consortium set up to implement the accord. Japan subsequently pledged to contribute $1 billion to the KEDO to defray the cost of supplying two 1,000-megawatt light-water nuclear reactors (LWRs) to the North, with South Korea picking up the tab for 70 percent of the estimated $4.6 billion project.

The most serious threat to Japan's security materialized in August 1998, when North Korea fired a three-stage rocket over Japan. Since

Japan lacked the capability to monitor the North Korean action, it relied on information provided by the United States; in other words, the U.S.-Japan alliance was a key factor in the unfolding of the crisis. Nonetheless, the Japan Defense Agency (JDA) made an independent analysis of all the data it had gathered, of which information supplied by the United States was pivotal. In a report published on October 30, 1998 the JDA said that the rocket North Korea launched from its east coast on August 31, 1998 was a "three-stage missile, based on the *Taep'odong–1* missile, with a range of more than 1,500 kilometers."[19]

According to the JDA report, the "first stage of the missile, which had a range of 1,300 kilometers, fell into the Sea of Japan." Its second stage, the report continued, "fell into the Pacific Ocean about 520 kilometers off the [Sanriku] coast." The third stage of the rocket was "equipped with a propulsion mechanism." "Although it flew for a short time, it failed to achieve a speed sufficient to attain orbit," the report concluded.

Upon learning of the rocket launch, the Japanese government promptly lodged a protest against North Korea through diplomatic channels at the United Nations. Chief Cabinet Secretary Nonaka Hiromu, the principal spokesman for the Japanese government, issued a statement calling the North Korean action "deeply regrettable." Saying that "this action directly affects Japan's security and . . . presents a very serious situation of concern . . . from the viewpoint of the peace and stability of Northeast Asia and of the nonproliferation of weapons of mass destruction," Nonaka stated that "Japan must reconsider its policy toward North Korea" and take "stern" counter-measures.[20]

The latter included: (1) suspending all inter-governmental negotiations with North Korea on the issue of resuming normalization talks, (2) not extending "food and other assistance" to the North "for the time being," (3) withholding signature on a cost-sharing agreement on the LWR project, (4) "canceling permission for charter flights between Japan and North Korea scheduled from 3 to 15 September" and (5) deciding "not to accept the applications [for] 14 further flights."[21]

North Korea flatly denied that it had fired a missile over Japan, claiming that it had actually launched a satellite named *Kwangmyongsong 1-ho* (Bright Star 1), which was orbiting the earth beaming patriotic songs. The North claimed that its rocket's third stage had used solid fuel, which, if true, would indicate a level of sophistication that is higher than had been previously estimated by outside observers.[22]

Pyongyang may have had multiple goals in mind when it launched the rocket over Japan on August 31, 1998. Internally, the launch may have been designed to enhance the legitimacy of Kim Jong Il, who was scheduled to be confirmed as the DPRK's supreme leader on September 5,

1998. Even though, contrary to expectations, Kim did not assume the position of the DPRK president (*chusok*), North Korea made it clear that as the chairman of the DPRK National Defense Commission, Kim was the country's paramount leader. The post of *chusok* was abolished and the president of the Presidium of the Supreme People's Assembly, North Korea's nominal parliament, became the ceremonial head of state under the newly revised "Socialist Constitution."[23]

A related goal may have been to boost the sagging morale of the North Korean people. By flaunting its rocket technology, the Kim Jong Il regime may have hoped to drive home both its determination and ability to turn the DPRK into a "great nation that is both powerful and prosperous" (*kangsŏng taeguk*).

Externally, Pyongyang's goals may have included: (1) jolting Japan to seek an early resumption of normalization talks and (2) showing to its clients in the global arms market what it has to offer. Acutely aware of the need to bolster its bargaining power vis-à-vis Japan, North Korea may have calculated that a demonstration of its missile capability, which now placed all of Japan within range, might serve to jump-start the stalled negotiations for diplomatic normalization.

As for a possible advertising function the launch may have performed, one must take note of the role of missile exports as a key source of North Korea's foreign exchange earnings. According to data collected by the ROK Ministry of Unification, the DPRK exported some 250 SCUD missiles to Iran, Syria, the United Arab Emirates, and other countries between 1987 and 1992, earning an estimated $580 million. In 1993, however, North Korea began exporting missile components for assembly in client countries such as Iran, Iraq, Pakistan, and Syria. When a staff member of the House International Relations Committee of the U.S. Congress asked the North Koreans to stop exporting missiles during his visit to Pyongyang in August 1998, the latter reportedly offered to do so for $500 million, which they claimed was equivalent to a third of what North Korea earns from missiles exports each year.[24]

An unintended consequence of the North Korean action was to strengthen Japan's defense capability, alliance with the United States, and trilateral consultations among Washington, Tokyo, and Seoul. Japan took steps to study the possibility of acquiring independent capability to monitor missile launches from adjacent areas such as North Korea, began to examine seriously the option of joining the United States in the development of theater missile defense, increased security cooperation with South Korea, and welcomed the institutionalization of consultations among the United States and its two Asian allies.

Two developments helped to accelerate all this. One was the discovery by U.S. reconnaissance satellite of a massive underground construction project in Kumch'angri, which Washington suspected might indicate the North's attempt to resume its nuclear weapons development program. The other was an intrusion into Japanese territorial waters of two high-speed boats, which, after being pursued by Japanese patrol boats, fled to North Korean territorial waters. Signs that the North might be preparing to launch a missile anew also served to increase the frequency of trilateral consultations. A Trilateral Coordination and Oversight Group (TCOG) was formed, serving as the channel of high-level consultations among the three countries on policy toward the North.

The appointment of former Secretary of Defense William Perry as U.S. North Korea policy coordinator and special advisor to the president and the secretary of state was another factor triggering stepped-up consultations among the United States, Japan, and South Korea. The report Perry submitted to the President and the Secretary of State in October 1999, while acknowledging that the interests of the ROK and Japan are "not identical to those of the U.S.," nonetheless underscores that they "overlap to a significant degree" (in the case of the ROK) or "strongly" (in the case of Japan).[25]

The "two-path strategy" recommended by the Perry report was devised "in close consultation with the governments of the ROK and Japan, and it has their full support." It is, the report stresses, "a joint strategy in which all three of our countries play coordinated and mutually reinforcing roles in pursuit of the same objectives." The first path, which "is clearly preferable for the United States and its allies and . . . for the DPRK," "involves a new, comprehensive and integrated approach to our negotiations with the DPRK." The United States "would seek complete and verifiable assurances that the DPRK does not have a nuclear weapons program." The United States "would also seek the complete and verifiable cessation of testing, production and deployment of missiles exceeding the parameters of the Missile Technology Control Regime, and the complete cessation of export sales of such missiles and the equipment and technology associated with them."

The United States "would, in a step-by-step and reciprocal fashion, move to reduce pressures on the DPRK that it perceives as threatening. . . . If the DPRK moved to eliminate its nuclear and long-range missile threats, the United States would normalize relations with the DPRK, relax sanctions . . . and take other positive steps that would provide opportunities for the DPRK." Since the first path depends on North Korea's willingness to "traverse it with us," however, there is a need for a second path, which, too, was devised "in consultation with our allies and with their full support." "On the second path, we would need to contain the threat that we have been unable to eliminate through negotiation."

Japan has removed all the sanctions it had imposed on North Korea in the wake of the latter's August 1998 rocket launch. It signed a KEDO cost-sharing agreement for the LWR project in October 1998 and resumed covert inter-governmental contacts with the North shortly thereafter. In December 1999, Tokyo announced that all the sanctions against the North would be lifted and that preparatory talks for the resumption of normalization talks would be held in Beijing. In March 2000, Japan unveiled a plan to provide 100,000 tons of rice to the North free of charge and an agreement with North Korea to resume normalization talks in April 2000.[26]

The ninth round of the talks finally opened in Pyongyang on April 5, 2000 after a seven-and-a-half-year hiatus. In two sessions, both sides exchanged their respective views, revealing a wide chasm in their priorities and perceptions. "Settling the past" was the North's foremost priority, which included an apology and a compensation for Japan's misdeeds during its colonial rule in Korea. Japan, on the other hand, placed a top priority on the issues of alleged abductions of Japanese nationals by North Korean agents and North Korea's missile development program. The joint press release issued on April 7, 2000 stated that the two sides had "held frank discussions on various issues" relating to diplomatic normalization but specifically mentioned only one—the "settlement of the past." Both sides, it added, agreed to hold the next round of their talks in May 2000.[27]

SECURITY COOPERATION
BETWEEN TOKYO AND SEOUL

As the preceding discussion makes plain, Japan and the ROK share two key factors in their respective security equations: a common alliance partner and a common source of threat. Security cooperation between the two countries, however, began slowly with modest personnel exchanges but has increased both in quantity and quality since the emergence of the nuclear issue surrounding the DPRK.

Military exchanges began in 1966, when the ROK established a military attaché office in its embassy in Tokyo; a Japanese military attaché office was set up in Seoul in the following year. In 1979, Japan's defense chief, the director-general of the Japan Defense Agency, visited South Korea for the first time. Eleven years were to lapse before another JDA director-general would visit Seoul.[28]

In April 1994, Lee Byung Tai became the first ROK defense minister to visit Japan. His meeting with his Japanese counterpart, JDA director-general Tamazawa Tokuichiro, occurred against the backdrop of escalating tensions on the Korean Peninsula fueled by North Korea's suspected nuclear weapons program. They agreed to expand exchanges of students, realize mutual port calls by training naval vessels, and hold dialogues between working-level defense officials.[29]

Ministerial meetings have since been held annually, alternating between Seoul and Tokyo. In June 1998, two months before the missile incident, Seoul hosted the first ROK-Japan Security Policy Committee meeting, in which high-ranking defense and foreign ministry officials of the two countries participated.[30] In 1999, the ROK Joint Chiefs of Staff and Japan's Staff Council held a dialogue, as did the ROK Navy and Japan's Maritime Self-Defense Forces. In August of the same year the two navies conducted a joint search-and-rescue exercise, a first in the history of Japan-ROK relations. Both countries, however, underscored the strictly peaceful purposes of the exercise.[31]

It is worth noting that Japan took pains to keep South Korea informed of the progress being made in the revision of the guidelines on U.S.-Japan defense cooperation. Following their adoption in September 1997, two high-ranking officials from the Japanese Foreign Ministry and JDA visited Seoul to brief their ROK counterparts. The latter reportedly asked Japan to display maximum transparency in preparing concrete measures for the implementation of the guidelines, and the two sides agreed to hold consultations in advance regarding matters that may affect ROK sovereignty.[32] On October 27, 1997, the ROK Defense Ministry announced that South Korea "will not allow the Japanese Self-Defense Forces (SDF) to operate in Korea's sovereign territory, though the revised defense guidelines . . . allow Japanese troops an expanded role in case of regional conflict." The ROK Defense Ministry said that it had informed Japan that "the Japanese forces, prior to their operations in international waters close to the Korea side and in the Korea air identification zone (KAIDZ) should consult with us in advance."[33]

In sum, while Japan and South Korea may be "quasi-allies," linked indirectly through their respective alliances with the United States, there still remains a considerable distance between the two. If the "de facto tripartite strategic alliance" among the United States, Japan, and South Korea is to operate with maximum efficacy, the degree of trust and dependence between Tokyo and Seoul will need to be upgraded, a process that may already be under way.

ROK President Kim Dae Jung's visit to Japan in October 1998 may have marked a turning point in Japan-ROK relations. His summit meeting with Prime Minister Obuchi Keizo produced the Japan-Republic of Korea Joint Declaration: A New Japan-Republic of Korea Partnership toward the twenty-first century. It proclaimed the "common determination" of the two leaders to raise to a "higher plane" (*shin jigen* in Japanese and *sin ch'awon* in Korean) the "close, friendly, and cooperative relations between Japan and the Republic of Korea." The declaration stressed the need for both countries to "squarely face the past and develop relations based on mutual understanding and trust."[34]

The declaration went on to list various measures aimed at translating the two leaders' commitment to usher in a new era of genuine partnership as elaborated in the supplementary "action plan." The measures encompassed five categories: (1) expansion of channels of bilateral dialogue, (2) cooperation to promote world peace and security, (3) strengthening cooperation in the economic field, (4) increasing cooperation on global issues, and (5) promotion of people's exchanges and cultural exchanges. Subsequent developments, including Obuchi's visit to Seoul in April 1999, suggest that the two countries are making notable progress in implementing the October 1998 joint declaration and action plan.

CONCLUSION

Will U.S.-Japan security cooperation continue to affect and be affected by the two Koreas? The answer will hinge on a multitude of factors, including the status of the U.S.-Japan alliance. As long as the interests of the two countries intersect, the alliance is most likely to endure. In his 1999 annual report to the president and the congress, Secretary of Defense William S. Cohen included the following discussion of U.S. defense objectives in East Asia:

> The United States seeks a stable and economically prosperous East Asia that embraces democratic reform and market economies. Central to achieving this goal are the United States' strong alliance relationships within the region, especially with Japan, Australia, and the Republic of Korea . . . The United States desires a peaceful resolution of the Korean conflict resulting in a non-nuclear, democratic, reconciled, and ultimately reunified Peninsula. . . . [35]

Cohen indicated that the "United States is committed to maintaining its current level of military capability in East Asia and the Pacific Rim," saying that "this capability allows the United States to play a key role as security guarantor and regional balancer." He saw North Korea's "continuing military threat" as the "most significant near-term danger in the region." In his words:

Due to forward positioning of its offensive military capabilities, its possession of chemical and biological weapons and their means of delivery, and the proximity of Seoul to the demilitarized zone, the North Korean threat to ROK security remains formidable. DPRK ballistic missile development, which may develop the potential to strike even the United States, remains a significant concern. The pressures imposed by increasingly dire economic conditions in the DPRK make this threat all the more unpredictable. The United States remains fully committed to its treaty obligations to assist the ROK in defending against North Korean aggression.[36]

"The U.S. security alliance with Japan," Cohen wrote, "is the linchpin of its security policy in Asia and is key to many U.S. global objectives. Both nations have moved actively over the past three years to strengthen this bilateral relationship and update the framework and structure of joint cooperation to reflect the security environment."[37]

This does not mean that the U.S.-Japan alliance is free of problems. Most recently, the issues of burden sharing and base relocation have emerged as sources of friction. Ever since Japan first offered 6.2 billion yen in 1978 to "pay for part of the salaries of Japanese employees at U.S. bases," its "sympathy payments" have steadily increased, covering "the cost of constructing housing for dependents of U.S. soldiers, and the utility, heating, and water bills of the U.S. forces." The payments for Fiscal Year 2000 (April 1999-March 2000) amount to 260.3 billion yen (about $2.5 billion). Since the Japanese government also spends 190 billion yen to "pay for base-related fees," the total comes to 450 million yen ($4.3 billion) a year. When Japan informed the United States of its plan to reduce its "sympathy payments" in Fiscal 2001 by about 10 percent, the United States strongly objected.[38]

Japan's rationale for its decision is that "economic and fiscal circumstances of both countries are now reversed compared with the situation in the late 1970s." The United States "highly praises the sympathy budget as proof of the strength of the Japan-U.S. alliance and proof that Japan is shouldering its share of responsibility in the bilateral security framework." It has also served to refute the "free-ride" argument.[39]

The other issue pertains to the relocation of the Futenma Marine Corps Air Station in Okinawa. Strong anti-base sentiments and politics in Okinawa have impeded progress in finding a site for the new base, thus preventing the 1996 U.S.-Japan agreement from being implemented. Pressure and monetary incentives from Tokyo, combined with local political dynamics, however, appear to have broken the impasse.[40]

Another factor in the equation is the U.S.-ROK alliance. According to the 1999 Defense Whitepaper published by the ROK Ministry of National Defense, the alliance is in "the best possible state." The ROK and the United States, it states, "always manage to reach a timely consensus on vital issues." It adds that the "two allies are now in search of ways to upgrade this alliance to a multi-dimensional, comprehensive security partnership, which will enable both states to respond to the new international security environment created in the wake of [the end of] the Cold War."[41] Such an upbeat assessment is shared by the United States. In the words of General Thomas A. Schwartz, the commander of the U.S. forces in Korea, "the alliance between the Republic of Korea and the United States has never been stronger. Our continuing cooperation and understanding is a success story in many ways."[42]

The two allies have held the ROK-U.S. Security Consultative Meeting (SCM) annually since 1968 at the ministerial level. At the operational level, coordination is achieved through Military Committee Meetings (MCMs). The ROK-U.S. MC is co-chaired by the chairmen of the ROK and U.S. Joint Chiefs of Staff. Immediately below this body in the chain of command is the ROK-U.S. Combined Forces Command (CFC), which has the "operational control" over the ROK-U.S. Combined Defense System. Until December 1994, the Commander-in-Chief of the CFC, who is always an American four-star general, exercised operational control over certain designated ROK units.[43]

South Korea, too, contributes to the cost of maintaining 37,000 U.S. troops on its soil. In 1991 Seoul "agreed to share the labor cost of Korean nationals working on U.S. bases and fund the ROK-Funded Construction (ROKFC) costs." The ROK and the United States concluded a defense cost-sharing agreement for the first time in January 1991, under which the ROK "agreed to pay one-third of the costs associated with maintaining USFK [U.S. Forces Korea], excluding salaries for U.S. forces and U.S. civilian employees." Under an agreement concluded in February 1999, the "ROK would provide 257.5 billion won plus U.S.$141.2 million in 1999, which adds up to approximately U.S.$333 million."[44]

General Schwartz told the House Armed Services Committee in March 2000 that "defense burden sharing is also a success story," saying that "South Korea has met Congressional goals in three [of the four burden sharing categories]—level of defense spending, outlays for foreign assistance, and provision of assets to multinational military activities." He said that "in the fourth category, cost sharing, the Republic of Korea paid $692 million out of $1.84 billion United States non-personnel stationing costs [in] fiscal year 1999," which "fell short of the 1999 goal of 62.5 percent." He hastened to add that South Korea "still provided a substantial contribution compared to other nations," if differences in Gross Domestic Product are taken into account.[45]

Finally, perhaps the single most important variable impinging on the evolution of the relationship between the U.S.-Japan alliance and the two Koreas is North Korea. The blending of a hardline and pragmatism in its external behavior is linked to both Pyongyang's strategic needs and internal political constraints. The former consist of security, legitimacy, and development, while the latter derives from the idiosyncrasies of the North's political system.

The North may now be in a pragmatic mode insofar as its external policy is concerned. Slow but steady progress is being made in its negotiations with both Washington and Tokyo. Even inter-Korean relations at the governmental level, which had remained dormant, while nongovernmental intercourse was expanding at a phenomenal rate, have entered a new phase. The historic summit meeting between Kim Dae Jung and Kim Jong Il and the joint North-South declaration of June 15, 2000 paved the way for a new era of reconciliation and cooperation on the Korean Peninsula. In a word, the DPRK may well opt for the first path in the Perry report, if it has not done so already.

No matter what happens in the months ahead, what North Korea has already done to America's alliances with Japan and South Korea cannot be undone. Pyongyang has single-handedly bolstered not only the two sets of bilateral security cooperation but trilateral strategic links among Washington, Tokyo, and Seoul as well.

NOTES

1. For an incisive analysis of Tokyo-Seoul relations utilizing the concept of "quasi-alliance," see Victor D. Cha, *Alignment Despite Antagonism: the United States-Korea-Japan Security Triangle* (Stanford, CA: Stanford University Press, 1999).

2. For the English text of the treaty, see the website of Japan Defense Agency: http://www.jda.go.jp/policy/f_work/anpo.htm. For the Japanese text, see Bōeichō (ed.), *Heisei 10-nenban Bōei hakusho* (Defense of Japan 1998) (Tokyo: Ōkurashō Insatsu-kyoku, 1998), pp. 346–47.

3. For the text of both the U.S.-ROK mutual defense treaty and the understanding attached to it, see Han K. Kim, ed., *Reunification of Korea: 50 Basic Documents* (Washington, DC: Institute for Asian Studies, 1972), pp. 28–30.

4. Bōeichō (ed.), *Heisei 10-nenban Bōei hakusho*, pp. 88–90.

5. Bōeichō (ed.), *Heisei 2-nenban Bōei hakusho* [Defense White Paper 1990] (Tokyo: Ōkurashō, Insatsu-kyoku, 1990), p. 265.

6. Bōeichō (ed.), *Heisei 8-nenban Bōei hakusho: aratana jidai eino taiō* [Defense White Paper 1996: Response to the New Era] (Tokyo: Ōkurashō, Insatsu-kyoku, 1996), pp. 314–315.

7. Japan Defense Agency, *Japan-U.S. Joint Declaration on Security—Alliance for the 21st Century* (Tentative Unofficial Translation), (Tokyo: JDA, April 17, 1996), http://www.jda.go.jp/policy/f_work/sengen_.htm.

8. Ibid.

9. Ibid.

10. Japan Defense Agency, *Guidelines for Japan-U.S. Defense Cooperation* (Tokyo: JDA, November 27, 1978), http://www.jda.go.jp/policy/f_work/sisin1e.htm; Japan Defense Agency *Completion of the Review of the Guidelines for U.S.-Japan Defense Cooperation* (New York: U.S.-Japan Security Consultative Committee, September 23, 1997); for the Japanese-language version, see Bōeichō (ed.), *Heisei 10-nenban Bōei hakusho*, pp. 394–403.

11. "Gaido rain kanren-hō seiritsu" [Laws Relating to Guidelines Enacted], *Yomiuri shinbun*, May 25, 1999; "Diet Enacts Defense Bills," *Daily Yomiuri*, May 25, 1999.

12. The White House, Office of the Press Secretary, *Press Conference of the President and Prime Minister Obuchi* (Washington, DC: White House, May 3, 1999), p. 2.

13. "Kankoku de keikaigan mo, gaido rain kanren-hōan" [Guideline-related Bills Trigger Apprehensions in South Korea], *Asahi shinbun*, April 28, 1999; "Il pangwi chich'im kwa uri ŭi taeŭng" [Japan's Defense Guidelines and Our Response], *Chungang ilbo*, April 29, 1999, editorial.

14. "'Chubyŏn sat'ae anjŏn hwakpo pŏban' ŭl pinan—Nodong sinmun" [*Nodong sinmun* Assails "Bills Bolstering Security in Situations in Surrounding Areas"], *Chosŏn chungang t'ongsin*, May 4, 1999, Pyongyang.

15. Gaimushō, *Nichi-bei anpo Q & A* [Questions and Answers on Japan-U.S. Security] (Tokyo: Gaimusho, February 2000).

16. Gaimushō (ed.), *Heisei 4-nenban Gaikō seisho: tenkanki no sekai to Nihon* [Diplomatic Bluebook: The World in Transition and Japan, 1992] (Tokyo: Ōkurashō Insatsu-kyoku, 1992), pp. 176–78; Gaimushō ed., *Gaikō seisho 1993: yori anzende ningen-tekina sekai o motomete* [Diplomatic Bluebook 1993: Toward a More Secure and Humane World] (Tokyo: Ōkurashō Insatsu-kyoku, 1993), pp. 16–17.

17. Gaimushō (ed.), *Gaikō seisho 1995: Nihon gaikō eno kitai—aratana jidai no sō zō ni mukete* [Diplomatic Bluebook 1995: Expectations for Japanese Diplomacy—Toward the Creation of a New Era] (Tokyo: Ōkurashō Insatsu-kyoku, 1995), pp. 19–23.

18. Bōeichō (ed.), *Heisei 8-nenban Bōei hakusho*, pp. 46–47.

19. Jieitai Bōeichō, *Oshirase: Kita Chōsen no misairu hassha no bunseki kekka ni tsuite* [Report on the Results of Analysis of North Korea's Missile Launch] (Tokyo: Boeicho, October 30, 1998).

20. Ministry of Foreign Affairs of Japan, *Announcement by the Chief Cabinet Secretary on Japan's Immediate Response to North Korea's Missile Launch* (Tokyo: Ministry of Foreign Affairs, September 1, 1998).

21. Ministry of Foreign Affairs of Japan, *Press Conference by the Press Secretary* (Tokyo: Ministry of Foreign Affairs, September 1, 1998, September 4, 1998).

22. *Nodong sinmun*, September 8, 1998.
23. For an unofficial English translation of the revised DPRK Socialist Constitution adopted by the first session of 10th Supreme People's Assembly on September 5, 1998, see *People's Korea* (Tokyo), September 17, 1998.
24. "Pukhan misail p'anmae, 93-nyn ihu hyŏnji chorip pangik ŭro chŏnhwan" [North Korean Missile Sales Change to Local Assembly Method Since 1993], *Chungang ilbo*, October 25, 1998; Kevin Sullivan, "N. Korea Admits Selling Missiles," *Washington Post*, June 17, 1998, p. A1.
25. U.S. Department of State, *Review of United States Policy Toward North Korea: Findings and Recommendations*, Unclassified Report by Dr. William J. Perry, U.S. North Korea Policy Coordinator and Special Advisor to the President and the Secretary of State (Washington, DC, U.S. Department of State, October 12, 1999).
26. "Seifuga Kita Chōsen eno seisai kaijō o happyō" [Government Announces Lifting of Sanctions on North Korea], *Asahi shinbun*, December 15, 1999; "Kita Chōsen eno kome shien nanoka nimo seishiki happyō e seifu" [Government Will Officially Announce Rice Aid to North Korea on 7th], *Asahi shinbun*, March 6, 2000; "Nitcho kosho 4-gatsu saikai, 10-man ton no kome shien mo seishiki kettei" [Japan-North Korea Negotiations to Resume in April, 100,000 Ton-Rice Aid Officially Approved], *Asahi shinbun*, March 8, 2000. For Pyongyang's confirmation of the agreement, see "Cho-il chŏngbugan pon hoedam, chŏksipja hoedami chinhaeng toenŭn kŏtkwa kwallyŏn han podo" [Report on Holding of Main Talks Between DPRK and Japanese Governments and Red Cross Talks], *Nodong sinmun*, March 8, 2000, p. 4.
27. "Nitchō kokkyō seijōka kōshō shuchō no hedatari senmeini" [Japan-North Korea Normalization Negotiations: Distance Between Positions Become Clear], *Yomiuri shinbun*, April 8, 2000; "Cho-il chŏngsang-hwa hoedam P'ŏngyang esŏ chinhaeng" [Korea-Japan Talks on Normalization Held in Pyongyang], *Chosŏn sinbo* (Tokyo), April 8, 2000; "Japan, North Korea Skirt Abduction Issue," *Daily Yomiuri*, April 7, 2000.
28. Bōeichō (ed.), *Heisei 3-nenban Bōei hakusho* (Defense of Japan 1991) (Tokyo: Ōkurashō Insatsu-kyoku, 1991), p. 320 and p. 332.
29. Bōeichō (ed.), *Heisei 6-nenban Bōei hakusho* (Defense of Japan 1994) (Tokyo: Ōkurashō Insatsu-kyoku, 1994), pp. 178–179.
30. ROK Ministry of National Defense, *Defense Whitepaper 1999* (Seoul, Ministry of National Defense, 1999), chapter 4; External Military Policy for Peninsula Stability and Global Peace, http://www.mnd.go.kr/mndweb/wpe/1999/242.html.
31. Ibid.
32. "Il, Hanguk e pangwi chich'im sŏlmyŏng-hoe" [Japan Holds Briefing on Defense Guidelines for Korea], *Hangyŏre sinmun*, September 30, 1997.
33. "South Korea Not to Allow Japanese Military Operations in Its Territory," *Korea Herald*, October 23, 1997.

34. Gaimushō, *Nikkan kyōdo sengen—21 seiki ni muketa aratana Nikkan patonashippu* (Tokyo: Gaimusho, October 8, 1998).

35. U.S. Department of Defense, *Annual Report to the President and the Congress, William S. Cohen, Secretary of Defense, 1999* (Washington, D.C.: U.S. Department of Defense, 1999), http://www.dtic.mil/execsec/adr1999/toc.html.

36. Ibid.

37. Ibid.

38. "Sympathy Payments," *Mainichi Daily News,* January 18, 2000, editorial.

39. "Discuss Sympathy Budget Coolly," *Daily Yomiuri,* March 5, 2000, editorial.

40. Michael J. Green, "4th Quarter 1999 U.S.-Japan Relations: Not Bad for Auto-Pilot," *Comparative Connections,* An E-Journal of East Asian Bilateral Relations, January 2000, http://www.csis.org/pacfoc/cc/994Qus_japan.html.

41. ROK Ministry of National Defense, *Defense Whitepaper 1999,* chapter 4.

42. U.S. Congress, House of Representatives, *Statement of General Thomas A. Schwartz, Commander in Chief United Nations Command/Combined Forces Command and Commander, United States Forces Korea, before the House Armed Services Committee* (Washington, D.C.: U.S. Congress, House of Representatives, March 15, 2000), p. 8.

43. ROK Ministry of National Defense, *Defense Whitepaper 1999,* chapter 4.

44. Ibid.

45. U.S. Congress, *Statement of General Thomas A. Schwartz,* p. 11.

CHAPTER NINE

CHINA AND JAPAN: RIVALRY OR COOPERATION ON THE KOREAN PENINSULA?

ROBERT A. SCALAPINO

Recent developments in Northeast Asia have underlined both the complexity and the vital importance of this region. Here, four major nations interact closely with each other, their bilateral and multilateral relations having a major impact on the three small nations in the area, the two Koreas and Mongolia. Thus, in exploring the influence of the Sino-Japanese relationship on the Korean peninsula, present and future, one must always be aware of the larger context influencing and, on occasion, shaping that relationship. In examining the current domestic conditions and the foreign relations of these two nations, therefore, we shall frequently refer to the United States and Russia, as well as to the relevant trends in the two Koreas.

Japan remains the second largest economy in the world, and there are indications that its lengthy recession is leveling out.[1] Some economic restructuring is taking place, especially in the high-tech fields. A new entrepreneur class is appearing, prepared to enter into serious competition both at home and abroad. Deregulation is also enlivening the financial sector. While growth rates will almost certainly remain low in the next few years, optimists see the Japanese economy turning the corner.

However, fundamental economic change in Japan involves culture as well as economics; hence, progress is slow and uneven. The old system of intertwined government-business corporatism, enterprises operating as enlarged families, and the emphasis upon import substitution–export orientation meshed well with traditional Japanese culture and provided the impetus for growth in Japan for decades. Japan also became a model for certain other Asian societies. But as events graphically illustrate, no economic strategy, however successful, is good forever. Recognition of that fact has come lamentably late in Japan.

Thus, economic uncertainties remain to render the future cloudy.[2] Will the *amakudari* system whereby retired bureaucrats moved into advisorial roles in industry (and conduits to government) and other collusive practices be altered to enable genuine domestic—and foreign—competition to prevail? Currently, extensive fiscal expansion continues in an effort to inflate the economy via public works and other programs. This has greatly increased government debt, with limited evidence as yet of the return of consumer confidence. Moreover, in two decades, more than 27 percent of the Japanese population will be 65 years of age or older, with extensive social responsibilities on the part of the state required.

Is Japanese political leadership up to the challenges? Since the end of the so-called 1955 system, whereby Japan had a one and one-half party system with the Liberal Democratic Party continuously in power and all other parties on the outside, Japan has experienced governance through fragile coalitions, with frequent turnovers.[3] No recent leaders have been able to acquire and maintain strong electoral support. Moreover, the quotient of cynicism and disillusionment with politics has risen, illustrated by low voting rates. Some observers have asserted that Japanese citizens suffer from a greater lack of self-confidence concerning their future and that of their nation than at any time in recent decades. Perhaps some of the features of contemporary Japan speak more broadly to the challenges faced by many democracies as the twenty-first century opens.

Despite domestic uncertainties, however, Japanese foreign policy has shown an increased involvement or assertiveness, especially in Asia, one sign of Japan's desire to be accepted as a major power, divested of the restraints of the past. Nationalism is ascendant in Japan as elsewhere, manifested in the desire to be a "normal nation;" in the official acknowledgement of the flag and the national anthem as symbols of Japanese nationhood; in the ongoing Diet discussions regarding constitutional revision; and in the changes underway in the U.S.-Japan relationship.[4]

The U.S.-Japan Security Agreement remains firm, with strong support in both societies, and in the recent guideline revisions, the sphere of American-Japanese cooperation has been enlarged. Current and former prime ministers as well as other leaders have continued to assert that the Japan-U.S. relationship is the cornerstone of Japanese foreign policy.

At the same time, however, the trend is away from the patron-client relationship that has prevailed for more than half a century, with Japan now calling for partnership, and seeking a more independent policy as witnessed by various economic proposals such as an Asian financial fund and earlier political initiatives with respect to Cambodia. The ASEAN (Association of Southeast Asian Nations) plus Three meetings are illustrative of the broad trends. Moreover, Japan has made it clear that it deserves permanent membership in the UN Security Council.

These developments have not greatly troubled the U.S.-Japan relationship. Indeed, those relations are stronger at present than at any time in the recent past. The United States has wanted Japan to do more in the security realm, although it has never been certain as to precisely what it wants Japan to do. Currently, a commitment to joint research on Theater Missile Defense (TMD) is in effect. And despite its opposition to a separate Asian financial fund, the United States has applauded, and indeed, urged Japan's economic assistance to troubled Asian states. Economic issues remain between the two nations, but the robust health of the American economy has served to soften concerns about the continuing high trade imbalance and Japanese protectionism in such fields as agriculture. For the present at least, the intensive U.S. hectoring so annoying to Japan has diminished. With respect to the Korean issue, moreover, Japan and the United States are now parties to a trilateral dialogue together with the ROK, conducted on a regular basis. In sum, as public opinion polls in both countries demonstrate, support for a close, trusting relationship between the two countries has rarely, if ever, been stronger.[5]

Japan's relations with China today are far more complex.[6] As is well known, the legacy of history still hangs heavily over the attitudes of the two peoples and their leaders despite some recent signs of improvement. In economic terms, Japan is a major investor and trading partner with China, involved in extensive technological transfer. Thus, after the ill-fated trip of Jiang Zemin to Tokyo in November 1998, when the Chinese president exhorted the Japanese to make more fulsome apologies for their past conduct, Prime Minister Obuchi, in his trip to Beijing the following year, concentrated on economic matters, and produced an accord supportive of China's entry into the World Trade Organization.

An increased number of high-level visitations have taken place recently, and in the latest joint communiqué, the preamble asserts "Japan is keenly conscious of its responsibility for the serious damage inflicted in the past on the Chinese people through war and deeply reproaches itself." In a Diet speech on January 28, 2000, Foreign Minister Kono Kohei asserted that Japan shared in the spirit of the joint communiqué statement, and advanced the thesis that China's stability and development were central to regional peace, and hence, of major importance to Japan.

Despite these conciliatory words, sentiment in Japan regarding China remains divided. A sizeable number of individuals, both in official circles and among the citizenry, view the possible rise of China as a major military and political-economic power in the region with apprehension. They note China's moves toward military modernization, and its sometimes strident approach to territorial issues centering upon Taiwan, but encompassing various islands from Senkaku (Diaoyutai) to Mischief Reef.

These concerns, while generally muted, figure in such policies as Japan's interest in missile defense, the creation of an independent intelligence satellite, and the initiation of an official discussion regarding constitutional revision. The Japan-China security dialogue was reopened in October 1999, after a two year hiatus, but the major issues remain contentious: TMD, the enlarged guidelines for the U.S.-Japan Security Treaty, and the People's Republic of China's (PRC) military modernization program.

With respect to Taiwan, Japan has officially adhered to a One China policy, and thus far, precluded Lee Teng-hui, Taiwan's recent President, from visiting Japan. Nor is Japan involved in weapons transfers to Taipei. Yet one fact makes China very uncomfortable. Japan is relatively popular in Taiwan, with this society being the one region of East Asia where the era of Japanese colonialism bequeathed a generally favorable legacy. Thus, not only is there extensive cultural interaction between Japan and Taiwan, but Japanese officials are frequent visitors. The 1999 trip of Tokyo Governor Ishihara (and his reference to Taiwan as a state) caused angry responses from Beijing.

Other statements from prominent Japanese and activities within Japan periodically rile Sino-Japanese waters. When then Vice-Minister Nishimura suggested that Japan consider possession of nuclear weapons, Chinese spokesmen responded with dire warnings. Another upsurge of Chinese anger took place over an Osaka conference of right-wing elements in January 2000, convened to deny official accounts of the Nanjing massacres.

The official PRC stance is to repeatedly warn Japan that the lessons of history must not be forgotten. Many Chinese appear to believe that Japanese militarism could easily be resurrected and cite the episodes noted here to bolster that view. It is true that Japan has the technical capacity to move rapidly toward a potent military force, one emphasizing the most modern weaponry rather than a greatly augmented size of armed forces. However, given Japan's domestic circumstances and priorities, it would seem likely that only the combination of two developments would be conducive to such a move: a greatly increased perception of external threat and the end of American credibility as a security ally. Since the latter at least is not in the offing, worries regarding Japanese militarism seem unwarranted. It is important to make a distinction between Japan's drive to be accepted as a major power with full sovereign rights and a decision to elevate military power so as to make it the prime instrument of foreign policy.

Meanwhile, in contrast to the high priorities given by Tokyo to Japanese-American and Japanese-Chinese relations, Japan's relations with Russia have remained largely stagnant, due in considerable measure to the uncertainties surrounding the Russian economy and polity.[7] As of early 2001, no progress has been made regarding the pledge to achieve a peace treaty between the two countries by the end of 2000, although high level discussions continue intermittently. Whether an agreement on the crucial issue of the Northern Territories (Southern Kurils) can be reached, however, remains to be seen.[8] Potentially, Japan and Russia—especially the Russian Far East—could build strong, mutually beneficial economic ties, and indeed, discussions to this effect have been ongoing in diverse circles. However, Russia must first get its own house in better order.

A recent poll reveals evidence of current Japanese attitudes toward the major nations. When asked with whom they felt close, those answering "Russia" totaled 15.8 percent, a slight increase over an earlier poll; toward China, 49.6 percent, also a small increase; toward the United States, 75.6 percent, a slight decrease but still a commanding statement. Clearly, Russia remains foreign and distant, not withstanding its geographic proximity, and the United States and China, in that order, receive primary attention. One overarching question, however, must be raised with respect to Japan's external relations. As internationalism becomes ever more important to Japan's future, can the strong elements of introversion and exclusiveness that have marked this homogeneous island society's past be further reduced to make Japan truly internationalist?

Turning to contemporary China, one is confronted with an intricate picture, at least as complex as the trends in Japan.[9] The extraordinary economic advances of recent decades show no signs of ending. Growth rates according to official figures remain 7–8 percent per annum, trade continues to be healthy despite the recent Asian economic crisis, and foreign investment substantial, with extensive transfer of technology. Hundreds of millions of Chinese have benefited from the reforms initiated under the leadership of Deng Xiaoping and continued by his successors.

It is widely predicted that within a few decades, China's GDP will exceed that of the United States, and exercise major regional and global influence. In addition, the drive for military modernization, with assistance from foreign purchases, will continue. Chinese military capacities will not equal those of the United States in the foreseeable future, but they are likely to exceed those of any other Asian nation. With nationalism now a more effective weapon of mobilization than Marxism-Leninism, the worry of many of China's neighbors is that the Middle Kingdom complex will be restored, with China demanding that it be recognized as the preeminent power and leader in East Asia, responding militantly to any perceived challenges.

Yet there are other possibilities. At present, a series of economic problems confront this massive nation: a fragile financial-banking system, greatly in need of further reform; ailing state owned enterprises, many of which still operate on old socialist principles despite recent reform efforts; large-scale and growing unemployment, with rural migration to the cities creating social as well as economic problems; a significant East-West gap in development; and massive corruption reaching to high levels.

The political challenges are also daunting. Can nationalism compensate for the declining appeal of socialist ideology, including "the thoughts of Mao" and "the words of Deng?" Can the shift from one-man dominance toward collective leadership, and the move from ideologues to pragmatically oriented technocrats preserve allegiance to the state despite the decline of charisma and religiosity? Is the move from hard to soft authoritarianism conducive to stability in a vast society with substantial ethnic and regional variations, and such new challenges to conformity as the Internet?

Whatever China's course in the decades ahead, it is certain to be some combination of strengths and weaknesses. In sum, China will be a major power with major problems. The gamble of other states including China's small neighbors, is that given the continuing economic problems to be confronted and its growing interdependence with others, China will match its words supportive of the Five Principles of Peaceful Coexistence with deeds.

There are some promising signs. In the recent past, China has worked intensively through high level visits and communiqués to strengthen its bilateral relations with all of its neighbors. Further, it has shown an increasing interest in participating in multilateral organizations and concerts, altering its earlier dependence upon bilateralism alone.[10]

One can assert that recent trends in Chinese foreign policy have been in part a response to a perceived American threat. Thus, the improvement in relations with neighbors represents the effort to create a buffer state system, and the "strategic partnership" with Russia, despite denial, is aimed at countering the U.S. "encirclement" of the Eurasian continent through NATO expansion and the strengthening of the U.S. alliance system in East Asia.

Certainly this factor is present, and the image of the United States in China at present is decidedly mixed at many levels, including at the grassroots level. The bombing of the PRC Embassy in Belgrade in May 1999 came against a background of repeated PRC charges that the United States was intervening in China's internal affairs (Taiwan), seeking to implant its political system on others (human rights issues), and aiming to be the sole superpower in a unipolar world (TMD and other evidences of strategic enhancement).

Similarly, the image of China in the United States as evidenced by Congressional and public opinion has been an increasing obstacle to improved relations. Whether the issue be human rights, Taiwan, military enhancement, or espionage, the attitudes of many Americans have ranged from skepticism to hostility.

Thus, while the leaders of both nations have seen a powerful need for positive and balanced relations, given the effect of that relationship upon every issue relating to Pacific-Asia, they have had political difficulty in sustaining that course. Progress has been made on certain fronts, such as approval of China's admission to WTO and the resumption of military to military talks, and a variety of efforts are underway to broaden dialogues at the NGO level. Meanwhile, by a strong majority, Congress accepted President Clinton's request to give China "permanent normal trading relations" (PNTR), a critical issue in the relationship.

Moreover, China has been a vitally important actor with respect to the Korean peninsula. Strongly supportive of President Kim Dae Jung's Sunshine Policy, Beijing has cautiously counseled the DPRK, and often engaged in dialogues with the United States and the ROK on key issues. Moreover, it is a party to the on-going Four Party Talks. Here, the United States and China have common interests. Yet it must be acknowledged that in overall terms, the PRC-U.S. relationship remains fragile.[11]

Most knowledgeable Americans do not worry greatly about China's relations with Russia today. The current ties between China and Russia are based upon shared apprehensions about Western, and especially American, power, together with the common commitment to fight against separatist efforts within their respective nations, and a mutual interest in Russian weapon sales to China. Yet the ideological glue is gone, the two economies are radically different despite future potentials for greater interaction in such fields as gas and oil, and the two cultures are deeply foreign to each other. In the Russian Far East, moreover, with its less than 8 million people, the specter of l.3 billion people to the South evokes apprehension. It is also significant that despite their grievances, both China and Russia need a favorable relation with the United States, and regularly manifest that fact.

The two Koreas are witnesses to, and participants in the drama of the intricate major power relations of this era.[12] It has been the fate of the Korean peninsula to be in the midst of larger, often contending external forces for centuries. Historically, Korea had three broad options in seeking security. The first was the maximum possible isolation. The second lay in accepting a special relationship with one power so as to protect itself against others. The third lay in the effort to balance relations with all major powers, striving to maintain a friendly neutrality so as to keep external threats to a minimum.

In this age, isolation is no longer a feasible policy, as the plight of the DPRK graphically illustrates. In seeking to pursue that course earlier (despite extensive economic dependence upon the Soviet Union and at times, China), it faced increasing economic obsolescence, being largely outside the modern world except in the military realm. Thus, the Korea of today and tomorrow—divided or united—must chose between the second and third alternatives, although some combination of these may be both possible and most desirable.

To explore present and future Chinese and Japanese positions with respect to the Korean peninsula, it is essential to examine briefly the current situation with respect to the two Koreas. The contrast between the ROK and the DPRK at present could scarcely be greater, whether the measurement be economic or political.

As a result of the reform policies initiated by President Kim Dae Jung and certain other factors, the ROK economy made a major advance in 1999, going from a decline in GDP of 6.7 percent in the previous year to a lo.7 percent gain. Advances continued in 2000, but by the last quarter of that year, certain warning signs emerged: two major *chaebol,* Daewoo and Hyundai, were in serious trouble, the former facing bankruptcy; rising oil and agricultural prices threatened inflation; and the financial system, burdened by large unredeemable loans, remained fragile. These and other concerns caused President Kim, under criticism for concentrating on foreign policies and neglecting the domestic front, to renew reform efforts.[13] However, opposition came both from labor unions and certain industrial sectors. Nonetheless, growth on a somewhat reduced scale seemed likely in the period ahead, and the ROK remained the third largest economy in East Asia, next to Japan and China.

In contrast, the DPRK remains a failing state in economic terms as the twenty-first century gets underway. The steep downward trend that started in the mid-1990s resulted in output reduction of some 50 percent by 1999.[14] In the latter year, the decline appeared to have ended, with Bank of Korea figures indicating a positive advance of over 6 percent, disputed in some circles.[15] Yet severe climatic conditions and mounting problems with aging industrial facilities as well as acute power shortages created new problems. At the end of 2000, the United Nations resident coordinator in the DPRK asserted that the North would need some 810,000 tons of food to provide the minimal needs of its population until the next harvest.

On the political front, the ROK continues with efforts to consolidate a democratic system against various historical and cultural obstacles. Regionalism remains a powerful force, with issues often secondary to an individual's birthplace. Personalism threatens to override institutions, with leader-follower groups constituting the central political force. Moreover, leaders—even those strongly committed to democracy ideologically— often operate in an authoritarian manner. And bitterness frequently dominates political debates, further evidence of the personalism imbedded in ROK politics. Yet South Korean democracy is less than two decades old, and it has shown surprising vigor despite the economic travails of recent years. Military coups, a drastic curtailment of freedoms, and unchallengable one-man rule appear to be matters of the past.

North Korea, on the other hand, is best viewed not as a revolutionary society but as one strongly traditional in its central characteristics.[16] The efforts to achieve maximum isolation resemble the historic "hermit kingdom," as Korea was once labeled. A dynasty has been created, with the monarch possessing near absolute power, wrapped in a religious aura. Moreover, dynastic succession has taken place. Only in the drive for mass mobilization and the effort to have the latest weapons of mass destruction has modernization been evident. Power is represented today by the tight bonds between Kim Jong Il and the military. Although there has been some evidence recently of greater attention to such bodies as the Supreme People's Assembly, most formal political institutions are readily dispensable, as their irregular meetings testify. Politics is highly personal, as it has always been. There is evidence that turf struggles take place, and in all probability, there are differences within the elite regarding such issues as the nature and timing of economic change. Yet there is no evidence that the DPRK is in serious risk of upheaval at present.

It is in this setting that North-South political relations have recently evolved. Under Kim Dae Jung, the ROK government has greatly stepped up its economic assistance and interaction with the DPRK. In his inaugural address in February 1998, Kim outlined his Sunshine Policy, focusing upon three broad themes: no toleration of DPRK military threats or actions; rejection of a policy of unification by absorption; and the promotion of exchanges and cooperation, returning to the Basic Agreement of 1991.[17]

Fortunately, Kim's new policy coincided with a growing interest on the part of the North in undertaking policy changes. Much earlier, Pyongyang had made its first effort to attract foreign investment, opening a free trade zone in the early 1990s at Rajin-Sonbong, on the northeast coast.[18] Yet the results proved to be very limited due to the North's lack of competitiveness. Other efforts followed, with the revised constitution of 1998 making some provisions for a private sector but with the emphasis still on *juche* (self-reliance) and the traditional economic order. By the time of Kim Dae Jung's presidency, however, the urgency of change had become acute. Economic decline had been continuous for at least five years.

Thus, out of a private meeting between Hyundai founder, Chung Ju Yung, and Chairman Kim Jong Il came the Mt. Kumgang tourist project, the first large venture by a South Korean company in the North. Other Hyundai projects followed. By the end of 1999, ROK companies had invested some $426 million in the DPRK, and trade in that year totaled $333 million. Much of the latter figure, however, reflected ROK aid.[19]

The North has remained cautious. Its leaders want economic change with minimal political alteration. Russia and even China serve as warning signals to them. Nevertheless, recent developments suggest that a point of no return may have been reached. Up to mid-1999, more than one hundred individuals had been sent abroad to undertake training or to garner information in such fields as economics, law, agriculture, science, and medicine. Interestingly, Kim Jong Il himself indicated to Chung in their second meeting an interest in the earlier development program of ROK President Park Chung Hee.

As these developments continued to unfold, President Kim Dae Jung delivered his Berlin Declaration in March 2000, advancing four goals: to dismantle the cold war structure on the Korean peninsula; to restart the visits of divided families; to resume inter-governmental talks between South and North; and to assist in the economic recovery of the North through inter-Korean economic cooperation.[20] Shortly thereafter, on June 13-15, the historic summit meeting between the two Korean leaders took place in Pyongyang, and while the communiqué issued was very general, it was also strongly positive. Subsequently, moreover, progress accelerated on many fronts. Trade and investment continued to advance despite economic difficulties. A growing number of small and medium ROK companies became engaged in "processing on commission" arrangements in the North, with additional companies applying for permits to ROK authorities. Plans for an industrial zone at Kaesong continued to be discussed.

Perhaps most importantly, an agreement was reached at the close of 2000 providing for investment protection, the avoidance of double taxation, procedures for the clearance of accounts, and the means for the settlement of disputes. To supervise the agreement, a joint committee for economic cooperation is to be established.[21] If properly enforced, this agreement could serve to greatly stimulate ROK investment in the North.

On the humanitarian front, long-time political prisoners who refused to recant their commitment to Communism were released in the South. Moreover, two visits of divided families—one hundred visitors from each side—had taken place by the end of 2000, with a third promised shortly.

Meanwhile, the first ministerial military to military meeting had been held on the South's Cheju island, with working level military talks subsequently held at Panmunjom. This represented the beginning of an answer to the long sought ROK efforts to move discussions into the security field.

Further, plans got underway in the fall of 2000 to reconnect the severed Seoul-Shinuiju railroad and to build a parallel highway. The UN Command gave the two Koreas permission to administratively control the section of the DMZ involved in the area targeted for construction, and work on mine clearing began in late 2000.[22]

In addition, cultural relations in a variety of fields—sports, music, and NGO meetings took place, with a highlight being the joint march of South and North Korean athletes under a single flag into the stadium at the opening of the Australia-sponsored Olympics in September 2000.

However, the DPRK has as yet exhibited little desire to tackle seriously the key security issues or to establish an official relationship with the ROK, probably because it has had few bargaining chips in dealing with the South on these matters, given its weak domestic and international situation. These issues have held more promise with respect to other governments, especially the major powers.[23]

Thus, high priority has been placed on improving relations with the United States, and secondarily with Japan. To obtain recognition from these two nations together with assistance in various forms would be to emulate the *Nordpolitik* policies of Roh Tae Woo who secured recognition from Russia and China at a critical point in the early 1990s, greatly enhancing the international position of the ROK.

In the meantime, progress has been made on other fronts. A number of nations including Italy, Great Britain, Spain, and the Philippines have established diplomatic relations with the DPRK since 1999, with Australia reestablishing official ties. The North gave further evidence of its commitment to move into the international community by joining ARF (ASEAN Regional Forum) and accepting a small OPEC loan to reconstruct dams and waterways so as to advance agriculture. Pyongyang has also made it clear that it would appreciate assistance from such institutions as the IMF and the Asian Development Bank. As further evidence of increased venturing abroad, according to a ROK National Intelligence Service report, 222 North Korean officials made overseas trips in 1999, compared to 134 in 1998, and 99 in 1997.

While DPRK efforts on the multilateral level have been of growing significance, the key developments have been at the bilateral level. Turning to DPRK-U.S. relations, numerous surges and retreats have taken place in recent years.[24] Thus, one must be cautious in evaluating the ongoing advances. The KEDO program, however, is again moving forward despite questions about the North's capacity to utilize the power to be produced, given its facilities.[25] Moreover, the delays in U.S. heavy oil shipments in the past have infuriated Pyongyang, with various threats issued. Nevertheless, the North's missile testing remains in abeyance, and the inspection of the suspected Kumganri site revealed no military operations. In the fall of 1999, moreover, William Perry, appointed by former President Clinton to review policies toward North Korea, submitted a report outlining two routes, one based upon the North's cooperation involving progressive U.S. interaction, and the other based upon the North's intransigence, proposing tightened restrictions.[26]

In the fall of 2000, two important events took place. In early October, Vice Marshal Jo Myong Rok, widely regarded as the second most powerful figure in the DPRK, came to Washington, meeting with former President Clinton and other key figures. Less than two weeks later, Secretary Madeleine Albright visited Pyongyang, discussing issues with Chairman Kim and others.[27]

A Clinton trip to the DPRK, once projected, did not materialize, with the former president asserting that there was not sufficient time for specific agreements to be reached. The key issues were North Korea's missile program and sales, and the related question of the North's support of "states of concern" as well as of individuals listed as terrorists like the former Japanese Red Army adherents. The North had issued a statement that it did not support terrorism either by states or individuals and groups, but specific concessions were absent. Reportedly, the North wanted sizeable monetary compensation for ceasing its medium and long range missile production and sales as well as U.S. guarantees of the launching of satellites for it, whereas the United States was prepared to provide economic assistance and access to international monetary agencies. The negotiations will continue, with the policy decisions of the Bush administration an important factor.

With respect to recent DPRK-Japan relations, less progress has been recorded although both sides recurrently show an interest in reaching some agreement.[28] Japan has had an unofficial link to the North via The Federation of Koreans in Japan (*Chochonryon*), the pro-DPRK faction of Koreans resident in the country who earlier provided much of the foreign investment and fund remittances to relatives in the North. In recent times, however, these activities have been reduced due to the North's economic woes and the recession in Japan.

In 1991 and 1992, eight rounds of talks between the two governments transpired, but the results were minimal, and the talks were broken off by the North. Subsequent Japanese political missions to Pyongyang took place on three occasions, but DPRK authorities refused to accept an open-ended agenda for official talks.

Finally, a multi-party mission of Diet members headed by former Prime Minister Tomiichi Murayama went to the DPRK capital in early December 1999, and after seven and one-half years, official talks were resumed in April 2000 in Pyongyang, in Tokyo in August, and in Beijing in November. In an effort to improve relations, Tokyo provided some food aid, and advanced funds to help the DPRK preserve ancient tombs on the outskirts of Pyongyang. Moreover, Prime Minister Obuchi publicly stated that he aimed to normalize relations between the two nations despite the numerous thorny issues to be resolved. Direct access to the North from Japan, suspended after the DPRK missile launch of mid-1998, was reopened.

Yet the only agreement reached in the course of the three meetings was to continue the effort. Fundamentally, the key issues have not changed: from the DPRK side, apology and compensation for Japan's colonial past, and from Japan's side, an accounting for the Japanese who were allegedly kidnapped by North Koreans in earlier times.

The sole concession by the DPRK to Japan in the past has been that of allowing Japanese women married to Korean men living in the North to visit their relatives in Japan on a selective basis. Behind the impasse, deep prejudices on both sides remain a major factor. Yet the hope of Pyongyang for extensive economic assistance and access to international financial channels provides impetus for an increased interest in normalizing relations with Japan.

Apart from its efforts to improve relations with the United States, the DPRK has made serious attempts to strengthen its relations with China and Russia, traditional, but more recently wavering allies.[29] Officially, the PRC and the DPRK have always been friends, their relation "sealed in blood," and cemented by a security agreement. Moreover, China has provided extensive economic assistance to the North during its recent troubles. Yet privately, Chinese authorities have taken a dim view of the DPRK. The North's refusal to learn from China and undertake major economic reforms has been seen as a serious blunder. Moreover, the Chinese have regarded the DPRK political order as bizarre. Until recently, high level visits had been minimal. The Chinese have insisted that their knowledge of the true situation in the North has been limited, and their ability to influence Pyongyang minimal.

In 1999, however, the visit of the second highest DPRK figure, Kim Yong Nam, to Beijing signaled a warming trend. Foreign Minister Paek Nam Sun also visited the Chinese capitol, and most significantly, Kim Jong Il visited the PRC Embassy in Pyongyang. Subsequently, his first foreign trip as DPRK leader to Beijing just prior to the summit meeting made clear the significance he attached to relations with China. Reportedly, in meetings with President Jiang Zemin and others, Kim expressed an interest in the Chinese economic program, a major step forward from the past.

This first visit, moreover, was followed by a second visit in mid-January 2001. After meetings with high officials in Beijing, the DPRK leader visited Shanghai, the nation's key financial and commercial center, touring high-tech plants and the stock exchange. The significance of this trip, as evidence of Kim's commitment to economic change, is obvious.

Turing to relations with Russia, these are also improving after being frigid since 1990. When Moscow signaled that it intended to establish relations with the ROK and to end "friendship prices" with respect to its DPRK trade, Kim Il Song was furious. China handled the transition in these respects in much more sophisticated fashion. Only in the past two years has a thaw in DPRK-Russian relations gotten underway, but recent developments have been significant. A new treaty was signed in February 2000 by Foreign Minister Ivanov in Pyongyang. Moreover, in July, President Vladimir Putin paid a two day visit to the DPRK capital, the first visit in history by a top Russian leader. Pledges to strengthen relations were given. It is important to note, however, that in the revised treaties with China and Russia, no pledge of military support in the event of conflict is given—only an agreement to consult.

Turning to the South, perhaps the most significant successes of the Kim Dae Jung administration have been in the field of foreign policy. Using the Sunshine Policy and a series of economic reform measures at home, Kim has greatly improved relations with the United States. Support for the Perry Report, and participation in the trilateral U.S.-Japan-ROK dialogue stand in contrast to the on-again, off-again policies of the Kim Young Sam government toward the North and toward U.S. policies.

At the same time, ROK relations with Japan have been strengthened. The visit of President Kim Dae Jung to Tokyo in 1998 produced strikingly different results than the Jiang visit. Japanese authorities presented a forceful apology for Japan's imperialist past, and Kim removed the ban on Japanese culture coming into the ROK as well as signing a fisheries agreement. Deeply implanted prejudices on both sides cannot be removed quickly, but the trend is now in a positive direction. In a recent Japanese poll, 48 percent of the respondents asserted that they felt closer to ROK citizens, with 46.9 percent feeling otherwise, the first time a majority has been positive. Moreover, 52.18 percent regarded Japan-ROK relations as in good shape, compared to 38.18 percent who viewed them negatively. While negative sentiments remain fairly high, the trends are favorable.

Success with respect to ROK-PRC relations have been at least equally impressive. Economic and cultural ties have greatly expanded, and the visit of PRC Defense Minister Chi Haotian to Seoul in January 2000, marked a major step in boosting ROK-PRC security relations, with a full range of subjects discussed, including an agreement that the Korean Peninsula should be nuclear-free. The PRC remains careful not to tilt toward the South unduly, since it wishes to keep a two-Koreas policy intact, and be able to serve as middleman in certain instances. There can be no doubt, however, that current PRC relations with the ROK, at least in the economic and cultural realms, dwarf those with the DPRK. Perhaps Kim Jong Il's visit to Beijing and Shanghai signals some change. Only time will tell.

Meanwhile, despite the fact that PRC-ROK relations are generally good, there are some troublesome issues. One relates to North Korean refugees or "food people" in the Yanbian Autonomous Region. While the earlier case of defector Hwang Jung Yop was finessed deftly by using the Philippines as a transit to the ROK, more recently, China—troubled by the influx of illegal personnel—has sent individuals back to the North, as it did with seven refugees coming from Russia. The ROK has protested without wishing to make the matter a major issue. China, in its turn has been unhappy about certain activities of South Koreans who have come to the region to interact with such individuals. Should the refugee flow mount significantly, these issues could assume greater importance.

ROK relations with Russia are satisfactory, if not extensive. Kim Dae Jung has made known his interest in seeing Russia and Japan join the Four Party Talks and in desiring the inclusion of the ROK in transnational oil and gas programs. Significant South Korean interest in investment in the Russian Far East, however, awaits an economic upswing there. Yet at some point, the development of a dynamic Natural Economic Territory (NET) in the East Sea region is very likely, with ROK participation akin to the NET existing between the ROK and Shandong province, currently expanding into Jilin.

As should now be apparent, Korea is presently the source of cooperation rather than contention among the major powers, including China and Japan. The Sunshine Policy should be given some credit for the ability of these powers to come more closely together. However, another key factor is the existence of common interests with respect to the issues. No outside state today wants a collapsed North Korea with its prodigious costs—economic and political—not only for the South, but for others as well. Nor does anyone want a nuclear North Korea. Moreover, another war on the peninsula would be catastrophic. Hence, there is a consensus among the powers that support for an evolutionary process bringing the DPRK into the world, seeking to improve its economy and reduce its paranoia, is the best of the available alternatives. No one can guarantee success. Much depends upon the attitudes and policies of the DPRK elite. Further, in South Korea, the United States, and Japan, opposition to policies labeled "appeasement" exists in considerable measure, and elections in any one of these states may cause policy shifts. Nevertheless, in the current setting, cooperation between China and Japan with respect to the Korean peninsula is at an all time high despite contention on other matters.

What if the situation with respect to the peninsula were to change, especially that pertaining to the DPRK? Perhaps there are five alternative scenarios for the North's future.[30] One is imminent collapse. While this does not seem likely, it cannot be totally discarded and clearly it would create multiple problems. A second, possibly more plausible scenario, is that of increasing factionalism within the North's elite, motivated by differences over both policy and power. In this scenario, at some point, one faction might turn outward for support—to China or possibly South Korea. Hence, it represents a dangerous possibility, with a domestic crisis suddenly being internationalized.

A third scenario is war—conflict on the part of a desperate leadership fearing absorption or as the result of an escalating incident. Again, the likelihood of this scenario seems slight. The objective of the DPRK elite is survival, not suicide—and whatever damage could be wrought upon the South, the North would be pulverized in the end by American and South Korean power. Yet the possibility, even if remote, must not be ruled out. With sea boundaries between North and South in rich fishing grounds still contentious, an incident might occur that suddenly escalated. A fourth scenario is minimal change, with military power playing an ever more forceful role in maintaining stability. This scenario has very limited long term potential. Finally, a fifth scenario is the evolutionary one outlined earlier. This is the scenario toward which a concert of powers is aiming.

Let the United States assume, however, that at some time, in some manner, Korean unification takes place. What is the likely impact upon relations among the major powers, and especially upon Sino-Japanese relations? Will history be replayed?

A central reason why China does not want Korean unification at this point is that it would likely be a unified Korea under the authority of Seoul. Today, the DPRK serves as a buffer state, and one with limited appeal to the several million Koreans living in China's Yanbian Autonomous Region. But a unified Korea might rekindle a longing to be part of an independent Korea among these people, as happened in the early years of the twentieth century.

Further, China participated in a war to prevent American power from being planted on the Yalu River, on China's border. China is not likely to willingly accept U.S. military forces once again near or on its borders. Thus, in the event of unification under ROK aegis, it would probably seek a neutral Korea, one nonaligned and offering friendship to all neighbors. In any case, should reunification come suddenly and as a result of the decline of the North, the key external issues are likely to involve China and the United States first and foremost, not Japan, at least initially. The current scene is vastly different from that of the late nineteenth and early twentieth centuries. In those years, China was in disrepair, Russia a loser in conflict, and Japan the clearly ascendant power. Events on the Korean peninsula were products of these conditions.

What if Korean reunification does not come swiftly, but is the result of a process, involving confederation or some similar interim steps, as both Koreas have advocated at various times? In such a case, the relationships of the major powers to the two parts of Korea are likely to follow patterns similar to the present trends. The North will at some point acquire recognition from the United States and Japan. Through the Four Party Talks—possibly widened later to include Japan and Russia—steps toward a peace treaty and arms reduction measures will be taken. China may continue to insure the North's security, at least informally. The U.S.-ROK security agreement will remain in effect, but with the revolution in military technology continuing, the presence of U.S. troops in the South may not be necessary at some point, given rapid deployment capacities. Japan's role will be primarily economic, with such interaction with the North expanding, and NETs established, economically integrating the region as a whole.

To be sure, this represents an optimistic scenario. Should reunification come hastily, the result of DPRK collapse or war, the complexities might be more difficult to resolve, especially as they relate to China and the United States. Yet Japan's role is likely to be principally an economic one, although in the event of any major conflict, its agreement with the United States for base use would become a serious issue.

In conclusion, the chances for intensive Sino-Japanese rivalry on the Korean Peninsula seem slight at this point, especially if division continues for a protracted period of time. Japanese expansion on the Asian continent now takes economic, not military forms, and that is very likely to continue. In the past, Japan served as an economic model for post–1945 Korea. Perhaps the relationship will in some degree be reversed, with a reformed South Korea serving as model. In any case, these societies can share in the high-tech and service fields toward which each is rapidly moving. Politically also, the two societies have much in common today, although the informal politics of each differ significantly. The historical legacy remains to be overcome. Many Koreans, North and South, fear the return of the old Japan, but as noted, there are numerous obstacles to such a course. Perhaps new generations, more internationalized in both communities, will look less to the past, more to the future.

There are risks in the currently rising Japanese nationalism, but such risks should not be exaggerated. This is the twenty-first century, not the twentieth century. Both the Asian continent and Japan are radically different than at the turn of the last century. This is manifest in Japan's present policies toward the Koreas. Its current aim is to play a role in supporting peace on the Korean peninsula through eventually establishing a presence in the North, supporting KEDO and other development-oriented programs while building closer economic and cultural ties with the South.

Will China be a rival or threat to Japan's newly cultivated policies toward the Korean Peninsula? At this point, in contrast to past history, South Korea is penetrating China rather than vice versa. Similar to Japan, it is cultivating an economic presence, especially in the Northeast. For its part, China is seeking to bolster its two Koreas policy while engaging in preventive diplomacy, hoping to serve as middle-man in strengthening the status quo. Conditions cause it to tilt in reality to the ROK, but it is making genuine efforts to restore DPRK confidence in it while cautiously rendering advice. As noted, many observers worry about the course of a strong China in coming decades, but one must pay homage to the restraints as well as the strengths—and place due emphasis on the degree to which the policies of others will influence the course of Chinese foreign policy.

Thus, under current conditions, the elements of cooperation between China and Japan on Korean issues are dominant. Since future events on the Korean peninsula are unpredictable, one can only note that the greatest risk is developments that would bring China and the United States into contention, with Japan as a U.S. ally unavoidably involved. Hence, the Four Party Talks should be deepened, and expanded to include Japan and Russia. The greater the degree of transparency among the major powers, and the more extensive the discussions regarding contingency plans, the better the prospects for avoiding unexpected emergencies that demand immediate, unplanned responses. In the latter possibility, danger lies. However, one can take hope in the fact that major power wars in this age are unwinnable. Even the "victor" will suffer irreparable losses, and leaders everywhere are coming to realize that fact.

NOTES

1. Recent studies of the Japanese economy of high quality include Kent Calder, *Strategic Capitalism: Private Business and Public Purpose in Japanese Finance* (Princeton, NJ: Princeton University Press, 1997); Ronad Dore, *Flexible Rigidities: Industrial Policy and Structural Adjustment in the Japanese Economy 1970–80* (Stanford, CA: Stanford University Press, 1996); and Robert M. Uriu, *Troubled Industries: The Political Economy of Industrial Adjustment in Japan* (Ithaca, NY: Cornell University Press, 1998). Earlier studies of continuing worth include Chalmers Johnson, *MITI and the Japanese Miracle: The Growth of Industrial Policy, 1925-1975* (Stanford, CA: Stanford University Press, 1982); Daniel I. Okimoto, *Between MITI and the Market: Japanese Industrial Policy for High Technology* (Stanford, CA: Stanford University Press, 1989); and Richard J. Samuels, *The Business of the Japanese State—Energy Markets in Comparative and Historical Perspective,* (Ithaca, NY: Cornell University Press, 1987).

2. For a sober analysis of Japan's problems, see a three-part series by Wasa Takahiro and Sonoyama Hideaki entitled "The Enigma of Japanese Capitalism," *Journal of Japanese Trade & Industry,* May/June, July/August, September/October 2000.

3. Excellent recent studies of Japanese politics include Gerald L. Curtis, *The Logic of Japanese Politics—Leaders, Institutions, and the Limits of Change* (New York: Columbia University Press, 1999); Masaru Kohno, *Japan's Postwar Party Politics* (Princeton, NJ: Princeton University Press, 1997); and Frank J. Schwartz, *Advice and Consent—The Politics of Consultation in Japan* (Cambridge, MA: Cambridge University Press, 1998). For earlier works, see George Packard, *Protest in Tokyo* (Princeton, NJ: Princeton University Press, 1966); Mark Ramsayer and Frances Rosenbluth, *Japan's Political Marketplace* (Cambridge, MA: Harvard University Press, 1993); and Robert Scalapino and Junnosuke Masumi, *Parties and Politics in Contemporary Japan* (Berkeley, CA: University of California Press, 1962).

4. See three instructive articles, Sasaki Takeshi, "A New Era of Nationalism"; Ito Kanichi, "The Meaning of Nationalism in Japan Today"; and Kitaoka Shinichi, "Is Nationalism Intensifying in Japan?" under the general title "Is Nationalism Surging in Japan?," in *Journal of Japanese Trade and Industry,* January 1, 2001, pp. 8–20.

5. For discerning essays on U.S.-Japan relations, see Ralph A. Cossa, ed., *Restructuring the U.S.-Japan Alliance—Toward a More Equal Partnership* (Washington, D.C.: Sigur Center for Asian Studies, 1999); and papers from the

March 1998 conference co-hosted by Nobuo Matsunaga and James A. Kelly, *The United States-Japan Relationship in a Year of Crisis*, (Honolulu, HI: Pacific Forum CSIS, 1998). For more extensive accounts, see Peter F. Cowhey and Mathew D. McCubbins, eds., *Structure and Policy in Japan and the United States* (New York: Cambridge University Press, 1995); Yoichi Funabashi, *Alliance Adrift* (New York: Council on Foreign Relations, 1999); and Michael J. Green and Patrick M. Cronin, eds., *The U.S.-Japan Alliance—Past, Present and Future* (New York: Council on Foreign Relations, 1999).

6. For two Japanese perspectives, see Tanaka Akihiko, "Obuchi Diplomacy: How to Follow a Successful Start," *Japan Echo*, April 1999, pp. 8-12; and Noda Nobuo, "Japan in a World of Rival Empires," *Japan Echo*, June 1999, pp. 8-11. Recent Chinese views are those of Jin Linbo, "Japan's 'U.S.-Centered Perception' and its Roots," *Foreign Affairs Journal*, The Chinese People's Institute of Foreign Affairs, June 1999, pp. 23–27; Xi Mi, "History speaks louder than lies," *China Daily*, January 22, 2000, p. 4; and Jing Xian, "Never forget infamous history," *China Daily*, February 26, 2000, p. 4.

7. A recent work, looking toward the future, is that edited by Vladimir I. Ivanov and Karla S. Smith, *Japan and Russia in Northeast Asia—Partners in the 21st Century* (Westport, CT: Praeger, 1999). See also the two volume work of Hiroshi Kimura, *Japanese-Russian Relations under Brezhnev and Andropov* and *Japanese-Russian Relations under Gorbachev and Yeltsin* (Armonk, NY: M. E. Sharpe, 2000; Gennady Chufrin, ed., *Russia and Asia—The Emerging Security Agenda*, (Stockholm, SIPRI: Oxford University Press, 1999), and Watanabe Koji, ed., *Engaging Russia in Asia Pacific* (Japan Center for International Exchange, Tokyo, 1999).

8. A comprehensive work focusing on the Northern Territories issue is the two volume study of Tsuyoshi Hasegawa, *Neither War Nor Peace, 1985–1998*, Vol. 2, *The Northern Territories Dispute and Russo-Japanese Relations*, (Berkeley, CA: University of California Press, 1998).

9. For an attempt to draw up a balance sheet on contemporary China, see this author's *The People's Republic of China at Fifty* (Seattle, WA: The National Bureau of Asian Research, October, 1999).

10. An official view of China's contemporary foreign policy is the statement of foreign Minister Tang Jiaxuan, September 22, 1999, reproduced in *Foreign Affairs Journal*, December 1999, pp. 6-12. For an excellent analytical study, see Quansheng Zhao, *Interpreting Chinese Foreign Policy—the Micro-Macro Linkage Approach* (New York: Oxford University Press, 1996).

11. Four recent works worthy of attention are Robert G. Sutter, *Chinese Policy Priorities and Their Implications for the United States*, (Boulder, CO: Rowman and Littlefield, 2000); Ezra F. Vogel, ed., *Living with China—U.S.-China Relations in the Twenty-First Century*, (New York: W. W. Norton, 1997); Lowell Dittmer and Samuel S. Kim, eds., *China's Quest for National Identity* (Ithaca, NY: Cornell University Press, 2000); and Michael D. Swaine and Ashley J. Tellis, *Interpreting China's Grand Strategy—Past, Present, and Future* (Santa Monica, CA: RAND, 2000).

12. An excellent overview is that of Don Oberdorfer, *The Two Koreas—A Contemporary History* (Reading, MA: Addison-Wesley, 1997).

13. For a recent evaluation of the ROK economic scene and the pressures on President Kim, see John Larkin, "Korea's Winter of Discontent," *Far Eastern Economic Review,* December 7, 2000, pp. 16–20). A useful broad survey of the ROK economy is *Korea's Economy 2000,* (Washington D.C.: Korea Economic Institute of America and the Korea Institute of International Economic Policy, 2000).

14. In addition to Nolin, cited earlier, see the well-researched, detailed analysis of Nicholas Eberstadt, *The End of North Korea* (Washington, D.C.: The AEI Press, 1999).

15. See the unpublished paper by Young-Kwan Yoon, "The North Korean Problem from a Political Economic Perspective: Why do We Need a New Approach?," 2000. For North Korean views, see the joint editorial of *Rodong Sinmun, Joson Inmingun,* and *Chongnyon Jonwi,* "Glorify This Year Greeting the 55th Anniversary of the Party Foundation as a Year of Proud Victory in the Frame of Great Chollima Upsurge," reproduced in *the People's Korea,* February 12, 2000, pp. 1–3. A discerning essay is that of Kongdan Oh and Ralph Hassig, "North Korea Between Collapse and Reform," *Asian Survey,* March/April, 1999.

16. See Robert A. Scalapino, *North Korea at a Crossroads,* (Stanford, CA: Stanford University, Hoover Institution, 1997).

17. Excellent essays on the Sunshine Policy are contained in Chung-in Moon and David I. Steinberg, eds., *Kim Dae-jung Government and Sunshine Policy: Promises and Challenges,* (Seoul: Yonsei University Press, 1999). See also Chung-in Moon, "The Sunshine Policy and the Korean Summit: Assessments and Prospects," *East Asian Review,* Winter 2000, pp. 3–36.

18. An optimistic appraisal of the project was given to this author and other members of an Asia Society delegation who visited the region in 1992.

19. For figures on ROK aid to the North through 1999, see Korea Institute for National Unification, *The Unification Environment and Relations Between South and North Korea: 1999–2000,* (Seoul: May 2000, pp. 146-151).

20. See "Address by President Kim Dae-jung at the Free University of Berlin," *Korea Update,* March 25, 2000, pp. 2–3.

21. Details are set forth in "North, South Agree to form Joint Committee for Economic Cooperation," *The People's Korea,* December 23, 2000, p 1.

22. See "Ground-breaking for the Seoul-Shinuiju Railway," *Korean Unification Bulletin,* no. 23, September 2000, pp. 1, 6.

23. For an excellent analysis of DPRK negotiation techniques, see Scott Snyder, *Negotiating on the Edge—North Korean Negotiating Behavior,* (Washington D.C.: United States Institute of Peace, 1999).

24. A first-rate overview is provided by Kongdan Oh and Ralph C. Hassig, *North Korea Through the Looking Glass,* (Washington D.C.: Brookings Institution Press, 2000). See also Ralph A. Cossa, *The U.S.-DPRK Agreed*

Framework: Is It Still Viable? Is It Enough? (Honolulu, Hawaii: Pacific Forum-CSIS, Occasional Paper, April 1999).

25. For an analysis of the 1994 Basic Agreement launching the KEDO program, see the task force report sponsored by the Council on Foreign Relations and the Seoul Forum for International Affairs, *Success or Sellout? The U.S.-North Korean Nuclear Accord,* (New York: Council on Foreign Relations, 1995).

26. For an evaluation of the Perry Report, see Ralph Cossa and Alan Oxley, "The U.S.-Korea Alliance," in Robert D. Blackwell and Paul Dibb, eds., *America's Asian Alliances,* (Cambridge, MA: The MIT Press, 2000, pp. 66–67).

27. Interesting coverage of these events from a North Korean perspective can be found in the article by Choe Kwan Ik, "New Millennium—Year of Diplomacy," *The People's Korea,* November 23, 2000, p. 4.

28. In addition to the sources already cited, see Hong Nack Kim, "Japan's Policy toward the Two Koreas in the Post–Cold War Era," *International Journal of Korean Studies,* Vol. 1, Spring 1997, pp. 131–158.

29. See Hung Yong Lee, "China and the Two Koreas: New Emerging Triangle," in Young whan Kihl, ed., *Korea and the World—Beyond the Cold War,* (Boulder, Colorado: Westview Press, 1994). In addition to the earlier works dealing with DPRK-Russian relations cited, see the account of Putin's visit to Pyongyang, "DPRK, Russia Declare New Era of Bilateral Friendly Ties," *The People's Korea,* July 22, 2000, p. 1.

30. These scenarios were first forth in my *North Korea at a Crossroads,* op. cit.

CHAPTER TEN

MULTILATERALISM AND KOREAN SECURITY IN TRANSITION

STEPHEN E. NOERPER

NEW ORIENTATIONS

In 1988, a newly democratic South Korea ushered in its *Nordpolitik*, or Northern Policy, marking a radical departure from decades of South and North Korea locked into a zero-sum, winner-take-all approach to international relations. Diplomatic recognition had long registered the relative success of the South and North in establishing legitimacy in the international arena.[1] The Northern Policy introduced new criteria, whereby South Korea encouraged external relations with North Korea and saw increased international activity and participation on the multilateral front as a means of drawing North Korea away from dangerous isolation and ultimately promoting change. In establishing relations with the former Soviet Union and China and in joining the United Nations with North Korea, South Korea orchestrated a heady diplomatic crescendo, which it followed with a steady internationalization campaign in subsequent years.

South Korean President Kim Dae Jung's Sunshine approach has built upon that opening, seeking to engage the North and draw it into the international community. Kim Dae Jung has coupled calls for international engagement and assistance with enhanced business and informal contacts from the South to the North. His March 2000 Berlin Declaration offered the promise of direct government-to-government assistance, leading North Korea to agree to a historic inter-Korean summit. North Korea, with the consolidation of the Kim Jong Il regime, appears to have tentatively embraced South Korea's approach and initiated new international contacts, perhaps out of increased trust but most certainly for economic viability reasons.

The *de facto* result is a new and historic orientation toward gradual integration that is reliant in part on enhanced multilateral activity. Unprecedented consensus exists over the need to maintain stability and curtail to what extent possible the tremendous costs akin to unification. The impetus lies in several directions. First and foremost, South Korean President Kim Dae Jung's Sunshine approach actively encourages key allies and the international community to embrace its former adversary. Secondly, North Korean leader Kim Jong Il's regime slowly, but increasingly, appears more responsive to the reality that the North Korean state will maintain itself only through opening to the outside. Third, external elements are uniquely aligned in their desire for peaceful transition on the peninsula.

GROWTH IN MULTILATERALISM

A more internationalist approach on the Korean peninsula is complemented by recent growth in multilateralism. Observers have declared Asia Pacific multilateralism "clearly a growth industry today," both at the official, or Track I, and nonofficial, or Track II, levels.[2] Dozens of institutional fora aimed at promoting political, economic, and security discussions exist in East Asia today. Although some of these fora date back to the 1960s and 1970s, many have taken off or come to light in the post–Cold War era. The latter are the most ambitious and potentially significant.

Foremost among recent Track I initiatives is the Association of Southeast Asian Nations (ASEAN) Regional Forum (ARF), which seeks "to foster the habit of constructive dialogue and consultation on political and security issues of common interest and concern."[3] The ASEAN Regional Forum has looked beyond its traditional ASEAN membership toward broader Asian concerns. Accordingly, the ARF Foreign Ministers have unanimously endorsed early resumption of the inter-Korean talks and South Korea's call for a subregional forum to address Northeast Asian security concerns.

A notable Track II mechanism is the Council for Security Cooperation in the Asia Pacific (CSCAP), which gathers academics, security professionals, and former and current defense and foreign ministry officials. CSCAP has concentrated recent efforts on providing direct support to the ARF, an interplay of Track I and II initiatives. ARF communiqués have seen concerns addressed through subsequent CSCAP working groups on confidence and security building measures (CSBMs), comprehensive and cooperative security, and maritime security cooperation. CSACP stands as one of the few multilateral organizations that include North Korea as a member.

The Northeast Asia Cooperation Dialogue (NEACD) is a prominent nonofficial initiative focused on the Korean peninsula. Hosted by the University of California's Institute on Global Conflict and Cooperation and bringing together officials, noted academics, and security professionals, the NEACD is aimed at enhancing mutual understanding, confidence, and cooperation among the two Koreas, China, Japan, Russia, and the United States through substantive dialogue in an unofficial setting.

The multilateral initiative that has taken the greatest institutional footing and provides something of a model is the Korean Peninsula Energy Development Organization (KEDO). KEDO was established in the wake of the 1994 Geneva Agreed Framework to finance and supply a light-water reactor (LWR) project to North Korea. Although government sponsored, with South Korea, Japan, and the United States comprising the Executive Committee, KEDO officially lists itself as a Track II initiative. Pacific Forum-CSIS Executive Director Ralph Cossa notes that KEDO served as an "innovative vehicle for the three founding members to deal directly with North Korea in the absence of diplomatic relations, demonstrating yet another service that Track II multilateral mechanisms can provide."[4]

Former KEDO Executive Director and U.S. Ambassador to South Korea and current Dean of the Fletcher School of Law and Diplomacy Stephen Bosworth suggested in an early *Annual Report* that "KEDO has become an important feature on the political landscape in Northeast Asia."[5] KEDO might well typify the sort of multilateral cooperation effort we're likely to see in the post–Cold War era: ad hoc, mission-oriented, temporary, and therefore cost-effective. A central aspect is that of the economic and security nexus, reflective of new realities in a globalized era.

KEDO's charter mandates that it: (1) contribute to the strengthening of the international nonproliferation regime while improving the prospects for lasting peace and stability on the Korean peninsula and beyond; (2) assist in implementation of the Agreed Framework between the United States and North Korea, under which North Korea agreed to freeze and ultimately dismantle its existing nuclear program, by (a) financing and constructing in the North Korea two LWRs; (b) providing North Korea with an alternative source of energy for heating and electricity production until the first of those reactors is completed, and, in doing so, meet or exceed international standards of nuclear and conventional safety, environmental protection, and ethical business practices;

and (c) serving as an example of how a cooperative and targeted international diplomatic effort can lead to a resolution of regional security or political crises, and provide a work environment where a multinational staff, with varied cultural, social, and professional backgrounds, can work harmoniously to accomplish organizational, professional, and personal goals.[6]

Such progress on the multilateral front beg consideration of fundamental questions:

1. To what degree might expanding the network of relationships assist in promoting cooperation and managing interdependence between the two Koreas and among them and other nations?
2. To what extent might multilateralism facilitate interactions and durable relationships between South Korea and North Korea and among other nations with North Korea?
3. In what ways might a more internationalist approach improve channels of communication with the isolationist North to identify areas of common interest and coordinate actions and strategies for North Korean development and enhanced regional security?
4. How might multilateralism instill trust and confidence, reducing asymmetries in information and making intentions more transparent between North Korea and South Korea and the international community?
5. How might bilateral and multilateral agreements and arrangements expand to ensure among parties observable compliance and agreement on the impact of non-compliance in arms control, conventional force rollbacks, and confidence-building measures?

Responses to Multilateralism

Northeast Asia is an area that has traditionally relied on a web of strong bilateral organizations, dominated by the United States in the post–World War II period. Observers cite the continued reliance on bilateralism as the rationale for the slow growth of formalized multilateral mechanisms in Northeast Asia. However, emerging regional security mechanisms generally are consistent with the national strategies of nations in Northeast Asia, thus enhancing regional security. The arguments of those who argue against multilateral initiatives for fear of undermining bilateral arrangements fail to realize that current efforts build upon existing bilateral security relationships, a phenomenon not seen as widely in other regions and one where the Asia Pacific sets the example.

Limits exist, and emerging arrangements serve more as confidence and security-building measures geared toward preventing the possibility of, rather than reacting to, aggression or crises. Gradualism, incrementalism, informality, and a process-oriented approach characterize multilateral cooperation in Northeast Asia. In tandem, these same characteristics condition South Korea's engagement policy.

The boom in multilateralism reflects new approaches among several nations. In the past half decade, the United States has embraced multilateralism more fully as a cost-effective and institutionally viable option. In remarks to the 29th International General Meeting of the Pacific Basin Economic Council (PBEC), former U.S. Defense Secretary Perry outlined four pillars of the U.S. approach in the Asia Pacific region, namely strong alliances, regional confidence building, comprehensive engagement with China, and counterproliferation.[7] Secretary Perry referred to U.S. alliances with Japan and others as the "linchpin" of the U.S. regional security strategy. Significantly, he held out the "promotion of multilateral security initiatives designed to reduce tension and build regional confidence" as the second pillar. In referring to the third pillar, engagement with China, Perry harkened back to then President Clinton's suggestion that "engagement means using the best tools we have—incentives and disincentives alike—to advance core American interests."[8] The fourth pillar entailed prevention of the proliferation of weapons of mass destruction and their delivery systems. He described the most notable success as the 1994 Geneva Agreed Framework, which aimed to curtail North Korean nuclear weapons ambitions.

Closely linked with the U.S. shift toward multilateralism was an orientation toward preventive defense. In *Foreign Affairs*, former Defense Secretary Perry suggested that "today the United States has a unique historical opportunity to foster peace through preventive defense. As preventive medicine creates the conditions that support health, making disease less likely and surgery unnecessary, so preventive defense creates the conditions that support peace."[9] He cited two similar opportunities earlier in the twentieth century, namely one missed in the form of an isolationist America's rejection of the League of Nations and one seized upon in a post–World War II "path of engagement" that entailed the Marshall Plan, the "epitome of preventive defense." In noting that preventive defense "employs a variety of tools that not only show nations how armed forces function in a democracy but also serve to build openness and trust between nations," Secretary Perry cited the Marshall Center in Germany and Asia Pacific Center in Hawaii as prime examples.[10]

Other great powers, China and Russia, appeared slow to embrace multilateralism. China was initially reluctant to participate in regional fora—preferring bilateral dealings and fearing that multilateral activities involving its neighbors threatened its sovereignty. Although Beijing still refuses to participate in Track II fora involving the South China Seas dispute, it has embraced limited participation elsewhere, including the Korean peninsula. China appears to increasingly regard multilateral mechanisms as useful for engaging with the international community in a constructive manner.

Russia views such opportunities as facilitating regional integration, and Moscow has signaled its desire to become directly involved in multilateral cooperation in Asia. Pacific Forum-CSIS's Cossa suggests that "bringing Russia into the Asian dialogue community costs little and also bolsters those in the Kremlin most committed to reform and international cooperation."[11] Moscow has bid for Asia Pacific Economic Cooperation (APEC) forum entry and expressed irritation over a lack of inclusion in the Korean peninsula Four Party Talks involving China, the United States, and North and South Korea, preferring a four-plus-two arrangement involving Russia, Japan, China, the United States, and the two Koreas.

Multilateral fora afford Japan a means to become involved more actively in regional security matters in a way that does not threaten other Asian nations. Those urging a more "normal" Japan—from both inside and out—wish to see an increase in international activity. Participation in ARF, CSCAP, NEACD, KEDO, and other activities allows Japan to cautiously, but positively, exert a more significant leadership role in the region. Coupled with a strong Japan-U.S. security alliance and Japanese participation in peacekeeping, Japanese engagement in multilateral cooperation is critical for progress in the Asia Pacific.

Mongolia too supports and actively engages in several multilateral fora. Couched between two giant neighbors, Russia and China, Mongolia recognizes the inherent economic and political benefits and increased stability akin to broader international cooperation. Given its unique cultural and historical ties, it has the potential to facilitate peaceful change and increased understanding on the Korean peninsula. Looking westward, Mongolia also exhibits support for Central Asian multilateral initiatives.

South Korea, an early supporter of the Asia Pacific Economic Cooperation (APEC) Forum, supports multilateralism as long as it is consistent with existing bilateral arrangements. South Korea has called for a Regional Security Forum and is extremely active in other multilateral arrangements. North Korea has committed, at least in principle, to multilateral dialogue as long as initiatives are not directed toward it. Its initial resistance in multilateral settings and varied attendance reflected resentment over delayed progress in normalization of relations with the

United States and Japan. Recent months have shown a dramatic increase in North Korea's willingness to engage multilaterally, engagement actively promoted by South Korea.

RESPONSES BY NORTH KOREA

North Korea has displayed slow, but positive movement on a number of fronts. North Korea has abided by IAEA safeguards and stands in seeming compliance with the 1994 Geneva Agreed Framework. It has worked with the Korean Peninsula Energy Development Organization (KEDO), even providing guarantees protecting South Koreans working on the light-water reactor project from prosecution, a compromise of some significance given prior staunch claims to sovereignty. Elsewhere on the multilateral front, North Korea has participated in the Four Party Talks with South Korea, the United States, and China, agreeing to committees on tension reduction and interim peace mechanisms.

The suspected development site at Kumchang-ri raised the specter of a noncompliant North, but subsequent United States inspections received "good cooperation" and alleviated some concerns. North Korea also has worked with the United States on locating remains from the Korean War and has engaged with the United States in discussion on missile issues.

Promotion of the Rajin-Sonbong Free Economic and Trade Zone, technocrats studying business overseas, a growth in local markets, and reported easing of internal movement reveal some limited positive movement on the economic front. A further sign of North Korean opening is its permitting international aid organizations to help meet the needs of the humanitarian crisis. The international aid community reports increased access and some success in stemming the tide of famine, malnutrition, and disease. Of course, there have been exceptions, with CARE, Oxfam, and Doctors Without Borders, prominent aid entities that have opted out of North Korea. North Korea has been more explicit in describing its most recent drought and announcing a 1998 mortality rate of 9.3 per 1000, a tacit acknowledgement of hundreds of thousands of deaths since the mid-1990s and the first time the DPRK has made such figures public. North Korean officials have afforded foreign media some exposure, albeit limited by the predicament of wanting to show the best of the worst.

TOWARD PREVENTIVE DIPLOMACY

Mirroring the evolution of multilateralism is adoption of preventive diplomacy efforts. A multilayered, multilateral approach toward North Korea is important relative to the unstable peace that has characterized the Korean peninsula. Encompassing actions between crisis and peace-time diplomacies, preventive diplomacy is critical in defining future approaches toward North Korea. With inter-Korean relations and those between North Korea and the international community having moved from confrontation toward rapprochement, preventive diplomacy efforts increasingly characterize this period prior to post-conflict peacebuilding. Such efforts lessen the likelihood of conflicts that might break out as the peninsula attains new stability and moves toward unification.

Definitions of preventive diplomacy vary. UN Secretary Generals Dag Hammerskjold and Boutros Boutros Ghali included peacekeeping, economic assistance, and other conflict management measures in their definitions. Michael Lund in *Preventing Violent Conflicts* defines preventive diplomacy as "action taken in vulnerable places and times to avoid the threat or use of armed force and related forms of coercion by states or groups to settle the political disputes that can arise from the destabilizing effects of economic, social, political, and economic change."[12] Lund suggests that preventive diplomacy is especially operative at the level of an unstable peace. Lund offers a preventive diplomacy "toolbox," a broad checklist that ranges from non-military approaches, including coercive and noncoercive diplomatic measure and development and governance approaches to conflict prevention, to military approaches, including restraints on the use of armed force and the threat or use of military force.[13] Such tools are used in deterrence and engagement on the Korean peninsula.

In the United Nations, member states attach increased importance to preventive diplomacy as the most cost-effective ways of dispute prevention and control. The Secretary General's office is engaged actively in implementing these political mandates in Afghanistan, Bougainville, Burundi, Cambodia, Cyprus, East Timor, El Salvador, Georgia, Guatemala, Haiti, Liberia, Myanmar/Burma, Sierra Leone, Somalia, Tajikistan, and the former Yugoslav Republic of Macedonia. Although preventive diplomacy is particularly favored by the international community, the UN experience in recent years has demonstrated several complementary forms of preventive activity: preventive deployment, preventive disarmament, preventive humanitarian action, and preventive peace-building, the latter of which may involve actions aimed at good governance, human rights, and economic and social development. In United Nations parlance, "preventive diplomacy" now falls under the broader rubric of "preventive action," and such action increasingly will characterize approaches on the Korean peninsula.

A challenge essential to structuring an effective multilayered, multilateral approach on the Korean peninsula concerns the range of appropriate action specific to regional, international, or nongovernmental organizations, each of which has comparative advantages and limitations.

Ruth Wedgewood in *Managing Global Chaos* suggests that regional structures build confidence and that regional leaders may be especially persuasive in preventing potential conflict. However, she cautions that regional structures (1) cannot effectively enforce sanctions on their own, (2) are traditionally reluctant to intervene in domestic conflicts within a neighboring state, (3) often have limited material resources to support mediation or intervention efforts, and (4) have not demonstrated the necessary political will to confront the most serious strategic problems, such as the North Korean nuclear problem. In short, difficulty surrounds the employment of coercive diplomatic tools such as sanctions, not to mention military intervention.[14] This appears true on the Korean peninsula, where the threat of U.S. sanctions against North Korea during the 1993–1994 nuclear crisis almost led to an outbreak of conflict.

That said, it is important to emphasize that cooperation between regional and international efforts may lead to more effective preventive diplomacy. Wedgwood observes that "in the last five years, there has been a salient pattern of double-teaming among international organizations; major powers with security interests and the UN Security Council have worked effectively with ad hoc regional groupings, formal regional organizations, and specific subregional groups to adapt their charters for new uses."[15] The Asia Foundation's Scott Snyder adds that "given the effectiveness of coordinated responses among international and regional organizations, the opportunity to effectively harmonize regional and international efforts at preventive diplomacy should not be missed."[16] Organizational double-teaming and a coupling of efforts among international, regional, and nongovernmental entities will assist in preventing conflict as the Korean peninsula moves toward new stability and facilitate relief, reconstruction, and unification efforts.

However, the notion of preventive diplomacy is not without, if not detractors, at least concerned observers. Dr. Robert Gates, former U.S. Deputy National Security Advisor and Director of Central Intelligence, outlined his requirements for preventive diplomacy, namely that (1) the "credible sanction of military force in the hands of those conducting the diplomacy;" (2) the "exercise of preventive diplomacy must involve integrated strategies," meaning the prospect of military power coupled with political and economic inducements; (3) "those managing the process must be seen to be willing to take actions—political, economic, or military—to deter aggression or bring the recalcitrant party or parties to the table;" (4) leadership is necessary. Although acknowledging that some Americans are "reluctant to pay the price of leadership," he views U.S. leadership as "critical to world peace." He cautions that "no multilateral organization anywhere can be effective in dealing with serious potential conflict" unless one country is willing to lead and others follow. For the time being in the Asia Pacific, that one country remains the United States.[17]

THE ROLE OF EXTERNAL FACILITATORS

South Korea is requesting external elements to commit to a new architecture on the peninsula. This marks a fundamental shift not only in South Korean ambition, but in the explicit handling of affairs on the peninsula, with Seoul firmly in the driving seat. Seoul has encouraged Washington to normalize relations with Pyongyang. Improving relations in exchange for DPRK missile and nuclear concessions figures prominently in the comprehensive approach toward North Korea urged by former U.S. Secretary of Defense William Perry in his review of U.S. North Korea policy.

Of course, challenges abound, not least of which is the absence of elements on Capitol Hill advocating engagement with North Korea. DPRK missile tests and suspicions about Kumchang-ri alienated conservatives and undermined liberal advocates, leading to difficult debate on funding for the Korean Peninsula Energy Development Organization (KEDO). The lead-up to the North Korea Threat Reduction Act spoke to further discord between the U.S. executive and legislative branches on engaging North Korea. Yet the Perry Process succeeded in tempering the most ardent opposition, and the resulting Trilateral Coordination and Oversight Group (TCOG) has muted concerns over a lack of a coherent and coordinated approach among the United States, Japan, and South Korea. TCOG represents the newest step forward on the multilateral cooperation front, although some observers prefer to label it a "minilateral" initiative.

Any long-term rift in Sino-U.S. relations also challenges forward progress, at least by way of coordinated responses on the Korean peninsula. Yet China has been consistent in its call for peaceful transition on the peninsula, a position fostered actively by South Korea. National Committee of the Chinese People's Political Consultative Conference (CPPCC) Chair Li Ruihuan's May 1999 visit to Seoul underscored China's commitment to the rapid development of Sino-ROK ties. Li observed to ROK President Kim Dae Jung that it is a matter of time before the DPRK and ROK unify and offered explicit support for Kim's engagement approach. China agreed to open a North Korean consulate in Hong Kong, albeit after the opening of a South Korean consulate in Shenyang.

China welcomed the DPRK Supreme People's Assembly President Kim Yong Nam to Beijing in June 1999 and committed to providing further food and fuel assistance—a move Seoul welcomed. The secret visit by North Korean leader Kim Jong Il to China in late May 2000, only weeks before the scheduled inter-Korean summit, speaks to China's significant role. China has fostered ties with South Korea's defense establishment, raising concerns in some circles in Seoul and Washington, but also has recognized the potential for cooperation with the United States in facilitating peaceful transition on the peninsula.

South Korean President Kim Dae Jung also has welcomed Russia's acceleration in contacts with both North and South Korea. During his visit to Russia, Kim expressed hope that Russia too would draw North Korea from its isolation. Russia resumed supplying the DPRK crude oil—some 400,000 to 500,000 tons in 1999. Russian Foreign Minister Ivanov's visit to Pyongyang resulted in a renewal of friendship arrangements, although notably not a security guarantee. ROK President Kim's meetings in Moscow featured common support for a six-nation summit on security in Northeast Asia.

As with the United States, South Korea has pressed Japan on normalizing relations with North Korea. President Kim Dae Jung's summit with Japan's late Prime Minister Obuchi led to Japanese agreement in considering compensation for North Korea, in line with events preceding the 1965 Japan-ROK normalization accords. Although talks resumed in the spring of 2000, little progress was made in the initial rounds, but the promise of further dialogue speaks to Tokyo's broader support for engagement. Concerns remain in Japan over the amount of remuneration requested by North Korea, the perceived missile threat in light of the August 1998 *Taepodong* launch, the visits by Japanese wives of North Koreans, and other unresolved issues of Japanese abducted by North Koreans in the 1970s. Yet Japan has committed significant food assistance to North Korea and progress will likely be in line with Seoul's and Washington's experiences.

Mid-level diplomatic powers and smaller powers both in and outside of the region also facilitate peaceful transition on the Korean peninsula. At the behest of Seoul and with Pyongyang responsive to overtures, a number of external powers have established contact with North Korea in an attempt to draw it into the international arena. Italy normalized relations in February 2000 and approved a Fiat license to a Unification Church automobile initiative in North Korea. Australia normalized ties in May 2000, advancing its contacts with and extensive analyses of North Korea. Britain, France, Belgium, the Philippines, Canada, and others have initiated discussions with North Korea, with a flurry of diplomatic recognition a tacit result in 2000 and 2001. Mongolia has had a political relationship with North Korea since the latter's inception and has a burgeoning economic and political relationship with South Korea. As host of the June 2000 Council on Security Cooperation in the Asia Pacific (CSCAP) Northeast Asia Working Group meeting, Ulaanbattar facilitated discussion on peninsular affairs. Mongolia has hosted visits by North Korean citizens groups, dialogued with South Korea on the issue of North Korean refugees, and offered support for a more formalized security dialogue mechanism, in keeping with South Korean President Kim Dae Jung's approach.

North Korea has expressed a willingness to engage in more international dialogue, most significantly in its 2000 bid to join the Association of Southeast Asian Nations (ASEAN) Regional Forum (ARF), a body geared toward political and security dialogue. The May 2000 Foreign Ministers meeting yielded approval of North Korea's desire to enter into the framework. For several years, the ARF has endorsed peaceful transition and reconciliation on the Korean peninsula.

North Korea invited the European Parliament to send a delegation to Pyongyang in late 2000, an invitation the Parliament's Foreign Affairs Committee agreed to in principle. North Korea's Ambassador to UNESCO suggested that a visit by a European Union (EU) delegation would assist in promoting understanding and cooperation at the parliamentary level.

Nongovernmental organizations (NGOs) also play a key role in enhancing multilateralism on the Korean peninsula. The Bay Area-based Nautilus Institute for Security and Sustainable Development initiated the Northeast Asia Peace and Security Network (NAPSNet) Daily Report, focused on peninsular concerns. It also launched a North Korea windpower project, designed to foster exposure to alternative energy sources, hosted DPRK energy specialists, and developed a water purification project. Agricultural training initiatives in California, Wisconsin, Georgia, and elsewhere have provided impetus for the development of a Korean peninsula Agricultural Development Organization (KADO), much in the guise of KEDO. An NGO-initiated Beijing-based business program orients North Korean technocrats toward the realities of international business and trade and underscores the importance of the rule of law in attracting foreign direct investment.

The East-West Center-based Northeast Economic Forum has advocated a Northeast Asian Development Bank (NEADB). This approach, borne of Track II dialogue, is aimed at financing eventual Korean unification, as well as development of Mongolia and the Russian Far East. Seoul views such a multilateral mechanism as easing its eventual burden and providing for costly infrastructure and other developments that the private sector would be less inclined to finance. Proponents of a new financial institution point to the tremendous cost, expertise, and focus of such development and cite limitations of the Asian Development Bank (ADB), the International Monetary Fund (IMF), and the World Bank. Regardless of the utility of new or existing organizations, the financial demands associated with transitioning North Korea are tremendous.

International consensus has moved away from scenarios of North Korean collapse and toward the probability of a North Korea remaining and in need of assistance. The United States Commander-in-Chief Pacific Forces reflected this new pragmatism in suggesting that one prepare for a range of futures on the Korean peninsula. This seems most appropriate, for under any reunification scenario, Koreans from the North will have an identity and history with which their brethren to the South and any peacekeeping entity—United States or otherwise—must reconcile.

U.S. TROOPS:
COUNTERWEIGHT TO MULTILATERALISM?

A continued U.S. troop presence on the Korean peninsula appears counterintuitive to the broader multilateral momentum. Yet South Korea and North Korea have expressed willingness to maintain at least some U.S. military presence for purposes of peacekeeping on the peninsula. Some analysts have suggested a rationale also based on long-term concerns about China and Japan. President Kim Dae Jung's call for the maintenance of U.S. troops was mirrored in the Pentagon's 1998 East Asia Strategy Report. However, the viability of such a presence must face the scrutiny of the U.S. and Korean legislatures, as well as the American and Korean publics—formidable hurdles to those favoring the status quo or that with slight revision. South Korean concerns about the perceived unfairness of the Status of Forces Agreement (SOFA), only recently amended, remaining questions about the Korean War massacre at Nogunri, and observances of the twentieth anniversary of the Kwangju massacre highlight continued difficulties in the U.S.-South Korean security relationship.

Externally, the call for a U.S. troop withdrawal has widened. In the United States, even a half-decade ago, the thrust was primarily libertarian. Within a few short years, more mainstream scholars have questioned the rationale for a continued U.S. force presence. Those defenders arguing strictly the benefits of continued deterrence are now met with arguments suggesting that South Korean capabilities provide overwhelming deterrence in and of themselves. Critics of a sustained U.S. troop presence also note the significance of U.S. arms sales on the peninsula, suggesting that decisions on weaponry are made more often in boardrooms in St. Louis than Seoul. These arguments suggest a U.S. military industrial complex actively engaged at the expense of peace on the peninsula. Russian Ambassador to South Korea Evgeny Afanasiev recently described the U.S. troop presence as a "legacy of the past," and such descriptions and calls for U.S. withdrawal will mount, especially with progress in inter-Korean dialogue and progress on the multilateral front. The Russian Ambassador couched his remarks in a call for enhanced multilateral security dialogue on the Korean peninsula and criticism of planned U.S. missile defenses.[18]

Further inter-Korean dialogue and multilateral activity, aimed at the eventual dissolution of the North Korean threat, have far-reaching implications for stability on the peninsula. They rob proponents of Theater Missile Defense (TMD) and National Missile Defense (NMD) of the fundamental argument of a North Korean "rogue" state threatening American shores. They call into further question the rationale for sustained U.S. troop presence and weapons sales on the peninsula and in Northeast Asia. Suggestions of the eventuality of U.S. troop withdrawal in turn raise questions of a security vacuum in Northeast Asia—the specter of which some observers fear could lead to an arms race or open conflict. Mirroring such issues are questions of demilitarization and demobilization of militaries North and South, the development of autonomous capabilities on and off the Korean peninsula, and missile and other power projection developments in a Confederate or United Korea. When weighing prospects for multilateral cooperation, these medium and long-term questions warrant careful consideration and debate, even at this transitional stage.

In the near term, revisiting the armistice and arriving at a peace treaty or interim peace mechanism appear ready challenges. A set of simultaneous nonaggression pacts between parties to the Korean conflict is one possible outcome, leading to a new, multilateral peacekeeping function for United Nations troops, rather than the military role of United States Forces Korea (USFK). Achieving normalization and a peace treaty are integral to North Korea's ultimate willingness to abandon nuclear weapons ambitions, including the resolution of processing discrepancies surrounding the 1990s nuclear dispute.

The need to transcend the armistice remains, and the Four Party Talks process, inter-Korean dialogue, and U.S.-North Korean normalization talks will advance the agenda beyond the once sacrosanct armistice arrangement.[19] The legal, logistical, and administrative dimensions of revisiting the armistice are fodder for continued academic and policy discourse and examination. New multilateral and bilateral arrangements will ultimately replace old prescriptions.

In closing, unique opportunity exists at this stage in peninsular affairs. Enhanced multilateral cooperation, engagement, measured change, and patient response constitute the only viable solution where alternatives could spiral dangerously out of control. The United States and other external powers need to abandon paternalistic instincts of the past and further multilateral initiatives as partners and facilitators. Danger exists in failing to do so, given the long and complicated legacy of external influence on the Korean peninsula. New multilateral approaches back a Korean solution to the Korean divide and will help lay to rest the last vestige of the Cold War.

NOTES

1. See Stephen Noerper, *The Tiger's Leap: the South Korean Drive for National Prestige and Emergence in the International Arena* (Sofia, Bulgaria: St. Kliment Ohridski University Press, 1996).

2. See Ralph Cossa, "Multilateralism and National Strategy in Northeast Asia," *NBR Analysis*, vol. 7, no. 5, December 1996, p .25. See also Ralph Cossa, "Security Multilateralism in Asia," IGCC Policy Paper No. 51, June 1999.

3. See ASEAN Regional Forum (ARF), *Chairman's Statement*, 1994.

4 ARF, *Chairman's Statement*, p. 4

5. Korean Peninsula Energy Development Organization, *Annual Report 1996/1997*, New York, p. 5.

6. Korean Peninsula Energy Development Organization, p. 1.

7. William Perry, "Preventive Defense in the Asia Pacific Region," prepared Remarks to the Pacific Basin Economic Council, Washington, D.C., May 22, 1996, p. 2.

8. "Remarks by the President to the Pacific Basin Economic Council," Washington, D.C., May 20, 1996, pp. 3–4.

9. William Perry, "Defense in an Age of Hope," *Foreign Affairs*, vol. 75, no. 6, November/December 1996, pp. 65–66.

10. Ibid., p. 69.

11. Perry, p. 6.

12. Michael Lund, *Preventing Violent Conflict: A Strategy for Preventive Diplomacy* (Washington, D.C.: U.S. Institute of Peace Press, April 1996), p. 37.

13. Ibid., pp. 203–205.

14. Ruth Wedgewood, "Regional and Subregional Organizations in International Conflict Management," in Chester Crocker et al., eds., *Managing Global Chaos: Source of and Response to International Conflict* (Washington, D.C.: U.S. Institute of Peace Press, September 1996), pp. 275–85.

15. Ibid., p. 281.

16. Scott Snyder, "Preventive Diplomacy in Southeast Asia," paper prepared for the Conference on Preventive Diplomacy, sponsored by IISS and the

Singapore Institute for International Affairs, Singapore, September 9–11, 1997, p. 15.

17. Pacific Forum-CSIS, *PacNet Newsletter,* no. 39, 1997, p. 1.

18. Young-Bae Shin, "N. Korea Missile Poses No Threat to U.S., Russian Ambassador Says," *The Korea Herald,* Seoul, May 25, 2000, p. 1.

19. See Peter Hayes and Stephen Noerper, "The Future of the U.S.-ROK Alliance," in Peter Hayes and Young Whan Kihl, eds., *Peace and Security in Northeast Asia: The Nuclear Issue and the Korean peninsula* (Armonk, NY: ME Sharpe, 1997), pp. 265–66.

CHAPTER ELEVEN

THE INTER-KOREAN RELATIONSHIP AND REGIONAL SECURITY*

SUNG-JOO HAN

The June 2000 summit between North and South Korea has changed the security dynamics of the Korean peninsula. The reverberations of that change reach across Northeast Asia, and beyond. The summit has also engendered exaggerated hopes and fears. On one hand, the appearance of a thaw in North-South relations has inspired great optimism among those who see it as an irrefutable sign of North Korea's intention to join the rest of the world as a constructive player. At the other extreme, it is seen as a masterstroke of deception by North Korea to reap economic gains and lower the guard of South Korea and its allies, principally the United States.

A more realistic assessment lies somewhere in the middle. Clearly, Kim Jong Il has not decided overnight to atone for all the regime's past ills. Nevertheless, his emergence on the world stage has started an inevitable process—intended or not—of North Korea opening itself to the rest of the world. The consequences, for the Koreas and for the major powers surrounding the Korean peninsula, are incalculable.

SIGNIFICANCE OF THE SUMMIT

The summit restores a certain symmetry to the Seoul-Pyongyang-Washington triangle, which had become especially lopsided following Pyongyang's announcement in March 1993 that it would withdraw from the Nuclear Nonproliferation Treaty (NPT). As a consequence of that decision, in March 1993, South Korean President Kim Young-Sam gave the

United States the green light to talk to North Korea about nuclear issues directly. Previously, South Korea had insisted on being a party to any such U.S.-North Korea talks or that inter-Korea talks should come first.

There were several reasons South Korea was willing to waive those conditions. First, it was necessary to secure Chinese cooperation on issues of Korean security. Second, North Korea at the time was adamantly against any direct North-South dialogue. Third, Seoul was confident that the United States would adequately represent its views and interests. Finally, it was important to engage North Korea in any way possible. Even so, the South Korean government was subject to much criticism at home about its exclusion from the talks. It was argued that U.S. and South Korean interests were different, that North Korea would now have no need to deal with the South, and that Washington and Pyongyang might reach a secret deal.

For the next seven years, such inter-Korean dialogue as existed usually required the United States to play the middleman. Even the aborted summit of July 1994 between South Korean President Kim Young-Sam and North Korean President Kim Il-Sung was brokered by former U.S. President Jimmy Carter. Both the United States and South Korea worked hard to mend the situation. It took much effort, for example, to include a paragraph on inter-Korea dialogue in the 1994 Geneva Agreed Framework (on the North Korean nuclear issue), delaying its signing for at least one week. The Four Party Talks between the United States, China, and North and South Korea were a mechanism to bring South Korea into discussion with North Korea on issues related to the Korean peninsula.

With the recent Pyongyang summit meeting between the two Koreas, the balance between inter-Korean and U.S.-North Korea relations has been restored. The summit was arranged and successfully conducted by Koreans themselves. Now, the United States is as interested in what goes on in North-South Korean dialogue as South Korea was interested in what went on in U.S.-North Korean talks. Inter-Korean dialogue is serving as the central dynamic for other relationships, especially North Korea's dialogues with the United States and Japan.

SUMMIT OBJECTIVES—SOUTH AND NORTH

What has South Korea hoped to gain from the June 2000 summit? In the short run, visible benefits should include family reunions and economic exchanges. In the longer term, South Korea aims to build trust. A diplomatic summit is more than a meeting between top leaders. The preparation leading up to it, the meeting itself, the follow-up process—

all these involve contacts and negotiations at many different levels on both sides. At the same time, South Korea is interested in increasing North Korea's exposure to and dependence on the outside world, and particularly its dependence on Seoul, thereby giving Pyongyang clear incentive to behave. South Korea's ultimate goal is to build a structure of peace on the peninsula and eventually bring about a fundamental change in North Korea.

As for the North, what moved Kim Jong Il to emerge from his seclusion? While it is possible that the North Korean leader suddenly converted to the cause of peace, a more plausible explanation lies in a rather more complex combination of motives. The first has to do with image. Kim Jong Il may have determined that if anyone can help North Korea escape its economic woes, it is South Korean President Kim Dae Jung. Kim Jong Il could have been grateful for his South Korean counterpart's Sunshine Policy of engagement with the North, and wanted to help shore up Kim Dae Jung's reputation. In so doing, Kim Jong Il probably saw the summit as a chance to present himself as a national hero in North Korea and as a reasonable and peace-loving man to the bewildered South Korean public.

The second factor concerns influence. Kim Jong Il must have reasoned that a show of Korean amity would further Pyongyang's efforts to improve diplomatic relations with other countries, particularly the United States and Japan. At the same time, he could have hoped to sow some discord between Seoul, on the one hand, and Washington and Tokyo on the other, as the three governments do not always agree on the urgency of such problems as missile- and nuclear-proliferation. As for China, it is no coincidence that only a few days before the inter-Korean summit, Kim Jong Il made a quick visit to Beijing to meet with the Chinese leadership, which had been urging closer cooperation with the South. In addition, North Korea's active diplomacy following the summit confirms that the dramatic meeting was, in effect, Kim Jong Il's own coming-out party.

Another possible motive was to gain tactical advantage. The North Korean leader may have decided that the goodwill generated by his public display of charm would enable him to avoid concrete concessions at the summit bargaining table: especially concerning such issues as weapons of mass destruction, on which the United States and Japan place much weight; and the reunion of separated families, politically very sensitive in South Korea.

One thing seems clear: the North's steps toward bridging the divide signalled a new confidence that it could maintain its regime internally even while reaching outside for help. Six years after the death of his father, Kim Jong Il must feel that he has succeeded both in consolidating his own position at home and in building a political system impermeable to outside influence.

Whatever the motivation, the appearance of harmonious relations can only have a positive effect on the political standing of both Kims at home and abroad. If symbolism was largely substituted for substance, the summit has at least opened a line of communication between the two leaders. It is conceivable that better communications could prevent the recurrence of such dangerous incidents as the Western Sea shoot-out of 1999 (in which North Korean naval ships fired on South Korean ships), while opening up the possibility of future summits, as well as expanded contacts between high-level government officials.

But it is too early to assume that trust and confidence have been established and that an era of cooperation has arrived. Neither is it realistic to expect that unification is imminent. On the contrary, the large-scale economic assistance that may result from the talks could help sustain and prolong the Pyongyang regime.

IMPLICATIONS FOR THE SOUTH

The South Korean government, even while reaping public approval for the successful visit, has much work ahead. It must maintain the momentum of the apparent goodwill established during the trip and push for concrete agreements, not only in the area of economic cooperation but, more importantly, on building a framework for peace and expanded people-to-people contacts. At the same time, the South must now contend with heightened expectations from the summit. These tend to lower the public's guard against the North Korean military threat, which remains undiminished.

Much will depend on how the evolving inter-Korea relationship affects the ideological configuration in South Korea. A quarter-century ago—about midway between the Korean War and now—I published a book, *The Failure of Democracy in South Korea.*[1] The main theme was the deep ideological divide in South Korean politics. As one side is normally predominant, this chasm is not usually apparent. But the differences do surface whenever political control loosens up.

It is difficult, and perhaps futile, to define "left" and "right" in Korean politics. In relation to the Korean War, however, the respective positions are straightforward. The right believes that North Korea's Kim Il-Sung instigated the war, causing millions of deaths and untold miseries for all Korean people, North and South. The left, by contrast, does not generally accept that Kim Il-Sung started the war and argues, in any case, that it is irrelevant. The left blames the United States for the division of the country and South Korean rightists for blocking unification.

The Korean War, which magnified the ideological divide that was already apparent before 1950, also helped mask the division because the orthodox right was able to silence dissenting voices. But the dissent emerged again in conjunction with the democratic movements that fought against the authoritarian governments of Park Chung Hee and Chun Doo Whan. It was noticeably amplified whenever the government relaxed its grip: in 1960 after the student uprising; in 1980, after the death of Park Chung Hee; in 1988, after the launching of the Roh Tae Woo government; and since the election of Kim Dae Jung in 1998.

Today, the left finds fertile ground to promote its interpretation of the Korean War and the U.S. role in Korea. Reasons for this include generational change, the change of leadership in North Korea, and a more permissive, if not indulgent, government in the South. The generational change is especially significant. The overwhelming majority of South Koreans were born after the Korean War. They seem not to know, or care, why Americans came to fight half a century ago, and rarely consider what would have happened if North Korea had taken over the South, or what has prevented another war. Instead, this generation questions why U.S. troops remain in Korea, and seizes on such controversies as Nogun-ri (where atrocities were allegedly committed by U.S. troops during the Korean War), Maehyang-ri (where the U.S. Air Force bombing range is located), and Status of Forces Agreement issues.

The right had its last hurrah in 1994 after the death of Kim Il-Sung. At that time, some leftist students set up memorial altars on campus for Kim Il-Sung while a few politicians suggested that South Korea send a mourning delegation to Pyongyang. This suggestion was denounced and blocked by the right, which was deeply angered by the idea of honouring a person the rightists considered a war criminal. Now, in the wake of the Pyongyang summit, the voice of the right rings discordant. The summit was a great success in boosting the image not only of Kim Jong Il, but of North Korea itself.

Those who counsel a more balanced approach are overridden by those who have fallen under the spell of Kim Jong Il. On the fiftieth anniversary of the Korean War, there was little enthusiasm for commemorating the event in any significant way. The war that has never for a moment been forgotten in Korea now threatens to vanish from the collective memory.

The South Korean attitude toward the United States could be described as a case of "familiarity breeding contempt." Not only is the United States blamed for the division of Korea and therefore for the war itself, but also for its acceptance of successive authoritarian regimes and its failure to prevent the 1980 Kwangju massacre in which several hundred protesters were killed by government troops. During the 1988 Seoul

Olympics, many Korean spectators cheered for the Russian basketball team over the American team. (If North Korean fans could choose their own favorites, they might well cheer for the Americans.)

ROK-U.S. ALLIANCE: TURBULENCE AHEAD?

Given the pendulum-swing of Korean ideology, it is impossible to predict how long the infatuation with Kim Jong Il and the North will last, or how it will affect the U.S.-Republic of Korea (ROK) alliance and the status of the U.S. troops in Korea. There is one obvious precedent. In the late 1980s, as the Cold War waned, Soviet negotiators at international conferences began to wield a new kind of threat: by showing a friendly face, they implied, the Soviet Union could deprive the United States of its key rationale for arms spending, military alliances, and troops in both Europe and Asia. As it happened, the threat did diminish, even before the Soviet Union collapsed. Although this collapse led to a significant reduction in U.S. troops in Europe, the end of the Cold War neither weakened the alliances nor caused U.S. forces to withdraw completely.

North Korea could now employ a similar tactic: threatening, as it were, to become less of a threat. Whether Pyongyang actually opposes, will "tolerate," or indeed prefers a continued U.S. troop presence in Korea, the fact is that simply by giving the appearance of peaceful intentions, the North can encourage complacency in the South. With the North Korean threat appearing to recede, South Koreans will begin to wonder whether they should put up with the inconvenience of U.S. troops. It should not be assumed that the U.S.-ROK alliance can survive as well as NATO has survived. In Europe, U.S. troops remain even though the Soviet threat has disappeared, while in Korea, their presence is increasingly questioned when the threat has *not* diminished. The perceived thaw between North and South Korea following the June 2000 summit has provided a convenient platform for those South Koreans who have always opposed the U.S. presence.

In response to these concerns, President Kim Dae Jung has been emphasizing the continuing need for U.S. troops. He has taken pains to remind South Koreans that the recent improvements in inter-Korean relations would not have been possible without the U.S. military alliance. He also rightly emphasises that the continued presence of U.S. forces in Korea is important not only for security, but also for South Korea's diplomatic and economic strength.

How widespread and serious is the anti-American sentiment? The South Koreans who protest against the U.S. presence can be divided into four broad categories. The first consists of ideologues who have always opposed the U.S. role in Korea. In their view, the United States is responsible for the division of the country and the outbreak of the Korean War. They consider U.S. troops an "occupying" force that should be removed at all cost and seek every opportunity to incite anti-American sentiment. A second group would like to see U.S. troops removed, not so much for ideological reasons, but because they have been persuaded that the security situation no longer requires them. For this group, the North-South Korean summit and the South Korean president's assurance that South Koreans need not worry about another war confirm that the North Korean military threat is simply an excuse for continued stationing of U.S. troops in the South. In the third category are people who believe U.S. troops are still needed for security as well as for diplomatic and economic reasons. However, they are convinced that American troops are in Korea to serve the United States' own interests; for example, to contain China and to bolster the U.S. troop presence in Japan. They believe U.S. troops will stay in Korea despite the protests, and that therefore it is safe to denounce the United States.

The fourth group is more concerned with immediate practical issues. They have no illusions about peace or an indefinite troop presence on the Korean peninsula. But they are unhappy about the existing Status of Forces Agreement, the slow pace of investigating war-time atrocities, the U.S. use of bombing ranges in Korea, and what they consider to be general U.S. insensitivity in dealing with Korea and the Koreans. In this group's view, it is necessary to deal constructively with these problems now to secure political support for maintaining a strong alliance with the United States.

Of the four viewpoints described above, adherents to the second and third are the most likely to be surprised. First, the assessment that security has been enhanced is at best premature. The summit has not put a dent in North Korea's military power and the potential for renewed hostilities on the Korean peninsula remains. The joint summit declaration scarcely touched on issues of peace and security. Neither was security on the agenda of the first ministerial-level meeting between the North and South after the summit. It is clear that Pyongyang wants to discuss security matters last, if at all.

Second, those who believe that the United States will keep its troops in Korea, no matter what, may also be in for a surprise. It will be difficult for the U.S. administration to justify the troop commitment to the public and the Congress in the face of rising anti-American sentiment in Korea. When the United States was asked by the Philippine parliament to close its bases, it confounded many expectations by promptly evacuating. The notion that the United States needs to keep its troops in Korea in order to maintain troops in Japan may have lost its validity. It is often assumed that the Japanese do not want to be "singularised" as the only major Asian host country for U.S. troops. Yet, despite problems and protests in Okinawa, the Japanese government and people are doing everything—from finance to legal arrangements—to keep U.S. troops. In fact, the withdrawal of U.S. forces from Korea could make Tokyo even more determined to keep them in Japan.

In order for South Korea and the United States to maintain their alliance, both governments must attend to it urgently. For Seoul, it would be unwise to present an excessively rosy picture of the security situation when peace is far from being assured. North Korea is not likely to give up easily its "ace" in dealing with the rest of the world: weapons of mass destruction, and, especially, missiles. And it would be unsafe to assume that the growing manifestation of anti-U.S. sentiment in South Korea is only a passing phenomenon. Fed with misleading information and unrealistic expectations, a point may be reached where events could become uncontrollable. Thus the South Korean government must make its citizens acutely aware that a strong alliance with the United States is necessary, not only for security, but also for economic prosperity, by providing security as well as continuing improvement in relations with North Korea.

The U.S. government, for its part, has to recognize that it is facing quite a different situation from the days of the Cold War and heightened North-South confrontation. The United States needs to understand a South Korean society that has undergone a generational change, matured in many ways, and become more confident and assertive. The anti-U.S. protests are a wake-up call. The ROK-U.S. relationship is entering a time of complex and difficult challenges and requires enhanced nurturing and protection, before it is too late.

KIM JONG IL'S PLANS FOR NORTH KOREA

Pyongyang states that it will continue its planned economy and adopt only minor changes to the existing structure. In practice, however, it is soliciting foreign investment, training its personnel in market economics, and changing the legal and organizational framework of the economy. Kim Jong Il's first objective must be to revive the failed economy with the assistance of South Korea and the rest of the world. A second, related, objective is to defend the regime and maintain the system. Third, North Korea will want to compete successfully with South Korea: if not economically, at least militarily and diplomatically. To this end, Kim Jong Il will want to limit exchanges to the economic area, permitting other exchanges, such as family reunions, only to the extent that they are absolutely necessary to sustain the new relationship with the South.

What kind of an economic model will North Korea pursue? The one that comes immediately to mind is China. However, it will be difficult for North Korea to emulate the Chinese pattern of development; China was in a much better position to adopt some aspects of a market economy. When it opened to the outside world, China did not feel its system threatened in the way North Korea probably feels threatened. Moreover, unlike North Korea today, China offered a much larger and more attractive market, which enabled it to attract foreign investment. China was also able to take advantage of the overseas Chinese who could provide capital, economic know-how, and connections with the outside world. In contrast, North Korea can afford only very limited opening and has to achieve economic development primarily with the help of South Korea. In the military and security areas, North Korea will find it difficult to change its existing policies in any fundamental way. There will be internal resistance, especially from the military sector, to changing its military stance. There may be a genuine sense of insecurity among North Koreans. More important, the regime will not want to relinquish the leverage it derives from its current military capability.

Within North Korea, there must be those who question the wisdom of embracing the South just as there are those in Seoul who have doubts about engaging Pyongyang. Kim Jong Il is taking an even greater risk than his South Korean counterpart. It could ultimately prove to be his and the regime's undoing.

Still, the gamble may pay off for both sides. For North Korea, the dividend would be in the form of a revived economy and regime survival. For South Korea, it could mean a less-threatening northern neighbour, increased North-South exchanges, and improved prospects for unification. In essence, the summit has given Kim Jong Il a stake in behaving well, if only to keep the economic assistance flowing and to sustain the profitable relationship with Kim Dae Jung, to whom his own political fortunes are now more or less linked.

POSSIBLE OUTCOMES

These considerations suggest four scenarios for the future. The first, and most optimistic, involves an evolution of the relationship based on reconciliation, cooperation, and expanded exchanges. North Korea becomes less threatening, leading to increased mutual confidence, arms reduction, and agreement on a structure of peace. In a second scenario, North Korea cannot cope with the sudden opening of society to the outside world and thus implodes as a result of ideological bankruptcy and economic collapse. A third scenario foresees the possibility of North Korea, after securing the maximum economic assistance from the South, sabotaging the reconciliation process. North Korea could do so either out of fear that continued exchanges with the South would weaken and ultimately undo its own system or in order to cause confusion and dissension within the South. The fourth scenario is the same as the third, but projected further into the future: an economically much stronger North Korea ends its reconciliation with a South Korea that has been weakened by the burden of assisting the North.

What is clear is that South Korea faces considerable risks. Security could be compromised as a result of friction with the United States, possibly leading to the withdrawal of U.S. troops. The economy might suffer from the burden of rebuilding North Korea, while foreign investors could be scared away by the deterioration of South Korean security. Society and polity may be hopelessly polarized on the issue of embracing and assisting the North.

THE INTERNATIONAL DIMENSION

The major powers with strong interest in Korea—China, the United States, Russia, and Japan—have all welcomed and supported the inter-Korean summit. But it is clear that they are reassessing their positions vis-à-vis the Korean peninsula, as the summit will surely affect their own interests in profound ways.

In the short- to medium-term, China has the most to gain diplomatically from improved relations between North and South Korea. China is back on center-stage in Korean affairs, as the secret visit by Kim Jong Il to Beijing a few days before the summit underscored. The Chinese have good relations with both North and South and do not seem to mind the prospect of improved relations between Washington and Pyongyang. A breakthrough in North-South Korean relations is consistent with China's other interests. These interests include peace and stability on the peninsula, a balance between North and South, and the avoidance of any conflict into which China could be drawn. China is particularly interested in preventing the collapse of the North. Improved relations on the peninsula, and the corresponding improvement in North Korea's economic position, will obviate the need for massive Chinese assistance.

For the United States, a sudden and radical change in the situation on the Korean peninsula could be a mixed blessing. Washington has pursued a "soft-landing" policy vis-à-vis Pyongyang, intended to bring about North Korea's peaceful transition to a relatively open and market-oriented society. This policy was affirmed in the high-profile report by former Defense Secretary William Perry, who concluded that bringing about the collapse of North Korea was neither feasible nor desirable under the existing circumstances.[2] A thaw between the two Koreas is consistent with this policy.

However, the United States is committed to preventing or at least curtailing North Korea's development of missiles and weapons of mass destruction. Washington would be concerned if the appearance of improved relations between the two Koreas diverted international attention away from this issue. Furthermore, as North Korea discovers alternative sources of economic support and assistance, the United States might lose some negotiating leverage.

It is a great irony that Korea today represents the principal strategic area where Chinese and U.S. interests coincide and the two countries cooperate. For Korea, of course, is where the United States and China once fought a war against one another. It was only with U.S. troops advancing on its border that China reluctantly entered the Korean War. The cost proved enormous: in addition to several hundred thousand casualties, China lost its hope of annexing Taiwan and gained an enemy in the United States. Declared an aggressor by the U.S.-dominated United Nations, China was hit with an embargo that prevailed for nearly two decades. This pushed China closer to the Soviet Union, until a rift emerged in the late 1950s. At that point, China was virtually isolated.

Only in the 1970s, almost 20 years after the end of the Korean War, did the United States and China improve their ties, largely because of mutual hostility towards the Soviet Union. Yet the end of the Cold War helped to alleviate further Sino-American rivalry over the Korean peninsula. The Bush administration withdrew U.S. tactical nuclear weapons from South Korea in the early 1990s, while China started to regard the U.S. troops stationed in Korea as a safeguard against both possible military conflict on the peninsula and a Japanese return to militarism.

Indeed, the overlap of interests is significant. Both countries want to denuclearize the peninsula and to limit Pyongyang's development of missiles. China has as much interest as the United States in curbing North Korea's missiles, since they could effectively reach anywhere in China. Moreover, Pyongyang's missile program provides justification for U.S. theater and national missile defense programs, and could also provoke a Japanese nuclear weapons program. Next, the United States and China share a concern about preventing a catastrophic collapse in North Korea, given the regional instability and high cost this would inevitably cause. Finally, neither wants North Korea to become a source of competition or a thorn in their relationship. The United States seemed untroubled when South Korea normalized ties with China in 1992. Similarly, China seems relaxed about the possibility of normalized relations between Pyongyang and Washington.

Russia's main concern on the Korean issue in recent years has been to avoid being left out of the process. In 1994, it proposed an international conference to tackle the North Korean nuclear issue. Like Japan, Russia had apprehensions about the Four Party Talks on Korea that excluded both countries. Until 1995, Russia's relations with Pyongyang worsened to the extent that Moscow decided not to renew its security treaty with North Korea. Since then, Russia has mended fences; the visit of President Vladimir Putin to North Korea shortly after the Korean summit constituted an emphatic gesture of return to the Korean question.

In addition to preserving peace, stability, and the status quo on the Korean peninsula, Japan seeks to maintain Korea as a buffer between China and itself. For this purpose, the continued presence of U.S. troops, both in Korea and Japan is deemed necessary. Japan also wants to ensure Korea's nonnuclear status and to curtail North Korea's missile program. In the long run, Japan would also be concerned about the possibility of Chinese dominance of Korea. So far, Japan has had only limited involvement in Korean matters, most obviously in the Korean peninsula Energy Development Organisation (KEDO) process. However, any large-scale economic rehabilitation program for North Korea will inevitably involve a contribution by Japan. Hence, Tokyo feels it has the need and claim to be actively involved in discussion of the Korean question. For this reason, Japan, together with Russia, supports the idea of a six-party (North and South Korea, China, United States, Japan, and Russia) mechanism on Korea.

CONCLUSION

The prognosis for North Korea is mixed. On the positive side, Pyongyang will continue to expand its diplomatic relations, not only with neighboring countries and the United States, but also with countries in Europe and elsewhere. It will actively participate in international organizations and multilateral mechanisms, as shown by its joining of the Association of Southeast Asian Nations (ASEAN) Regional Forum (ARF). Despite the confidence of its leadership that any change can be controlled, North Korea will undergo an inevitable process of political and social evolution. On the negative side, Pyongyang is not likely to change its basic military policies toward South Korea and will continue to pose a threat to stability on the peninsula. Likewise, it will be an economic basket-case for a considerable period to come, despite large-scale foreign assistance, mostly from South Korea.

Seoul's expanded relationship with North Korea will give rise to increasing domestic tension in South Korea, not only political, but economic, as South Korea takes on the burden of transforming the failing Stalinist economy. As the two Koreas move closer together, or at least manage their relationship with less third-party mediation, the United States will reassess its respective distance from each country in the trilateral relationship between the two Koreas and the United States. How this will affect the U.S. forces in Korea will depend on the behavior of North Korea as well as on the internal dynamics of both South Korea and the United States.

In regional terms, an improved inter-Korea relationship is likely to have a positive rather than negative effect on U.S.-China and China-Japan relations. China, despite its strong opposition to the deployment of National Missile Defense (NMD) and Theatre Missile Defense (TMD), will refrain from demanding the complete withdrawal of U.S. forces from Korea and Japan for fear that it will prompt the remilitarization of Japan. As the presence of U.S. troops also suits Japan's interests, even if they are withdrawn from Korea, Japan could be even more determined to keep its own U.S. troop presence, despite general expectations of most experts to the contrary. Both Japan and Russia, which have been largely sidelined in Korean affairs, will increasingly assert their roles in relation to those of China and the United States.

Overall, the change in North-South Korean relations will make the regional situation more fluid and will involve major-power reassessment of policies and interests and a reconfiguration of alignments and alliances. The chances of achieving multilateral dialogues and mechanisms will increase. There is a whole new game developing in Northeast Asian regional politics, one in which each country is trying to secure a place for itself in determining the future of Korea as a whole. North Korea will try to take advantage of this major-power competitiveness; however, the simple fact that it is beginning to engage the rest of the region is a positive step. South Korea, for its part, must distinguish between appearance and reality, and between short-term impulses and long-term interests. It should devise and pursue a diplomatic policy that permits making new friends while keeping old allies.

NOTES

* This chapter originally appeared in *Survival*, vol. 42, no. 4 (Winter 2000–2001), pp. 85–95 as "The Koreas' New Century."

1. Sung-Joo Han, *The Failure of Democracy in South Korea* (Berkeley, CA: University of California Press, 1974).

2. The non-classified portion of the review is available at http://www.state.gov/www/regions/eap/991012_northkorea_rpt.html.

INDEX

9 780312 238742